Consumer Rights

Perspectives and Experiences

Consumer Rights

Perspectives and Experiences

Major Suresh Goel (Retd)

MD Publications Pvt Ltd
New Delhi
www.mdppl.com

Published by :

MD Publications Pvt Ltd
"MD House", 11, Darya Ganj,
New Delhi-110 002
Phone : +91-11-41563325 (Customer Service)
+91-11-41562846 (Editorial)
E-mail (orders) : order@mdppl.com
Website : www.mdppl.com

ISBN : 978-81-7533-211-9

Published and Printed by Mr. Pranav Gupta on behalf of **MD Publications Pvt Ltd** at Printext, New Delhi.

PREFACE

Consumer rights are now an integral part of our lives like a consumerist way of life. They have been well documented and much talked about. We have all made use of them at some point in our daily lives. Market resources and influences are growing by the day and so is the awareness of one's consumer rights.

These rights are well-defined and there are agencies like the government, consumer courts and voluntary organisations that work towards safeguarding them. While we all like to know about our rights and make full use of them, consumer responsibility is an area which is still not demarcated and it is hard to spell out all the responsibilities that a consumer is supposed to shoulder.

Consumer protection laws are designed to ensure fair competition and the free flow of truthful information in the marketplace. The laws are designed to prevent businesses that engage in fraud or specified unfair practices from gaining an advantage over competitors and may provide additional protection for the weak and unable to take care of them. Consumer Protection laws are a form of government regulation which protect the interests of consumers. For example, a government may require businesses to disclose detailed information about products-particularly in areas where safety or public health is an issue, such as food. Consumer protection is linked to the idea of consumer rights (that consumers have various rights as consumers), and to the formation of consumer organizations which help consumers make better choices in the marketplace.

Consumer interests can also be protected by promoting competition in the markets which directly and indirectly serve consumers, consistent with economic efficiency, but this topic is treated in Competition law. Consumer protection can also be asserted via non-government organizations and individuals as consumer activism.

Consumer protection law or consumer law is considered an area of public law that regulates private law relationships between individual consumers and the businesses that sell those goods and services. Consumer protection covers a wide range of topics, including but not necessarily limited to product liability, privacy rights, unfair business practices, fraud, misrepresentation, and other consumer/business interactions. Such laws deal with credit repair, debt repair, product safety, service contracts, bill collector regulation, pricing, utility turnoffs, consolidation, personal loans that may lead to bankruptcy and much more.

One of the greatest achievements of the Indian consumer movement is the enactment of the dynamic consumer law: COPRA. Coming 39 years after Independence, it has acknowledged the rampant consumer abuses, including those of the government owned public utilities like telephones, transport, power etc. These utilities, in the first place, were created as state monopolies ostensibly to protect consumers.

I am very grateful to Mr. Pranav Gupta, Director, MD Publications Pvt Ltd, New Delhi, for his cooperation and support for this book.

Major Suresh Goel (Retd)

CONTENTS

	Preface	*v*
1.	Consumer Rights : An Introduction	1
2.	Marketing in a Transitional Economy and the Consumer Attitudes	57
3.	The Consumer and the Manufacturer	127
4.	Consumer Protection Act	157
5.	Consumer Protection and Competition Policy	183
6.	Consumption : Expanding the Discourse on Social Change	221
	Bibliography	265
	Index	269

1

Consumer Rights
An Introduction

Consumer rights are now an integral part of our lives like a consumerist way of life. They have been well documented and much talked about. We have all made use of them at some point in our daily lives. Market resources and influences are growing by the day and so is the awareness of one's consumer rights. These rights are well-defined and there are agencies like the government, consumer courts and voluntary organisations that work towards safeguarding them. While we all like to know about our rights and make full use of them, consumer responsibility is an area which is still not demarcated and it is hard to spell out all the responsibilities that a consumer is supposed to shoulder. In this chapter, we will give an overview of the 8 consumer rights, their implications and significance for a developing country like India, and also define the various aspects of consumer responsibility.

Media managers are complaining heavily about piracy. Although the scale of losses claimed by their representative bodies should be accepted with caution, it can still be seen that the dimension of content piracy is substantial. The significant decrease in revenue cannot be explained in terms of ageing demographics, the excess revenues generated during the vinyl-to-CD conversion cycle and greater competition for the disposable income of young consumers, but rather is to a significant extent attributable to copyright infringements. In the 20th century, the presence and influence of the market grew dramatically in consumer life. We began to purchase things from the market for a price. Soon, mass production and industrial production came into being, giving the consumer world an entirely new dimension. Have you ever wondered how much urban consumers depend on the market for fulfillment of even their basic needs.

This over-dependence on the market and the inherent profit motive in mass production and sales has given manufacturers, and dealers a good reason to exploit consumers. As a consumer, you would know how market products are constantly under-weight, of inferior quality and do not prescribe to quality standards specified by quality-control agencies. Consumers not only do not get value for their money but also often have to suffer losses and inconvenience due to market manipulations.

THE 8 CONSUMER RIGHTS

In order to safeguard consumer interest, 6 consumer rights were initially envisioned by consumer rights activists of the West, namely:

- Right to Safety
- Right to Information
- Right to Choice
- Right to be Heard
- The Right to Redress
- The Right to Consumer Education

The Techno-legal Paradigm on Strong Protection

In a situation with extensive intellectual property piracy, where current legislation fails to provide the necessary security, media companies are developing self-help mechanisms in order to safeguard sustained sources of direct revenue. The content industry is determined to address this critical situation by seeking techno-legal means of preventing the uncontrolled redistribution of content. *Technical strategies* aim to protect the economic interests of media companies through the deployment of Technical Protection Measures based on key technologies such as encryption, watermarking and rights expression languages. In this context, Charles Clark has stated that "The answer to the machine is in the machine"; in other words, the survival of the media industries presupposes the development of suitable technical infrastructure. Technical strategies are effective only when accompanied by contract-based *legal strategies* (e.g. mass market licenses or technology licenses) and by an appropriate legal framework that supports the use of DRMS solutions by ensuring the protection of technical measures.

In fact, the technological and legal approaches provide mutual support for one another, thereby constituting a protective unity. Technology prevents infringements, while legal measures provide deterrents regarding circumvention of the technology.

In the quest to safeguard their means of existence, the media industries have been focusing on techno-legal content protection in an isolated and excessive manner and neglecting consumer interests in their profitability calculus. Numerous voices support the so called "Napsterization" threat model that assumes that one crack is sufficient to enable a pirate to inject the content into P2P networks, leading to the perfect public good problem, a phenomenon also referred to as "ROCE". Therefore, in accordance with the Napsterization model, the DRMS security design selected must be absolutely bullet-proof in order to prevent a single attack which threatens the entire economic value of the content.

A Paradigm based on Consumer Needs

However, this would not make sense, either from a technical or from an economic perspective. From a technical viewpoint, it will never be possible to implement complete protection. Even if technological protection measures can remain a step ahead of the attack techniques and tools of the hacker community, the fundamental problem of the "analogue hole" will continue to exist. This refers to the possibility of digitising high-quality analogue copies and distributing at least one copy in media networks, with the resulting snowball effects (due to the problem of the "digital hole"). Thus, sooner or later, the availability of unauthorized copies must be expected. In economic terms it is not necessary to increase protection levels excessively or to make technical installations bullet-proof. DRM systems have a substantial price attached to them. The costs of setting up, deploying and maintaining the technical infrastructure seriously erode revenue potentials.

Therefore, in some situations weaker protection may be preferable to stronger forms of content protection. Shapiro and Varian summarise this by stating, "The important thing is to maximise the value of your intellectual property, not to protect it for the sake of protection". The need to fine-tune the level of content protection is a well-investigated research issue. Empirical case studies show that liberal download sites with a low protection level, such as iTunes, have proven successful in the marketplace, while many strong content protection systems, such as Sony´s Key2Audio system, have been outright commercial flops. Thus, economic reasoning shows that the reflection of consumer needs in the design of DRMS is of pivotal importance. Therefore, this contribution seeks to show that decision makers in the media industry must analyse and integrate the notion of consumer utility in their overall strategy.

The technical design of DRMS and the scope of content protection must be aligned to consumer interest and the given competitive situation. For this purpose, more abstract industrial organisation-models are helpful to determine this optimal level of protection and understand how this level depends on the given market structure.

The following arguments demonstrate that a lower level of technical content protection can both satisfy consumer needs and increase profits. Thus, consumer requirements are reconciled with the economic imperative. The corollary is that hurting consumer interests can lead to a depression of profits. Therefore, consumer-friendly technical installations should be desirable, not in order to demonstrate excessive civil responsibility on the part of the media industries and concede to consumers their well-deserved legal freedom. Instead, the idea is to selfishly maximize profits by ac-counting for the needs of honest and potentially illicit consumers.

Paradox of Profitable Piracy

The pirating of copyright materials is considered harmful to the interests of the copyright owner. However, some economists argue that the toleration of certain levels of piracy can enhance profits and accommodate consumer demand for more liberalized usage, a position which may appear counterintuitive at first sight.

Three factors associated with "profitable piracy" have been identified in the economic literature: indirect appropriation, experience effects and network externalities.

In the case of *indirect appro-priation*, the copyright owner is able to obtain revenue from unauthorised copies by charging a higher price for the original media products from which unauthorised copies are made.

The logic behind this approach is straightforward: If the copyright owner knows which originals will be used to make copies, a higher price can be charged for these originals. This allows the copyright holder to capture some of the revenues that could have been appropriated through ordinary sales if unauthorised copying had been prevented.

Experience effects can also lead to profitable piracy. Information goods can be considered to be experience goods, since consumers are not perfectly informed about the characteristics of media products prior to consumption.

Copies provide information concerning the value of a product, and this in turn promotes the purchasing decision. Network technologies, such as Peer-to-Peer (P2P) systems, can help copyright owners by making it easier for consumers to inspect the media products (e.g. by sampling songs), so as to facilitate the purchasing decision. If P2P systems were merely used to "try out" content, then their use would be complementary to retail purchasing, rather than a substitute for it. In addition, the exchange of media products stimulates demand by allowing consumers to sample content that is subsequently bought. Finally, *network externalities* are highly relevant in markets for information goods in cases where consumer valuation of a good increases when more consumers have purchased it. For example, in the case of online games, network effects emerge from the liquidity of the player pool. Both legal and illegal copies of the game application can expand the "network" of consumers of that online game. Due to the existence of network effects, unauthorised copying and consumption provide value to legitimate buyers. It thus seems reasonable that illicit copying may benefit rights holders for information goods that exhibit network effects.

Effects of Content Degradation

Media companies can also engage in content degra-dation activities, by focusing on ways to increase the utility difference between original and pirated products. An important parameter is the degradation factor that represents the utility discount of the media product vis-à-vis the original product. A low degradation factor means that the pirated product is only slightly degraded and provides almost the same utility to the consumer as the original product. Conversely, a high degradation factor reflects substantial degradation and consequently a significant loss of utility vis-à-vis the original product. The concept of content degradation can be interpreted in two ways:

First, it can be interpreted as the quality discount of the pirated product in relation to the original product. In the case of analogue reproduction, copies represent poor substitutes for originals (e.g. "screener" copies produced illicitly in cinemas). Although this does not apply to digital reproduction, original content often provides consumers with a higher level of utility, to the extent that it is bundled with valuable additional services, which are unobtainable or difficult to obtain from pirates. For instance, software products are often supplied with manuals and support services, such as technical support; and discounts on upgrades may be provided. Alternatively, it can be interpreted as a transaction cost disadvantage incurred when purchasing the product from a pirated source. In this interpretation, a high degradation level means that the transaction cost is prohibitively high when purchasing from a pirate, with the result that the valuation of the original media product is reduced almost to zero. For example, in the case of highly degraded media product, a consumer who wishes to purchase from an ori-ginal content provider can simply buy the content legally via a known (online) retailer. If instead the customer wishes to purchase from the pirate, it is first necessary to find the pirated product, which implies higher search costs and possibly greater download costs than in the case of purchasing the original product. Thus, the overall tran-saction costs of purchasing from a pirate may be much higher than are those for purchasing from a legal source. This reduces the level of utility of pirated products.

Content Degradation Strategies

Content degradation strategies assume that the media company can determine the level of degradation of competing pirated products. While network effects are inherent in a media product and therefore constitute a given exogenous parameter, it can be argued that the quality difference between a pirated product and the original is something that can be deliberately designed into the competing products. In fact there are at least three strategies which could cause customers to have a reduced willingness for pirated as opposed to original products. First, media companies can combine their information products with (physical) services that are difficult to copy. For example, this could take the form of more sophisticated (including individualised) artwork accompanying audio CDs, or bund-ling media products with promotional activities, such as sweepstakes.

Secondly, media companies could increase transaction costs for illegal purchases. One approach would be for legal companies to penetrate P2P networks and supply illegal downloaders with fake pirated goods. This would greatly increase the search costs involved in finding genuine pirated goods. This has occurred in the case of Madonna's "American Life" album, where fans seeking tracks from P2P networks have downloaded files which are blank except for Madonna delivering a message to those attemp-ting to download her new songs. This could at least provide a fresh approach to the problem of music piracy and file-trading. Thirdly, through fear campaigning, media companies could highlight the ethical and legal problems associated with piracy. This could result in a psychological devaluation of pirated media products. It can be seen that there are various ways to deliberately increase the degradation level, which can also be used in combination.

In all these cases, media companies have to incur additional costs in order to increase the utility difference between original and pirated products. Related costs include production costs for additional physical components, server and broadband capacity to infiltrate P2P networks, and advertising costs. The benefit of "homemade" content degradation is that it reduces the need for technical protection. This means that content degradation is in some sense a substitute for a higher protection level. Therefore, with a bundle of degradation measures, the need for high-security, illiberal DRMS can be reduced. Honest consumers are not hurt but - instead - benefit from this downward adjusted level of protection. However, efforts to increase the quality difference between original and pirated products (e.g. by means of content individualisation) also imply costs which should not be unreasonably high.

CONSUMER RIGHTS AND ITS EXPANSION

Rights and Responsibilities

India has been observing 15 March since 1989 as the National Consumers' Day. This day has a historic im-portance as it was on this day in 1962, when the Bill for Consumer Rights was moved in the US Congress. During his speech President John F. Kennedy had remarked:

"If a consumer is offered inferior products, if prices are exorbitant, if drugs are unsafe or worthless, if the con-sumer is unable to choose on an informed basis, then his dollar is wasted, his health and safety may be threatened, and national interest suffers."

John F. Kennedy had equated the rights of the ordinary American consumer with national interest. He gave the American consumer four basic rights:

1. The Right to Safety - to be protected against the marketing of goods which are hazardous to health or life.
2. The Right to Choose - to be assured, wherever possible, access to a variety of products and services at com-petitive prices: and in those industries where com-petition is not workable and Government regulation is substituted, an assurance of satisfactory quality and service at fair prices.
3. The Right to Information - to be protected against fraudulent, deceitful or grossly misleading information, advertising, labeling, or other practices, and to be given the facts s/he needs to make an informed choice.
4. The Right to be Heard - to be assured that consumer interests will receive full and sympathetic consideration in the formulation of Government policy, and fair and expeditious treatment in its administrative tribunals.

Kennedy recognised that consumers are the largest economic group in the country's economy, affecting and affected by almost every public and private economic decision. But they were also the only important group who were not effectively organised, whose views were not heard.

Therefore, the Federal Government, by nature the highest spokesman for all people, had a special obligation to the consumer's needs. Thirteen years later President Gerald Ford felt that the four rights constituted in Kennedy's Bill of Rights were inadequate for a situation where most consumers are not educated enough to make the right choices. So he added the Right to Consumer Education, as an informed consumer cannot be exploited easily.

While these rights served the interest of the American consumer well enough, they did not cover the whole gamut, because a global consumer did need, apart from them, other well-defined rights like basic needs, a healthy environment and redress. The Consumers International (CI), former International Organisation of Consumer Unions (IOCU), the umbrella body, for 240 organisations in over 100 countries, expanded the charter of consumers rights contained in the US Bill to eight, which in a logical order reads:

1. Basic Needs,
2. Safety,
3. Information,.
4. Choice,
5. Representation,
6. Redress,
7. Consumer Education and
8. Healthy Environment.

This charter had a universal significance as they symbolised the aspirations of the poor and disadvantaged. On this basis, the United Nations, in April 1985, adopted its Guidelines for Consumer Protection.

Birth of Consumers' Day

Considering the importance of Kennedy's speech to the US Congress on this day, and the resultant law, the CI took a decision in 1982 to observe 15 March as the World Consumer Rights Day from 1983. Peculiar though it may sound, 15 March is not observed as a special day in the world's largest and most pulsating consumer society - the US. But at home in India the Government, adopted 15 March as the National Consumer's Day. India is a country, which never fell behind in introducing progressive legislation - we were among the first in the world to introduce universal adult franchise for women.

Gandhi had rightly said:

"A customer is the most important visitor on our premises. He is not dependent on us. We are dependent on him. He is not an interruption in our work - he is the purpose of it. We are not doing him a favour by serving him. He is doing us a favour by giving us the opportunity to serve him."

Birth of Copra

The right to redress lead to the passing of the Consumer Protection Act (COPRA) in 1986 in India which has been defined as the Magna Carta of consumers but, it recognises only six of these eight rights:

1. Safety,
2. Information,
3. Choice,
4. Representation,
5. Redress and
6. Consumer Education.

Besides this statutory recognition, COPRA has succeeded in bringing about revolutionary judicial reforms by providing juristic quasi-judicial courts solely for redressal of consumer grievances (where a price has been paid), for adjudication within a limited time frame of 90 to 150 days.

The rights of basic needs and healthy environment could not be provided in COPRA as these symbolised the aspiration of the poor and the disadvantaged, and were not the subject matter of priced commodities and services available in the market place. However, these are the backbone of peoples' movements in both the developing and the developed worlds.

Yet, in spite of pulsating movements, the rights of consumers could and were trampled on and often. There existed a vacuum in the definition of rights. It was often seen that boycotts would be spontaneous or organised in an adversarial situation, examples of, which are numerous. On an occasion in Calcutta a boycott of fish was successfully organised and the marketing cartel had to bow down, by cutting the inflated prices, rather than store rotting fish.

Right To Boycott

Taking a leaf out of India's freedom movement, when Mahatma Gandhi had successfully organised various boycotts of foreign cloth, salt etc. we at CUTS, declared and adopted the 9th Consumer Right on India's Independence Day - 15 August 1990: "The right to resist and boycott any person, goods or services in the event of conflict with consumer's interest". This right was the ultimate one, to be used when all methods fail. And many a times they do: the seller does not heed, the administration does not listen, and the judiciary fails. This right inherently signifies consumer unity as an individual consumer can be helpless or even apathetic, and it is a collective action that succeeds.

While the right to boycott epitomises the enability of consumer rights, the right to basic needs remained abstract. It only defined a consumer's necessities required to survive and live a dignified life but it did not demand the means to obtain them - the right to work. However, the right to work is also vague, as this colloquially meant easy jobs, and did not feature in the existing charter of Consumer's Rights. In the interlude, a new Union Government in India raised a debate to recognise the right to work, as a fundamental right on the one hand, and advocating self employment schemes for everyone, including the poor, on the other.

Observing the societal disarray created by government job and dole schemes, whether permanent or temporary, and how they maim the spirit of enterprise which prevails in the mass humanity of India, 'CUTS' was inspired to declare and adopt the 10th (enabling) Consumer Right on 26 January 1991: "The right to opportunities to acquire basic needs which will enable one to work and to earn a living, without exploitation." This inherently demands execution of the state's singular responsibility to provide productive infrastructure, work ethos, job opportunities, social justice and economic equity. Both these rights were adopted at the Third National Convention of Consumer Activists at Calcutta during 1-3 November 1991, calling and urging the now (CI) IOCU to recognise and take suitable steps in expansion of the Consumer Rights internationally.

India's Global Reputation

Laws, rules, regulations and orders (for which India has unparalleled distinction in the Guinness book of records) alone do not protect consumers, but it is the rights' movement of people which produce results in a democracy. One of the greatest achievements of the Indian consumer movement is the enactment of the dynamic consumer law: COPRA. Coming 39 years after Independence, it has acknowledged the rampant consumer abuses, including those of the government owned public utilities like telephones, transport, power etc. These utilities, in the first place, were created as state monopolies ostensibly to protect consumers.

Critics of COPRA rightly conclude that it can't do anything about rising prices, but it has succeeded in bringing about fairplay in the supply of goods and services available in the market place, giving substance to the adage: Customer is King. Also, COPRA has encouraged active consumer bodies to demand, and perhaps see in the near future, independent Public Utility Regulatory Commissions to debate costing, pricing and promote competition. This confidence emanates from the empowerment of voluntary organisations in COPRA and other consumer laws. While right to information is enshrined in COPRA, addition of the enlarged Right to Know in the fundamental rights chapter of the Indian Constitution would only result in meaningful empowerment - no more tight rope walking, but total glasnost. In fact the Central Consumer Protection Council has recommended to the Government to enact a Freedom of Information Act on the pattern of a similar law in the US.

Another major achievement of the Indian consumer

movement in the context of the world scenario, was to get the government in 1989, to adopt 15 March, the World Consumer Rights Day, as the National Consumers' Day. Unlike the Labour Day on 1 May, this has roots in the US, the Consumer Rights Day, which also has roots in the US, is not even observed there. Today India is the only country in the world, which has exclusive courts for consumer redressal. At the IOCU's 13th World Congress held in Hong Kong during 7-13 July 1991 it came in for praise and developed countries were called upon to emulate. In the same year, these developments inspired Jim Sugarman, a noted US consumer activist and a close associate of Ralph Nader, to candidly observe: "India is getting a global reputation for the rapid development of its consumer movement."

Bureaucrat's Revenge

COPRA, which was amended by an ordinance in June 1993, is a mixture of sad and happy tidings. And tragic because of one surprise which our bureaucrats sprung onto the bill, a matter which was not even discussed in the high power working group of the Central Consumer Protection Council. The law then proposed a limitation of one year to file complaints, where none existed. An utter nonsense, which goes beyond the principles of our well established Limitations Act of 1963, wherein courts cannot be approached after the expiry of three years of the last cause of action.

Since there was no limitation period prescribed under COPRA, in one matter, the apex consumer court, the National Commission had pronounced that the principles of the Limitations Act do not apply but can be relied upon, though not religiously. This proposal would not only have put consumers at a terrible disadvantage but also annoy them badly. Most warranties and guarantees on goods expire in one year, and manufacturers often drag on many consumers during this period by attending to complaints, instead of setting it right or replacing or refunding the price of the defective goods. They will thus be deprived of the easy redressal avenue by this one-year 'deadline'.

Consumers will be angry because the rules on the time limit of 90/150 days provided in COPRA for disposal of cases are practiced more in the breach, and cases drag on for years. Under this situation, expecting consumers to meet a deadline will be very irritating. Granted that delayed complaints can be entertained, but that would mean a set of lengthy arguments on just the admissibility of the case. Fourthly, the law also enables consumers to file class action complaints, which incidentally always existed, but there can be no basis to determine the deadline in such matters. For instance, if the Motor Vehicles Act, 1988 provides for certain mandatory safety features which have been ignored by manufacturers; after research, we decide to file a complaint what would be the limitation period? Due to these arguments and lobbing the time limit was revised to two years, when the ordinance was put on the table of the parliament.

Belying Expectations

The law belied the consumer affairs Minister, A K Antony's note in the statement of objects and reasons, wherein he says the working of the redressal agencies has helped to arouse the expectations of the people on several other grounds as well. Housing by way of plots or flats or houses has been covered under the definition of 'services' under COPRA. Rather than adopt the words: 'real estate', as defined under the MRTP Act, 1969 from which the whole definition clause of services was borrowed in the first instance, a new jargon: 'housing construction' is added. This would mean that the consumer courts will only entertain complaints relating to: flats, land, houses purchased or to be purchased.

In a beacon case involving a plot: Garima Shukla vs. UP Avas evam Vikas Nigam, the National Commission had held that the dispute is covered as a deficiency in the service of housing. The Supreme Court upheld the orders of the National Commission. Among several other recom-mendations of the Central Council, another major one has also been diluted. In view of several protests by consumers, the council had agreed to recommend incorporation of an open, democratic and a transparent process of selection of the non-official members of consumer courts. The recommendation was that a selection committee headed by the minister and consisting of the secretary in charge of the department, a nominee of the chief justice of the state high court and two consumer activists (one a woman) would be the right form.

The bill now proposes a committee headed by the President of the state commission and the consumer affairs secretary and the state law secretary. It is thus heavily loaded against transparency. I have seen many a president of the State Commission sitting in the chamber of the secretary, especially when s/he is a retired high court judge. By and large the secretary has to follow the minister's orders, therefore the transparency sought in the selection process will be doubtful. Presence of two activists would have perhaps changed the odds.

However the president of the State Commission can only be appointed after consultation with the Chief Justice of the concerned high court, but those who know, consultation does not mean consent or concurrence. On several occasions, in spite of opposition, people have been appointed, after the so-called con-sultation.

The Broom Stick

The Council had made several other vital recommen-dations after long deliberations and critical debates, but they have been given the broomstick. These were:

1. Consumer rights were to be put in a separate chapter so that violations of the same could be an additional ground, if not the basis of a complaint. These will now continue as decorations in COPRA, for the central council to 'talk, about - only once in a year, as against twice as recommended'.
2. Services rendered by public health care system and civic bodies were to be covered, as they are not charities but are run from the taxpayer money. So that consumer could get value for money and these white elephants are brought

to heel. The union health ministry prevailed.

3. Lawyers were to be debarred except when the complainant had engaged one, or with his consent or if the consumer court directed the parties to engage lawyers, when questions of law were involved. This was recommended because lawyers often delay the settlement of cases by court craft etc. Apparently the belligerent lawyers lobby proved stronger.
4. Writ jurisdiction of high courts has to be excluded by bringing COPRA under Article 323B of the constitution as their interference, particularly the Calcutta High Court, delays the proceedings especially when an hierarchy of appeals is provided under COPRA where the Supreme Court is the ultimate arbiter.
5. Empowering Consumer Courts by giving them the authority to order cease and desist, or interim injunction or take suo motto action (of its own accord and on its own information) like the MRTP Commission, so as to meet the ends of justice have not been incorporated. For, bureaucrats felt that it would give unbridled power to over 450 district fora and 30 state commissions and that would have created havoc.

Some readers might remember the case of ITC LTD's Wills brand being injuncted by a Gangtok district judge, which cost ITC a large sum of money to get it vacated from the Supreme Court under its extraordinary jurisdiction. This type of case is a freak but without such power our consumer courts will be hamstrung in protecting the consumers interest, as it were.

Section 1(4) of COPRA says this Act will apply to all goods and services, therefore under the definition of services, where illustrations are given, it was understood that it was an all inclusive definition and exclusions had to be specified. To correct the anomaly, especially in view of the hectic lobbying by the medical fraternity and other professional groups, it was proposed to put a semi-colon, and add, "not limited to" before the illustrations. But this has also not been inserted in the amendment bill.

Recalling Unsafe Goods

So much so for the bureaucratic revenge and/or sabot-age. However there are many welcome steps, though confused as well, which will take the consumer movement considerably forward. These are:

- Enhancement in the scope of relief under COPRA to stop the sale of and/or order withdrawing the marketing of hazardous goods. This will entitle consumers and consumer groups to challenge harmful goods, provided a law says so, like the BVO case when this toxic chemical was banned but continued to be used in soft drinks like Limca, Gold Spot etc.

But the clause does not empower consumers to challenge hazards in services. For instance the Electricity Act provides for certain safety measures to be adopted by the suppliers, but consumers may not be able to challenge it. This is more so surprising when in all the consumer rights in COPRA 'services' have been added along with 'goods', and under the relief section power has also been given to consumer courts to remove defects and deficiencies in services.

- A major beneficial change has been added to cover agreements for purchase, as against the earlier pro-vision for only goods or services actually purchased. This would cover disputes relating to booking of flats, cars, scooters and similar contracts, where delivery has not been made.
- Restrictive trade practices have been added, also enabling the courts to stop these, as well as unfair trade practices. This means that there would be a mini-MRTP Commission in every district.
- Monetary jurisdiction of a district forum has been raised to Rs. 5 lakh, while that of a state commission to Rs. 20 lakh. Beyond this, the National Commission. Age limit of the members of the state commissions has been fixed at 67, while that of the national commission at 70. No mention of the age limits of members of the district forums.

Complaints against goods purchased for commercial purpose will ordinarily not be adjudicable under COPRA save and except where such goods in dispute have been purchased by a self-employed business-person like a taxi owner-driver.

Costs would be awardable to consumers or their organisations that win cases. Simultaneously consumers who file frivolous or vexatious complaints could be penalised with a fine of up to Rs 10,000. And if they don't pay up, they could face a worse fate of paying a further fine of up to Rs 10,000 and/or undergo imprisonment of up to three years like other offenders.

Following the Supreme Court order, in the Common Cause Vs Union of India case, administrative control of district fora will now be under the state commissions, who will in turn report to the National Commission. A proper reporting system and procedures will also be incorporated.

Lastly, a quiet change has been incorporated to redefine the department of civil supplies as consumer affairs, which is what we in the consumer movement have been shouting for a long time.

RIGHTS AND RESPONSIBILITIES OF CONSUMER

Liberalization is paving way for a market-driven economy, where the manufacturers seek to maximise profits. Manufacturers are not often concerned about the quality of goods and services and their impact on the health of people and the environment. Instead of the consumer guiding the producer about what should be produced, it is the producer who decides what the consumer should want. The plight of a consumer is further worsened by the use of advertising techniques.

Consumers are saddled with the problem of choosing between too many products with too less information. With the concentration of market in the hands of a few large corporations, it becomes important that the consumers are aware of their rights in order to ensure proper standards for the goods and services for which they make payment. There are many goods which are sold in the market without much information about their quality, quantity and purity. In case of goods meant for mass consumption like, food, milk products, edible oil etc. the ingredients are not known.

Manufacturers or producers seldom follow the safety regulations in the products like, lamps, batteries, footwear, electrical equipments, wires, cement, LPG cylinders, stoves, switches, plugs, sockets etc. leading to many fatal accidents. Adulteration of food is another major problem. Milk can contain detergent, refined oil, caustic soda or urea. Mustard oil can be adulterated with argemone oil and arhar dal with yellow colour. Vegetables and fruits are artificially coloured. Indis-criminate use of pesticides by farmers and untreated ef-fluents by industries, have led to the problem of food contamination by pesticide residues and toxic heavy metals. Although in Kautilya's *Arthashastra*, strict rules were set for the trade and industry and punishments for exploitation were prescribed. But, there was no organised and systematic movement safeguarding the interests of the consumers in India. Rampant food shortages, hoarding, black marketing, adulteration of food and edible oil gave birth to the consumer movement in an organized form in the sixties.

Consumers started voicing their concerns and demanding better products and services. Till mid seventies, consumer organisations were largely engaged in writing articles and holding exhibitions. They formed consumer groups to work on the malpractices in ration shops and overcrowding in the road passenger transport. The eighties witnessed an upsurge in the number of consumer groups. The battle for consumer protection has to be fought by many agencies.

The Government has to play an important role, by enacting suitable laws and enforcing them effectively. India has been observing 15th March since 1989 as the National Consumers' Day. This day has a historic impor-tance as it was on this day in 1962, that the Bill for Consumer Rights was moved in the US Congress. Steps have been taken by the Government of India by way of enactment of various Acts and other measures to help consumers. Indian Penal Code, Standards of Weights and Measures Act, Motor Vehicle Act, are some of the Acts. Despite these Acts, the fact remains that very little could be achieved in the field of consumer protection.

A major breakthrough came during 1986 when Parliament passed a law for Consumer Protection Act -1986. Three-tier quasi-judicial machinery at the district, state and national levels was set up with a view to provide speedy and simple redressal to consumer disputes. The District Forum deals with the cases involving claims up to Rs. 20 lakhs, the State Commission between Rs.20 lakhs to one crore and the National Commission deals with the cases involving claims exceeding Rs. one crore.

The objective of the consumer courts is to ensure speedy justice to the con-sumers against various malpractices and negligence without involving any cost, as no court fees is charged. Consumer courts have been set up as special courts, as it was expensive and time consuming to get justice through civil courts. The Consumer Protection Act, which has been defined as "the Magna Carta of Consumers", spells out six consumer rights: Right to Safety, Right to Information, Right to Choice, Right to Representation, Right to Redress, and Right to Consumer Education. India has the biggest consumer movement today due to the efforts of consumer organisations and the establishment of consumer courts. India is the only country in the world which has exclusive courts for consumer redressal.

This has been internationally praised including the developed countries. The Consumer Protection Act (COPRA) has succeeded in bringing about fair play in the supply of goods and services to a large extent. The Act applies to almost all goods and services. Still, the present scenario is not very encouraging. Unfortunately the consumer courts have become replica of legal courts, as the procedure is no longer simple and quick. The consumer redressal process is relatively cumbersome and more expensive and time- consuming than desired. The process involves engaging a professional personnel, requires time for filing the case and attending the court proceeding and certain other formalities like producing the bill, warranty cards etc. These procedures need to be made simpler and quicker for making the process more meaningful and realistic.

Consumers have the social responsibility of exposing the manufacture/supplier or the service provider for resorting to illegal trade practices. Unethical notings like "Goods once sold will never be taken back" are in sharp contrast to the practice in some of the developed countries, where the sellers declare, "In case you are not fully satisfied with our product, you can bring the same to us within a month for either replacement or return of your money." This is the result of consumer consciousness. Consumers have to realize their role and importance. The consumer movements can be winner movements only with our active involvement by knowing our rights and enforcing them. It requires a voluntary effort involving the participation of one and all. If the consumers remain passive, they will continue to be exploited. It is necessary that consumers take action with solidarity to get a fair deal and timely redressal. An alert consumer is a safe consumer.

CONSEQUENCES OF "IDEAL" CONSUMER BEHAVIOURS AND ETHNO MARKETING

The Cultural Dimension of Marketing

According to new tendencies viewing marketing as a social process, a broad epistemological trend supported by the relativistic paradigm has emerged. Culture has been recognized as the main backstage where consumption behaviours are assumed and where certain products have acquired a particular symbolism. As a result, beyond instrumental, sociological, social, mutual benefice exchanges and strategic, administrative and market engineering considerations, a tendency in the academic and research community worldwide to think about marketing in a cultural framework has emerged in the last few decades. In contrast with the one-country paradigm, this propensity suggests that societies are sub culturally determined to a large extent and that almost all countries consist of distinct subcultures (Japan, is an exception).

In fact, the past 20 years have witnessed increasing interest in cross-cultural differences between ethnic groups and their implications for marketing strategy using ethnicity and culture as segmentation criteria. Apart from some research in multicultural Australia, very little has been done to conceive and develop the marketing process in countries with cultural diversity in their historical traditions. There is a lack of cultural marketing studies in the majority of Latin American countries, where there is a convergence of native, African and European ancestry with different shades and mixture). Faced with the necessity mainly experienced by small and medium size organisations to incorporate culture in their process of conception, implementation and control of marketing activities as an organisational philosophy, ethno marketing has emerged as an alternative approach.

Reaffirming marketing's contextual character, in which culture is assumed to conduct and guide the entrepreneurial success, the main ethno-marketing characteristics are presented. First, ethno-marketing's principal features are described emphasizing its four epistemological foundations: ethnicity, ethno consumerism, cultural dimensions of markets, and marketing-oriented organisational culture. Second, postulates of ethno marketing are mentioned. Third, ethno marketing strategic matrix elements are shown, highlighting the three marketing functions to be fulfilled: to comprehend consumers, to conquer customers and conserve clients. Fourth, ethno marketing and organisational relationship are formulated. Fifth, ethno marketing and ethnography's mutual influences are stipulated. Sixth, the main strengths of ethno marketing are presented. Seventh, some ethno marketing research implications are suggested.

Ethno marketing begins by recognizing culture as the frame and the essence driving contemporary businesses. In the same context, consumer behaviour, organisation decisions and the market dynamism in which an enterprise develops its activities, are analyzed under cultural dimensions. Anthropological and ethnographic contributions characterizing consumption cultures are also considered. Under the revealing lens of culture with all its symbolic charges printed over human conduct, consumers, customers, clients, entrepreneurs, employees, government agents, intermediaries, and artifacts, products and mutual benefice exchanges, ethno marketing discovers the hidden predominant values and beliefs supported by an in-depth underlying world located at the heart of our cultural roots. Under the former cultural approach, it is plausible to accept marketing as a cultural expression rather than a technical one. Products (artifacts) are exchanged (marketed) between persons.

Products are charged with symbolic meanings installed in the culturally constituted world. Consumers, customers, and clients (market demand agents) are linked to entrepreneurs, employees, and competitors (supply market agents) through agents and distributors (intermediary market agents), regulated by persons who work for private and public institutions (regulation market agents). All of them act as human beings, rather than commercial beings, prompted by their values and beliefs, and by their deeper underlying world. In this sense, ethno marketing has been visualized as the social process in which, from the point of view of the human groups, it conceives and implements the three main functions of marketing: to comprehend consumers, to conquer customers (buyers) and to conserve clients. Thus, the consumer is a person for whom every product is conceived, the customer is a person who acquires a product, and the client is a person who routinely purchases a product. All of these functions are grouped in a strategic matrix where the dispersed efforts of the modern businesses are accumulated. Ethno marketing is conceived as marketing for homogeneous ethnic groups under the great cultural diversity that characterizes current cultures.

Accepting this revolutionary and irreverent way of seeing the fundamentals of marketing, ethno marketing breaks the traditional and ancient marketing view from the classic marketing mix approach into thousands of fragments (4 P's model). Under that old marketing concept much damage has been caused both to businesses and academic worlds when trying to reduce marketing processes to a universal formula with superficial variations in its four main ingredients, without paying enough attention to the radical adjustments having to do with considering current competitive surroundings. The ethno marketing proposal has been supported on four central grounds: first, the extensive debate around the historical-temporal ethnicity construct with two sets of principles operating within every human group: the inclusionary-exclusionary principle, and the difference-identity principle; second, Ethno consumerism understood as the study of consumption from the point of view of the social group or cultural group that is the object of study; third, markets' cultural dimensions where objects, norms and exchange parts acquire meaning only within a certain culture, and fourth, market oriented organisational cultures (MOOC model) in which marketing assumes a prominent role as the main axis of every enterprise strategy, as supported in different prior work.

Ethnicity

Several approaches developed in the social sciences involving ethnic topics are vast and complex, although from a marketing point of view in-depth anthropological and sociological perspectives on ethnicity as a social phenomenon are preferred. Thus, ethnicity is a concept of individual and group identity that "embraces differences identified by color, language, religion or some attributes of common origin". As a theoretical construct ethnicity has acquired a central position in cultural studies establishing separate status for people operating within differentiated groups. Despite the undeniable importance that ethnicity has gained in marketing, there are still some questions about who defines it and what its borders are.

Several researchers affirm that the basis of ethnicity is self-identification of the members mediated by the per-ception of the others. From a marketing perspective most of the ethnicity studies deal with ethnicity as a complex social structure wherein the distinct ethnic values of a group are linked to consumer behaviour. The majority of these studies involve ethnic groups living in developed country markets. Often these studies deal with processes of acculturation. Within the marketing discipline, literature, training, and epistemological paradigms, the focus is on learning to assess what is, in fact, culturally relevant outside the researcher's own culture. As a result, much of the litera-ture has tended to be parochial and/ or ethnocentric in its perspective.

Ethno Consumerism

Putting together cultural, social, and individual aspects under the same analytical framework, Venkatesh (1995) the "Ethno consumerism" construct is proposed. It is conceived as the study of consumption from the point of view of the social group or the cultural group to which one belongs. This new paradigm about consumer behaviour uses theoretical categories originated within a given culture. Ethno consumerism is envisioned as the study of consumption from the point of the cultural order in question, using categories of behaviour and thought that are native to the culture. Ethnos means nation and people, and consumerism is used in the classical sense of consumption as a set of cultural practices. Consumerism is not to be mistaken for concepts such as consumer activism, consumer rights, and so forth.

Ethno consumerism follows the intellectual traditions of comparative methods and cross-cultural studies, but it differs from existing versions of these studies in several aspects. Ethno consumerism is not a method, as the others tend to be, although cross-cultural comparisons can and must be made. Ethno consumerism begins with basic cultural categories of a given culture and studies the actions, the practices, the words, the thoughts, the language, the institutions, and the interconnect-ions between these cate-gories. After reviewing many research experiences developed by several ethnic and cross-cultural studies, Ethno consumerism forces the researcher to contemplate the person not as an individual but as a cultural being, as being a part of a culture, a subculture and other group affiliations. Ethno consumerism combines the study of the consumer with value systems, symbolic beliefs systems, rituals and daily practices.

All of them are intertwined in a holistic consumer vision. The Ethno consumerism approach has several levels:

1. The study of the cultural level (symbolic and beliefs systems and, norms and ritualistic practices).
2. The study of the social level (social organisation, social institutions, etc.).
3. The study of the individual level (personality, cognition, behaviour, mental constructs, etc).

CULTURAL DIMENSIONS OF MARKETS

Undoubtedly postmodern thought yields ideas that help to foster a better understanding of markets; in particular, of the dynamism of markets, and the interplay between firms and their environments on which this dynamism is based. The basic ideas of postmodernism are that the individual does not have an autonomous con-sciousness but needs communicative interaction with others to develop his or her own identity; that meanings are not given prior to communication but arise from it and are context-dependent; that there is no universal and permanent meaning, but at best only a local and temporary unity of meaning and consensus on the rules of the game, which are continually broken and shifted in an ongoing process of differentiation and change. Under this approach the markets are like processes in continual construction and must be seen from the perspective of assigning meaning to the objects in the exchange process (commodification and decommodification), to exchange parties (markets social imaginary), and to the norms of market exchanges.

- Cultural construction of objects of market exchange. Although this process tends to be taken for granted by economists and some economic sociologists, the goods and services that can legitimately be sold in markets vary widely both historically and cross-culturally. These products have suffered cultural commodification or decommodification processes from their original conception. This legitimating social process differs among the different existing cultures in the world and corresponds unequivocally to values, beliefs, and dominant cultural assumptions. It is conceivable that the execution of this process of meaning assigned to a product – a good, service, or idea – by the set of people who use it, maintains a narrowly prescribed relation with the predominant cultural patterns. It has to be understood that this legitimating social process is related to the cultural dynamics in which these products are situated. Likewise, the existence of a series of symbols in the culturally constituted world, allows marketing professionals to define some of the symbols to be used to introduce, conserve, or take a product out from the market.

- Cultural construction of parties to market exchange-Spillman has labeled this social construction process of creating meaning by the parties to market exchange: "The social imaginary of the market". Contrary to the general thought and practice on marketing, it suggests that transactions are not carried out by the individual alone but within groups (organisational, corporations, sections, nations, families, committees of purchases, for example) or by people who represent a given group. Most importantly, but simultaneously less recognized, is the ranking that traditionally has been assigned to this social imaginary of the "other" as the counterpart to the transaction in the market. These potential counterparts can be implicitly or explicitly delimited by geographic, demographic, ethnic, or racial aspects, as well as gender, nationality, and based on existing social networks and social classes. In regard to social classes, perhaps this is the most used marketing category through the well-known concept of social mobility with which potential "others" can acquire those products that symbolically allow them to see themselves as becoming better, almost as being part of a more elevated social class with more privileges and with greater refinement. This is a component of Veblen's conspicuous consumption (emulation).

- Cultural construction of norms of exchange - This construction refers to the interpretation of the norms as well as to the ways in which, formally or informally, these norms are judged or used to sanction or to award someone. Specifically it refers to that which is con-sidered "natural" in a given market as well as to those things that symbolize success and failure. Typically within a market exchange activities should be charac-terized as a clear competition between buyers and salesmen. These parties to the same transaction within lucrative organisations are directly related to market agents who interpret and evaluate any transactions carried out under the social protection of such rules. What is implied by this prescriptive optics is that through the prizes and punishments scheme it is possible to construct rules that impose and establish the limits of every executed transaction. It is expected that rituals associated with such norms of behaviour symbolize this regulation of conduct and human acts. These norms, in their turn, have been stereotyped by people who use and practice them, and also come to be seen as laws of implacable application within which no opposing claims are permitted. Market agents' behaviours–supply, demand, regulation, and inter-mediation– are watched by society members who in an open or a hidden way are in charge of fortifying and defending them.

MARKET ORIENTED ORGANISATIONAL CULTURES

Studying organisational culture as a source of sustained competitive advantages, Barney analyzed such cultures as a valuable, rare and imperfectly imitable resource. Consequently, the implementation of a specific organisational culture can become a source of superior sustained financial performance for the organisation that manages, consolidates and maintains it. Among the modern forms of organisational cultures emerge those with a specific market orientation, suggesting that a business with an increased understanding of market requirements can improve its global performance. It seems to be clear that during the development of the change processes carried out within any organisation symbols can acquire new and potential idiosyncratic connotations. These symbols like language, besides being itself an inte-grating force of values and beliefs and expressions and forms to make things, allow that every member of any organisation shares strategies, processes, and policies. It is for that reason why it becomes essential to construct a common language among the employees with respect to which a market oriented organisational culture implies in contrast to which traditionally has been believed.

To establish a market orientation within an organisational culture is related, definitively, to the implementation of the marketing concept in the whole organisation. In other words, trying to create or to drive a market-oriented organisational culture implies efforts to instill the marketing concept as always present in every functional unit that comprises the organisation. This means that in order to be successful, a market oriented organisation needs to construct long term relationships, implementing strategies that allow potential consumers to be converted into loyal clients, one of the essential postulates of the marketing concept. In order to achieve this state of client loyalty, an organisation must have a close knowledge of its counter-parts' needs in each of the different moments in which the organisation builds exchange relationships: before (pre-transactional exchange), during (transactional exchange) and after (post -transactional exchange) the process is executed.

Accepting the former approach, any market-oriented organisation must operate by considering the three components of behaviour–client, competition, and inter-functional coordination–, and the two decision criteria–long term and profitability– that characterize all kinds of market orientation. Thus a market oriented organisational culture is defined as "a set of behaviours, myths, rites, rituals, symbols, beliefs, assumptions, and mainly values, that allow the organisation to place the client in the center of its activities, to know its present and future competitors, to coordinate suit- ably its internal activities, to make the decisions in a long term perspective and not to forget its agreed profitability according to its own plans and needs previously determined".

Postulates of Ethno Marketing

Within the framework of uncertainties and multiple paths to cope with the consumer, ethno marketing (as a discipline of thought and organisational action in which culture, understood from an anthropological and an ethnographic perspectives) and is taken as an overwhelming mechanism that stimulates and answers commercial relationships and produces almost unconquerable market segments. It is supported on the following postulates:

- Marketing conception and practice are inscribed in the relativistic scientific paradigm, in open opposition to - not complementary with - the positivistic paradigm predominant in current marketing schools. That is, marketing, as a discipline has a contextual character and the validity of its truth depends completely on detected, analyzed, and interpreted environmental conditions. The essence of any context is totally determined by patterns and dominant cultural schemes.
- The 11 postulates of Ethno marketing are ratified:
    a. Two systems conform the marketing system: one, is the study, analysis and interpretation of the organisational surroundings, and the other, the definition and implementation of the strategies and the programs in concordance with such reality;
    b. The marketing study object are the mutual benefits of exchange between company and market;
    c. Consumer sovereignty prevails;
    d. Consumers need to have freedom and in making decisions are driven to choose the best alternative;

e. Companies must make attractive, differentiated and competitive offerings so consumers can exert their freedom of election;

f. Consumption precedes to purchase act-occasional or repetitive;

g. Desires put dynamism into demand and are their permanent motor;

h. Market segmentation is a marketing imperative not a strategy of discretionary usage;

i. Information is the raw material for decision making;

j. Service is inherent to marketing and finally,

k. Marketing's final mission is to construct permanent relationships with clients.

- The market structure formed by the different market agents involves demand (consumers, customers, clients), supply (organisations, competitors), inter-mediaries (agents, distributors), and regulation (public and private institutions).
- Products - goods, services, and ideas, convey a high symbolic meaning.
- Anthropology, with its most recognized method, ethnography, is the social science most capable of comprehending, conquering, and conserving partici-pant market agents.
- Market research must be supported on diverse methodologies where the consumer can be contemplated in natural scenes. Participant observation, in-depth interviews, hidden client techniques, consumption vestiges analysis, and film or audio registers, among other data compilation techniques, can be used.
- Consumption phenomena that form symbolic meanings rather than merely functional ones must be the starting point of any marketing effort.
- Any entrepreneurial organisation must have a clear and powerful market oriented organisational culture to create superior values for the client.

- Marketing's basic functions are synthesized in the three strategic foundations to reach organisational objectives: to comprehend consumers, to conquer customers, and to conserve clients. The consumer comprehending process is to contemplate, to collect, to categorize, to calculate, and to characterize them. The customer conquest process includes to coincide, to coordinate, to compete, to communicate, and to allocate all the organi-sational efforts.

The client conservation process aims to consult, to classify, to consent, to cultivate, and to consolidate relation-ships with them.

- Market segmentation identification processes should be conducted under a symbolic perspective approach in which authentic consumption reasons are factors that envision potential consumers groups rather than relying on demographic, geographical, or socioeconomic bases.
- As human beings, consumers belong to different market segments at the same time in relation to a given category of product.
- Organisational communication must assure that it is aimed at a specific market segment, hopefully in a one by one relationship.
- Enormous organisational efforts should be made to build efficient and dynamic market information systems.
- Market audits must be practiced routinely within any organisation.

ETHNO MARKETING STRATEGIC MATRIX

Next, using culture with all its complexities rooted in tradition and the history of each market as an airdrop platform, the ethno marketing strategic matrix (ESM) is presented. It is expected that this ESM will become an ordered, systematic, and coherent body of knowledge with which to practically face the typical consumption phenomenon of our present societies. There are three fundamental functions in the ESM that must be undertaken from marketing perspective in order to be successful in terms of reaching the objectives of mutual benefits for the organisation and its markets. These benefits must be established in order to achieve permanent exchange relations-hips. To facilitate greater recall and memorization of the 15 activities to be carried out, they have been synthesized in a 15 C's matrix, five for each of marketing principal functions. That is, this is the most fundamental ethno marketing function related to the processes of comprehending consumers and utilizing the most effective sources of market intelligence that allow us to decide on a strategic course, and develop tactical plans to be implemented.

Later, and armed with the information with which tastes, preferences, and consumption trends were comprehend, the entire organisation must get ready for conquering customers (buyers), who at that time are being attacked by all classes of attractive and differentiated market suppliers. In order to close the marketing cycle that will serve as starting point for the new one. The central preoccupation is focused on the client conservation function either by adjustments to the given offerings, or by client requests, or simply, because of client loyalty. Is vital for the organi-sational survival within current scenes of competition so competed as those we are living in this moment. Let us see in detail each one of these functions and the activities that ethno marketing proposes.

Comprehend Consumers

Support for consumer sovereignty is one of the key postulates that ethno- marketing recognizes. This first function, is related to the necessity to comprehend consumers without any excuses. Consumption profiles, consumption trends, tastes, and preferences, for instance, should be deeply known. Based on contemplation of con-sumption phenomena, expressions, contexts, and rituals, it will be possible to know consumers, to categorize them, to calculate them, and mainly to characterize future marketing strategies and programs to be implemented to satisfy their most in-depth yearnings. Understanding consumers must be translated into clear and convincing explanations of the human complexities facing consumers. With this information it is possible to draw up the path to transform these consumers into clients who are the end target of all organisational efforts in the market.

Thus, the different consumption types inherent to this era will have to be made apparent, and their motivations enlightened by the ethno marketing approach will need to be conceived in order to attend and service the human groups–ethnic groups. For instance, profane and sacred consumption must accurately be delimited in order to discover if the profane or the sacred has prevailed in certain social circles. Emulation-based consumption also will have to be defined in terms of the insistent imitation processes of certain public people located in the superior layers of the society that many potential consumers carry out. The materialism thought to be typical of these times will also have to be considered given the remarkable influence that it has in the acquisition of certain type of products (luxury products, vehicles, jewelry) mainly those of greater social visibility which make them a self-extension. Things are not as they are; they are as we are. Possessions as a way to reaffirm many consumers' personalities. For these consumers life turns around those things that can be acquired, and through these things they attempt to be seen as successful individuals and consequently worthy to be emulated.

This, too, must be considered. Similarly, consumption rituals must clearly be identified in terms of artifacts used, learned and faithfully repeated scripts, roles to be fulfilled, and the intended audiences for the which role is being executed. Likewise, it is indispensable to find the con-nection cultural values–terminal values– through which consumers try to materialize their consumption objectives, and those product attributes with which consumers assume that their expectations can be satisfied. Executing the five activities associated with the initial function to comprehend consumers in their own context corresponds to pre-transactional exchanges of expectations by consumption profiles typical of this phase. The following activities must be implemented:

- Contemplate- The complexity of expressed human behaviour in the form of consumption is so deep that any orthodox approach is insufficient to explain it. The consumption symbolism translated into behaviours that are not always appreciated at first glance demands audacity and risk to break with traditional forms in order to conte-mplate consumers in their own realities. To develop a singular task, it emerges that consumer contemplation processes do not from a passive and distant attitude in which the researcher involvement does not exist. On the contrary, based on human nature that tends to hide such behaviour that can hurt individual images built in human relationships, it is necessary to use anthropological methods, particularly the ethnographical. Doing so, it is possible to study human beings in their complex dimensions with the deliberate intention to decipher the most recondite aspects of their personality. Participant observation, non-participant observation, in-depth interviews, hidden client techniques, film or audio recordings, and even analysis of vestiges –such as sweepings– have arisen as powerful alternatives to scrutinize, sometimes in the shadows, hidden consumer behaviours relegated to the subconscious world, avoiding discovery.
- Collect- As a result of the contemplation process there appears an urgent necessity to know consumers in all their confused and particular human dimensions. For doing so, ethno marketing proposes the continual adding of information from highly diverse sources. Imagination and creativity to find this kind of information are needed and may require access to different archives and diverse official and private databases. The usage of different information systems is recommended, such as reading general or specialized newspapers and magazines, revision of some native films, even some stories presented on T.V where certain lifestyles are is characterized, information transmitted through other mass media, T.V commercials, adver-tising advises, radio spots, formal

and informal conversation with experts or consumers of products under study or substitutes, and so on.

- Categorize- Equipped with all the collected information taken from secondary or primary sources, the ethno marketing is ready for looking for those mechanisms that allow grouping consumers into compatible categories, toward which it is possible to direct mar-keting efforts the company considers advisable. In other words, consumers belong to different segments entering or leaving them according to the particular consumption symbolism they seek. These situational segments should be accurately identified. It is possible to utilize different instruments to analyze the available information. From the most refined multivariate tech-niques to find statistically significant differences involving measured variables, to intuition and intros-pection process is carried out by the marketing decision maker/manager, transformed into the means to analyze, to interpret and consequently, to recommend the strategic path to be followed. Categorizing discovered groups; it will be possible to concentrate all the organi-sational potentialities to differentially serve each identified market segment.
- Calculate- Accepting that the ultimate goal of any marketing effort is to obtain profits –the essence of a capitalist system– it is essential to measure the market to know the volume of potential transactions. Here, the attempt is to be concrete, to have enough information, and to define a marketing strategy. In order to obtain this measurement it is necessary to determine each market segment size in terms of potential demand and current consumption volumes, to establish the amount of the market that is being served by diverse supply agents, and primarily to measure either the actual company market share or its target penetration. This need "to measure all that is susceptible to be measured," (misestimates) the insights that are provided by the relativist epistemological approach in which ethno marketing is enrolled with respect to the assumed disdain for the quantitative aspects that comprise

human behaviour. It is clear that no marketing strategy can be sustained in the long sun without having absolute clarity of the company market position, its competitors, the market size, and mainly the market portion that is being taken care of by the whole sector in which the company is involved.

- Characterize- Having collected data about tastes, desires, preferences, tendencies and in the consumption phenomena market segments to be taken care of, market size, and sector and target shares, ethno marketers have all of the judgmental elements needed to determine the strategy and marketing programs to implement. Diverse scenarios and different alternatives that imply acting in each of them, the human, financial, administrative and marketing resources demanded will then have to be brought to bear. It is here when organisational abilities and capacities that are put into action to delineate the way to "walk the walk" as well as potential difficulties that can impede reaching its goals.

This is a crucial time since the company faces the obligation to make decisions with respect to the markets to be take care of, and to the business in which it wants to participate. In this sense, it is important to understand the role of the border definition –ample or narrow– because it is going to limit the market to pursue. This crucial definition has many critical consequences. Competitors and the business in which the company is going to unfold all its potentialities depend on it. For instance, if the company decides to be within the general transport sector –including all types– or if it prefers to be within a narrower sector or within interregional passengers, the business scenarios will be different. According to this definition competitive forces that are to be faced and the level of confrontation demanded in order to comprehend consumers and turn them into clients will be identified.

Conquer Customers

Inspired by several marketing postulates that serve as conceptual nourishment to the ethno marketing approach, this function is related to the conquest of customers (buyers) and emerges as one of the key actions to be undertaken by an organisation that looks for word to maintaining itself in the market in a profitable manner. The urgent necessity to display attractive, dirferentiated, and competitive offerings, in the market so that the consumer has true freedom and will in decisions, an organisation must develop a package of actions that help it to become the best market alternative.

This offering, unlike many, is created not solely by basic products -goods, services, ideas- that are processed; on the contrary, the offering includes the organisation that makes presence in the market as a whole. It is for this reason, supported by the previous consumers' comprehension process, that it is important to make those decisions to be implemented coincident with the detected reality, to coordinate all the areas within the company, to establish the characteristics of potential competitors, to communicate such particularities, and finally to coordinate any offering in the adequate channels in an opportune and profitable way. It is in fulfilling this marketing function that mathematical models appear for the decision-making by marketing engineering professionals. The development of these five activities under ethno marketing's customer conquest framework puts the organisation en route to fulfill the transactional exchange process in which the organisation delivers products and by which it receives profits within pricing politics in return.

- Coincide - This is one of the most critical marketing activities that need to be developed in order to reach the organisational objectives. Experience has demonstrated the tragic inconsistency between known, studied, analyzed, and interpreted data with respect to the decisions made. Making all those detected realities concordant with the strategic program executed, it is possible to avoid wasting organisational efforts in constructing exhaustive and detailed situational diagnoses that are almost never considered in the mar-keting strategy formulation and implementation process. With the accomplishment of this activity it is desirable to connect the circumstances of the surroundings with the decisions implemented. That is, the essence of marketing is to find a clear answer according to market expectations.

- Coordinate- Following the same path to consistently link the detected market information with strategy and programs to be implemented, a market-oriented organisational culture must be built within a company interested in reaching its ethno marketing goals. Inside that organisat-ion a set of values, beliefs, and some work assumptions created around the development of superior values for the client must prevail atmospheres and organisational climates in which rituals, informal networks of information, heroes, and actions linked to the socialization, and stimuli processes should be created with thought given to fostering pro-social behaviours. This means encouraging certain cultural practices (improvement of labor conditions for those employees who have better relations with clients) around companies' intentions to work with the clients, for the clients, and by the clients.
- Compete- Facing the unquestionable freedom and will that consumers have to prefer one of the multiple products that are offered in the market, the company must know clearly that in the business arena it will be in front of a series of competing forces that also fight to win the potential consumer's pocket. For that reason, without remaining exclusively watching itself in the mirror of the present and potential competitors, the organisation must have the ability not only to identify them–directly or indirectly, but also know them in their trajectories, entrepreneurial spirit, strengths and weaknesses, strategies, programs, and in their daily activities.
- Communicate- These same competition levels per-ceived in each market segment, induce not only designing supplies competitively superior to those of the competition but also communicating them in an efficient form. It should be ascertained whether all of messages

be delivered to the market target actually arrive. It is advisable to know at which corners of national or international geography the messages are arriving. In this sense, the different forms and the different means used have to guarantee that the audience towards which the competitive and attractive supply has been offered is receiving the message without obstacles or barriers. On this matter, the traditional and wasteful formula of emitting a series messages to by channels of which little is known about their true impact must be discarded even though advertising professionals and communication agencies assert the opposite.

- Collocate- It is here where a good part of the efforts directed at accomplishing the two first functions of ethno marketing takes place. Having understood consumers in the specific surroundings in which they live, and established the strategy in concordance with the detected market data and with the internal forces, everything is prepared to implement all activities so carefully planned to this point. To place the offering does not mean anything more than to execute all of the directed activities to start up the organisational operation, beginning with distribution to gain greater impact. The channels planning process in which the brokers are going to fulfill their intermediation role between the company and the market emerges here.

Conserve Clients

Guided by the financial precept that it is cheaper conserving clients than conquering new ones, ethno-markering proposes the idea of structuring a package of activities conceived to retain and to maintain those people who have somehow been in contact with the organisation or a part of it. In doing so, it is suggested that most of the organisational resources should be devoted to creating internal systems that guarantee to consult, to classify, to consent, to cultivate, but mainly to consolidate the relation-ship with the clients. All of these activities under the permanent feedback philosophy that characterizes organi-sations, are intended to facilitate the enterprise policy to adjust and to fit the chosen strategic path or, at least, to look for optimum ways to avoid wasting resources in useless enterprise actions. To implement this set of activities means in one way or another to make specific the ethnomarkering function rooted in the mutual benefits exchange looked for in the post-transactional phase where satisfaction is given in order to receive in return the loyalty of clients forever.

- Consult- Among the activities more widely accepted by persons interested in doing business although unfortunately the least practiced ones in real terms, is to investigate true attitudes assumed by current clients. And this is worse when in spite of knowing complaints, reclamation, and exigencies formulated by the clients, they are then sent to visit all the company areas (for instance through transferred telephone calls) or are simply the ignored. The attempt here is to test com-pany's ability to listen to the market voice, particularly to its specific market segment it has targeted. Imple-menting schemes of marketing audits that watch the fulfillment of the elaborated plans and programs, allows the creation of systems that guarantee to gather input from this restlessness and expectations.
- Classify- It would be absurd and quite myopic not to understand that one of the intentions to consult clients, is to classify them in order to analyze the possibility of consenting, cultivating, and mainly consolidating the relationship with these clients. This qualifying activity can be developed in varied forms. It is possible to have clients grouped by different loyalty levels based on the number of times periods those clients repeat their purchase in certain. It is also necessary to analyze the character of the product and its perishable nature. With this criterion, loyalty degrees can be established: completely loyal, moderately loyal, and intermittently loyal clients, for instance. Likewise, it is possible to use other equally important criteria. For example, depe-nding

on their proximity to company former clients can be seen as present, lost, recoverable and non-recoverable clients.

- Consent- Having clarity about groups and the content of their complaints, it is obligatory to create the conditions to start a recovery plan, for example, of those people who had contact with the company in a given time. The decision must be compelling and accurate. The policies must make some processes flexible empowering employees who are going to be related to those clients who occasionally have been hurt by some company decisions and some organisational conveniences. The doors of the dialogue, the assumption of mistakes, and the payment of indemnification –if there is place for them– must characterize this rational activity conceived to conserve clients.
- Cultivate- A great deal of the transparent spirit re-flecting a true vocation in serving and protecting the client interests involves an organisation understanding some key realities. Every action carried out will be reflected on in the long run. Those permanent mutual benefit exchanges today surely will be the "culture broth" of future relationships for those involved. The clients' cultivation must be fed by an enterprise policy conceived to surprise the clients, giving them something unexpected, but which stimulates them in unimaginable dimensions.
- Consolidate - Structuring an adequate ethno marketing program to conserve clients must include all the necessary mechanisms to feed these relationships to consolidate loyalty and attachment to the company, its programs, and its brands. This process of consolidation must put particular emphasis on long run relationships to be established with different market agents, especially with those on the demand side. It must be accepted that the ultimate goal of ethno marketing is to look for potential consumers through developing the comprehension function until transforming them into clients to be conserved until having

someday conquered them like customers.

This consolidation process seems to close the infinite circle of consumer-customer-client-consumer. This is possible if a company as a whole can consolidate its relation-ships with the remaining market agents. Having developed the three different and complementary ethno marketing functions, it is clear that we are attempting to rescue what classic thinkers of modern administration as Peter Drucker affirmed with respect to the importance of creating clients, as the only reason of being of any organisation. This former way of thinking, characterized by challenging the entire organisation to comprehend the market, conquer it, and conserve it satisfactorily for everybody, has impelled this intellectual effort. Putting together a series of reflections in regard to marketing's professional job in spite of making it more complex has rendered it simplified by the enormous technological advances.

This undoubtedly one the most relevant ethno marketing contribution. In the 1940's, experts coping with the ENIAC computer -more than 30 kilos of weight and more than 18,000 vacuum tubes- elaborated a general and quite wrong prognoses with respect to the future of computers. They never understood the possible system developments around computation advances. As we now know, these systems have allowed us to process and to analyze data and help turn it into useful information. Also, they have facilitated the process of consultation and classification of clients to be consented, cultivated and consolidated for the general welfare of all of the involved people.

Ethno Marketing and Organisation

Taking into consideration the role-played by ethno marketing in this process of revolutionizing and shaking the current organisational structures, this effort would be incomplete if the relationship between this proposal and its effect on the organisation was not considered. Culture has invaded the whole sphere of current businesses without requesting permission from anybody. Its presence is perceived everywhere: In the market where the three culture levels are reflected (artifacts and conduct, values and beliefs, and underlying world), as well as inside the organisation where the cultural patterns prevailing during the life of the company have also been transformed into the dominant ones.

As indicated before, the consumer's comprehension process is developed through its five activities through and the pre-transactional exchange of expectations by consumption profiles takes shape. The customer's conquest process by means of these five activities allows us to make concrete the transactional exchange of products by utilities. And, finally the client's conservation process materializes the post-transactional exchange of satisfaction by loyalty.

Ethno Marketing and Ethnography

Knowing and interpreting consumer behaviour, and entrepreneur is and employees' attitudes from an ethno marketing perspective, signifies seeing humans as social beings and not in the solitary optic according to the pre-dominantly social research tradition. It implies resorting to ethnography in order to analyze the content of human actions attempting to find explanations for evident human irrationalities. This inevitably entails considering marketing from a contextual perspective, as group, cultural and symbolic manifestation to which the consumer belongs and/or has belonged during his/her existence. In this sense, marketing as an expression of a certain culture must be seen from an anthropological and social optic, where beliefs, values, and traditions of participant agents determine the behaviour of individuals who, as cultural beings, participate in the different marketing exchange processes. Starting on detailed and in-depth studies about those determinant factors of human beings' behaviours involved in the marketing process, it is possible to see the true contributions of cultural anthropology and its ethnographic methods to the conception and implementation of marketing postulates within a determined context. And this is possible with the present ethno marketing proposal.

It is assumed that the process of studying, analyzing and interpreting the market environmental reality to give answers to the detected needs, implies in one or another form approaching the cultural surroundings. Consequently, these cultural circumstances could only be approximated by appealing to the ethnographic method of cultural anthropology to reveal the symbolic world that is hidden behind actions and commercial decisions of each studied community. The ethnography from its own epistemological perspective becomes a form not to learn culture but to live it within the perspective to experience it within certain groups according to their socially established and shared norms of conduct. Thus, not only does ethnography establish the context and subjective meaning of the exper-ience of a group of people, it looks for explaining the cultural meanings of this experience in a comparative and interpreted way.

In order to fulfill its assignment, ethnography uses different methods to collect and process data in a full concordance with the clear ethno marketing intentions to give life to the culture and its different ethnic expressions. In order to obtain it the next four characteristics of ethnography guide the practice of the research work of ethnographers and consequently of ethnomarketers:

- To give special primacy to the systematic process of gathering and registering information about human actions in natural settings in which the consumer expresses his/her deeper and rooted socio-cultural patterns.
- To involve the vast and experiential researcher participation in specific cultural contexts, particularly through participant observation.
- To generate interpretations of human behaviour that participants find credible and acceptable.
- To incorporate multiple sources of intelligence in a search to find different approaches to the phenomenon under study, in contrast to pursuing traditional con-vergence in obtained results.

Some Ethno Marketing Strengths

Undoubtedly, it could be affirmed that ethno marketing can be transformed into the clearest expression of a cultural encounter of several worlds that is worth being explored in order to understand the depth of its own complexities. On the one hand, the historical and social antecedents that bring both consumer and entrepreneur appears, and on the other hand traditions and market segments customs in which many agents are all going to encounter in search of the their own satisfaction emerge. Everyone conscious or uncon-sciously is taking part in the permanent exchanges properly planned by the organisations. The advantages to approach marketing with this cultural perspective in mind are quite reasonable because it allows:

- Exploring in greater detail the cultural dimensions of marketing activity.
- Taking sectors like analysis unit with special emphasis in the representation of production in speech and marketing activities.
- Transforming a method of markets research in a source of meaning in the market.
- Considering effects experienced by the development of market activity by marketing professionals.

Some Ethno Marketing Implication in Research

It seems obvious that a revolutionary proposal like ethno marketing will produce a rough shaking movement within traditional views of marketing conceptions and implementation. It is expected that classical ways to approach consumption phenomena and strategic paths to face it, will be changed. Thus, comprehending consumers, conquering customers, and conserving clients should be challenging marketing functions to be carried out under predominant cultural patterns within each market segment. In this sense some implications for marketing research can be mentioned:

- According to the emergent relativistic paradigm in the

contemporary marketing approach, it is necessary to accept the exclusive contextual validity of each conclusion to be obtained from any marketing research effort.

- Culture should not be seen simply as another environmental condition influencing organisational decision-making processes. Rather culture has to be considered as the central issue to be permanently researched in each type of mutual beneficial exchanges carried out between an organisation and the chosen market seg-ments to be served.
- In consumer market research it is necessary to accept consumption symbolism as the main marketing study object which has revolutionized traditional research thinking within the majority of business schools throughout the world.
- If market segmentation is accepted as a contemporary marketing imperative it is necessary to develop marketing efforts to approach the symbolic segmentation identification process.
- During marketing strategy implementation, process market research should be focused on following relationships among the underlying world, values, and beliefs, and conducting an artifact symbolism according to Schein's cultural levels.
- In the post-transaction, marketing function research activity should emphasize the symbolic relationship established between the organisation and its market segments.
- In the post-transaction marketing function research activity should emphasize the symbolic relationship established between the organisation and its market segments.

CROSS-CULTURAL COMPARISON

When the 'World Consumer Day' is celebrated on the 15th of March every year, it's an apt time to pause and review the relationship between consumers and businesses. The discipline of marketing makes consumer the focal point of all business actions and the satisfaction of customer needs has emerged as the holy grail of marketing strategy and a key to marketing success. Customer satisfaction with marketers has been declining over the years and service failures are commonplace, in spite of the increased focus on con-sumer satisfaction. Customer response choices to service failures range from no action to direct complaints to the marketers or even third parties. At times, customers have gone to the internet with their complaints and received worldwide attention. Which of these responses is better from the perspective of the business organisation? While it may appear to the uninitiated, that customer complaints requiring the organisation to expend resources for redressal, are less desirable than 'no action' on the part of the customer, the consensus among the marketing scholars is to the contrary.

Several of these scholars have in fact suggested that organisations must actively encourage customers to complain in case of service failures, as it provides them with yet another opportunity to satisfy customer needs and win their loyalty. An intriguing research question arising out of the service failure-customer complaining behaviour domain concerns the nature of appropriate customer response. Should the customer complain actively and publicly, or, take no action? Even more interestingly, which of these behaviours should be considered 'ideal' from the point of view of the service business organisation?

A few years ago, a Consumer Association in Singapore conducted a contest to identify the 'ideal' consumer, by asking businesses to nominate ideal consumers. The selection of a tourist who chose not to complain when she was stranded in New York City in the middle of the night on her arrival from Singapore, due to a foul-up in her hotel reservation by the travel agency as the ideal consumer, caused some controversy and generated a heated debate regarding the characteristics of an 'ideal' customer. The concept of an 'ideal' state is not alien to the services marketing literature. 'Ideal' expectations or desires which represent the hopes and wishes of the consumers constitute the highest level of customer expectation in the service quality model. Analogously, 'ideal' consumer behaviours are proposed in the present research, as the best, wished for responses of consumers in case of service failures. The available evidence suggests that only a small percentage of unhappy customers complain and that demographic and psychological characteristics of customers play a role in determining their response. The influence of cultural differences on customer complaining behaviour has been examined in recent research. Compared to customers in Singapore, American customers can be expected to be a lot more assertive and likely to launch a complaint in case of a service failure.

The proposed research develops hypotheses relating personal and cultural characteristics to ideal customer behaviours on the basis of prior research in customer complaining behaviour (CCB) and empirically tests them using data collected from the culturally distinct nations of U.S.A. and Singapore. The contributions of this study include the introduction of the concept of 'ideal' customer to the marketing literature and the systematic examination of its antecedents and consequences in a cross-cultural context. On the basis of an extensive review of CCB literature, Singh suggested that in future research, personality/attitudinal characteristics of customers be utilized to explain variations in complaining behaviour among customers. The present research proposes that national differences in complaining behaviour are attributable to cultural variables such as collectivism/individualism. A brief summary of the literature focusing on the consumer responses to service failures and the major cultural and personal characteristics affecting them is presented here.

Consumer Responses

According to Hirschman , a dissatisfied customer has three potential options: exit (termination of the relation-ship), voice (consumer complaining) and loyalty. Research in the area of marketing has augmented this framework through the identification and testing of several behavioural and non-behavioural responses and attempted to organize them into hierarchical frameworks. The parsimonious framework offered by Singh categorized the voice responses into active (complaints directed towards the seller), private (word-of-mouth directed towards friends and relatives), and third party (such as formal complaints to government agencies) responses. There is general consensus on the question of multiple responses as researchers have recognized the tendency of consumers to produce multiple responses to a dissatisfying experience.

Individualism/Collectivism

An analytical dimension that captures the relative importance that people accord to personal interests and to shared pursuits. Individualism is the condition in which personal interests are accorded greater importance than the needs of the group. Collectivism places the interests of the group above those of the individual and promotes cooperativeness and harmony among members. Individualists, according to Furrer *et al.,* are more assertive and demanding of service providers. Consequently, when service is inade-quate, they are likely to complain more in comparison to the collectivists and even switch to alternative providers. The Liu *et al.,* study found that the individualistic customers had a higher intention to switch and engage in negative word of mouth.

Assertiveness/Aggressiveness

Focusing on the consumer-marketer interactions, Richins has identified two interaction styles that have crucial implications to CCB. Assertiveness is defined as the behaviour which enables a person to act in his/her own best interest, whereas aggressiveness is defined as a 'response that delivers noxious stimuli to another organism.' Assertive behaviours would include standing up for customer rights and complaining when necessary. Aggressive behaviours on the other hand, might include rudeness, abusive language and even physical violence. Richins developed scales for the interactive styles of assertiveness and aggressiveness and validated them through extensive testing. Her results indicate that while aggressiveness correlates negatively with attitude toward business and positively with the number of actual complaints made over the past few months, assertiveness correlates positively with the attitude as well as complaint behaviours.

Consumer Alienation

A lack of acceptance of market institutions, practices and outputs by the consumer is how marketing scholars have defined alienation. Allison conceptualized consumer alienation from the marketplace as a multi-dimensional construct composed of powerlessness, normlessness, social isolation and self-estrangement, but his empirical results indicated support for the one-dimensional structure of the scale he developed. In relating the construct of consumer alienation to CCB, Singh and Wilkes proposed an inverse relationship between alienation and the various types of voice responses. Their empirical results supported the hypothesized inverse relationship and they concluded that exit and negative word-of-mouth might be the favored responses of alienated consumers. Kim *et al.*, (2003) proposed similar effects of alienation on attitude toward complaint and the perceived value of complaint. According to their results, alienation had no effect on perceived value of complaint, but the negative effect on attitude toward complaint was strong.

Culture

There is a growing body of research on the influence of culture on personal characteristics and the effects of cultural factors on service expectations of customers. The differences in the behaviours and expectations of Asians and Westerners in service interactions have been identified by Winsted. Ferrer et al have examined the link between cul-ture and the relative emphasis placed on service quality dimensions. Mattila and Peterson tested the effects of interactional and distributive justice perceptions as well as culture on customer satisfaction in multiple countries and concluded that while perceptions of both types of justice had significant effects, culture (country) had no direct effect. The effects of culture on personal characteristics and the constraints it places on consumer responses to service failures have been recognized in the relevant literature. A survey of consumers in two distinct cultures, namely, Singapore and the U.S., was conducted for empirical testing of the hypotheses presented earlier. A survey instrument has been developed on the basis of prior literature and pre-tested. Apart from items measuring cultural and personal characteristics, the questionnaire presents a scenario involving service lapse in the context of travel booking and asks the respondent to indicate how an "ideal consumer" would respond. Cultural and personal characteristics of consumers were measured using 5-point Likert scales. The items used in the present research are adapted from scales employed in prior research cited earlier. All items mea-suring consumer responses to service failure employ 6-point semantic differential scales, with the responses 'least likely' and 'most likely' serving as anchors. Exit response was measured through a single item. Data collection was done by university students as part of their coursework.

Cronbach's alpha was computed to assess the reliability of each variable. These coefficients were calculated separately for the Singapore and the U. S. samples. The reliability coefficients are within an acceptable range for all variables except alienation and assertiveness. The items measuring assertiveness display especially low reliability in the case of U.S. sample and the results of any statistical tests must be interpreted with caution.

Variable scores were computed by summing across the items measuring each variable. Prior to the summing, responses to any negatively worded items were reversed. These summated scores were used in the statistical analyses undertaken for the purpose of hypothesis testing. Correlation analyses and t-tests were considered appropriate for testing the hypotheses developed earlier. SPSSX 13.0 version was used for conducting the statistical analyses. The results of these analyses are reported in the following section.

Correlations among the study variables were computed separately for the U.S. and Singapore samples. The results indicate partial support for our hypotheses. The first hypothesis, linking individualistic orientation to the active voice response in case of service failure received support from the U.S. data. The hypotheses linking assertiveness with voice and exit responses similarly received support from the U.S. sample alone. None of the other results were statistically significant at the alpha = 0.05 level.

The results were however, in the predicted direction except for the two hypotheses involving alienation. The correlation coefficient between alienation and voice response is positive in Singapore data, contrary to our hypothesis. Further, the relationship between alienation and exit response is negative in both countries, a direction contrary to the one proposed in our hypothesis.

While a considerable amount of research has accumulated in the area of consumer responses to service failures, the present research introduced the concept of an "ideal consumer" and tried to elicit from consumers in two countries, ideal consumer responses to lapses in the service provided.

The results indicate partial support for the hypothesis focusing on individualistic/collectivistic characteristics of consumers. Individualism correlated positively with voice response only in case of the U.S sample. The hypotheses linking consumer assertiveness to the voice and exit responses received support among American consumers, but rejected in the sample from Singapore.

The results of the present study show no statistically significant differences in the service failure responses of consumers from the two countries, but it is interesting to note that the voice response is lower and exit response is higher for Singaporeans in comparison to their American counterparts. Recall the notion expounded by Liu *et al.,* regarding the restraining influence of culture.

Drawing from cross-cultural research, they suggested that cultural traditions might give rise to norms limiting behavioural responses. Given the earlier comments regarding Asian cultures, it is quite likely that consumers from these cultures are not as vocal or direct in their complaints to the service provider.

While statistical significance is lacking, the direction of the results from the present study appear to support the notion that voice response might be more restrained in Asia in comparison to the U.S. consumers. While the present research proposes the role of personal and cultural characteristics on the responses of ideal consumers and the results validate the framework partially, further research is needed to more fully confirm it. Future research could expand the study to other countries - especially other Asian countries, since none of the results were statistically significant in the Singapore sample. The present study employed only one scenario involving travel service.

In future research, the framework needs to be tested across an array of service scenarios to capture differences across service types and assessing its robustness.

2

Marketing in a Transitional Economy and the Consumer Attitudes

In the last two decades, a quarter of the world's population in countries including China, Eastern and Central Europe, has been in a historical transition from central planning to rely on market forces. Reforms and economic development have led to the adoption of modern marketing practices, the emergence of consumer societies, and a growing middle-class. Concomitant with the development of these economies has come the growing power of consumers, as evidenced by consumers' rising awareness of their rights and increasing willingness to engage in disapproving behaviour such as protests and lawsuits against companies that they consider to be unethical, including many multinational corporations. Flourishing marketing activities and burgeoning consumerism have made understanding consumer attitudes toward marketing increasingly important for both the businesses and governments in these societies.

Since consumer perceptions of marketing activities represent vital knowledge for management decisions and public policy making, marketing researchers and practitioners have long been interested in the genesis of consumer attitudes toward marketing, and how they affect consumers' experiences in the marketplace. Existing studies in various countries suggest that consumer attitudes toward marketing vary greatly due to demographic and psychographic factors, and that they may be influenced by their ethical ideologies. Several cross-cultural comparisons have found some differences in consumer attitudes toward marketing between developed economies in Europe and North America, newly industrialized countries such as Hong Kong, and less developed economies such as India. While economic development, consumerism, and cultural values were used to explain such variations, the findings about the sources of these differences remain inconclusive. In transitional economies that once relied on central planning, "let the buyer beware" was the rule and consumer sovereignty was not an ultimate goal of economic activities.

In the last two decades, however, consumers in these societies have been exposed to a great variety of modern marketing practices brought about by economic reforms and the influx of foreign businesses. How these consumers perceive marketing and its specific functions remains largely unknown and may be different from their counterparts in advanced economies. Therefore, research is especially needed to shed light on this important subject in transitional economies. First, the reliability and construct validity of previous research instrument need to be tested for transitional economies. Second, the predictive validity of the instrument, i.e. whether consumer attitudes toward mar-keting affect their satisfaction, has received scanty treatment and need to be established. Third, replication of previous studies would provide interesting comparisons in consumer attitudes between developed countries and transitional economies and meaningful implications for businesses and governments. Mainland China, a transitional economy that has been experimenting with the free market philosophy in the last two decades and that has attracted increasing attention in marketing and consumer research, provides a unique context for examining these issues.

In a survey of consumers in mainland China, we gauge consumer attitudes toward marketing by adopting the Consumer Sentiment Toward Marketing scale that was developed by Gaski and Etzel and test its reliability in the transitional economy. Second, we examine the construct validity of consumer attitudes toward marketing as a second-order latent factor using confirmatory factor analysis (CFA). Furthermore, based on Fishbein and Ajzen's attitude model, we explore the predictive validity of the construct by assessing its effect on consumer satisfaction along with other independent variables, including the importance of the marketing mix variables and consumer beliefs about business. Finally, we compare the findings of the survey with those of previous consumer studies in other economies, explore the implications for marketing management and public policy in transitional economies, and suggest directions for future research.

Consumer attitudes toward marketing activities are important from both a theoretical and a managerial standpoint. The advent of an organized consumerism movement in the USA during the 1970s led to tremendous interest among researchers in studying the attitudes of consumers toward business. As consumer perceptions significantly affect their behavioural responses to marketing activities, consumer attitudes toward marketing have been found to be linked to several key macroeconomic variables and have been used in economic forecasts.

Such information can also help in the formulation of effective strategies for companies and the development of policies by government agencies to regulate industries and to protect consumers' interests. While some researchers have assessed the overall attitude of consumers toward marketing, others have dealt with consumer attitudes toward specific marketing activities such as advertising and pricing. In general, researchers have asked the following three questions:

1. How do consumers perceive marketing in a specific economy?
2. Are there significant differences in consumer attitudes toward marketing?
3. And if so, what factors explain such differences?

Barksdale and Darden pioneered the research on consumer attitudes toward marketing in the USA and replicated their study for a number of years in the 1970s. They measured consumer attitudes toward the four marketing mix variables, consumerism, government regulation, and consumer responsibility. Overall, they found that consumers had rather negative attitudes toward marketing practices. Later, Gaski and Etzel modified the Barksdale scale and labeled it as the Consumer Sentiment toward Marketing. They found that although the attitudes of US consumers toward marketing were negative, the reputation of marketers had shown improvement over time. Their results also suggested that women perceived marketing more positively than did men. In another study, Web-ster found significant differences in consumer attitudes toward various marketing practices including product, pricing, advertising, and retailing or selling; however, many of the differences remained even after social class and income effects were removed. Therefore, the factors that explain the differences in consumers' attitudes need clarification.

Recently, several researchers have found that a number of other factors influence consumers' attitudes toward marketing. Treise *et al.*, examined the perceptions of familiar advertising controversies: targeting practices and message strategies. Their results show that consumers believe that advertising often violates broad ethical norms. In addition, the degree to which consumers judge advertising as ethical or unethical varies as a function of their ethical philosophies, such as relativism and idealism. Nwachukwu *et al.*, found that perceptions of individual autonomy, consumer sovereignty, and the nature of the product played significant roles in consumers' ethical judgment of advertising and marketing.

CROSS-CULTURAL COMPARISONS

Due to the rapid globalization of business in various regions of the world, rigorous measures of consumer attitudes toward marketing are needed for cross-cultural comparison. One of the important research questions is the relationship between the level of consumerism and consumer attitudes toward marketing. Barksdale *et al.,* surveyed six countries: Australia, Canada, the UK, Israel, Norway, and the USA. Although they found that con-sumers in all of these countries exhibited critical attitudes toward marketing, they placed the six countries on a life cycle of consumerism development. Overall, economically advanced countries such as Norway, the USA and Canada have a higher level of consumerism. Thus, consumers in these countries tend to be more satisfied with the status quo and are less likely to want additional government regulation. In a study of India, which is a developing nation, Varadarajan and Thirunarayana examined the attitudes of consumers toward marketing practices, consumerism, and government regulations using the Barksdale scale. They found a high level of consumer skepticism regarding the operating philosophy of businesses, discontent with marketing practices, and support for the consumer movement and greater government regulation.

To provide additional empirical insights into the validity of the consumerism life cycle concept, Varadarajan and Thirunarayana compared the responses of consumers in India with those of consumers in the six countries that were surveyed by Barksdale *et al.,* Their findings suggested that consumers in countries that were in the "crusading" stage of the life cycle, such as India, appeared to be more dis-satisfied with the current status and strongly favored more government intervention on behalf of consumers. This is especially true for advertising. Despite wide variations in the volume of advertising and different levels of government regulation of advertising from one country to another, negative views about advertising seem to be a universal phenomenon, and perhaps more so in developing economies. Some believe that with less experience in consumerism than those in developed economies, consumers from industrializing markets may have more favorable attitudes toward various marketing activities.

One study seems to support such a proposition. Wee and Chan examined consumer sentiment about marketing practices in Hong Kong by measuring attitudes toward product, price, advertising, and retailing using the Consumer Sentiment toward Marketing scale. Their results showed a more favorable consumer sentiment toward marketing than did a previous study in the USA. Wee and Chan offered two possible explanations as to why marketing was doing better in Hong Kong than in the USA: either the US population was more skeptical about marketing or marketers in Hong Kong were indeed faring better than their counterparts in the USA. In another comparative study, Chan et al. found that Australian consumers had unfavorable attitudes toward marketing, in contrast to the more favorable attitudes among Hong Kong consumers.

Chan *et al.,* cast doubt on the proposition that con-sumer attitudes toward marketing are positively related to the level of consumerism development. Instead, they argued that consumer attitudes might be affected by cultural values. Their explanation for these differences is that people in individualistic societies such as the USA and Canada tend to be more dissatisfied with the market environment. Consumers in collectivist societies such as Hong Kong place greater emphasis on harmony and relationships, and thus tend to be less critical of marketing.

Transitional Economies

In transitional economies, after decades in a seller's market that was under-supplied, consumers have come into contact with many marketing practices that are new to them, such as television advertising and sales promotion. Although the movement toward the market economy has been mostly beneficial, the transition has not been free from controversies, and cases of questionable marketing practices and consumer discontent have become more frequent. Meanwhile, consumerism is still at the developing stage in transitional economies, and consumers are less experienced in protecting their rights and interests. Government regulations, public policy, and the legal infrastructure for protecting consumer interests in these countries are still underdeveloped. Studies of consumers and marketing in mainland China highlight the need for further investigation. Since the beginning of reforms in the late 1970s, the country has witnessed phenomenal growth in household income and accumulated savings. Both businesses and consumers have embraced various marketing practices with great curiosity and enthusiasm.

In two separate surveys in mainland China, Zhao and Shen measured audience attitudes and behaviour regarding commercial advertising. Their results indicated that Chinese consumers supported the return of advertising. Their findings also suggested that Chinese consumers paid more attention to the information content than the entertainment features of advertisements, which suggested that Chinese consumers looked for cues about product quality and features in advertising. In another study, Crellin found a significant generational split between those who were receptive and those who were unreceptive to advertising from an audience study in mainland China. Those under-35 felt positive toward advertising, whereas those over-35 had the traditionally hostile attitudes toward advertising. However, public opinion regarding commercial advertising remained quite reserved.

Mainland China, as a huge potential consumer market, has been flooded with domestic and imported goods. For a growing number of consumer products, over-capacity has led to a buyer's market. Meanwhile, the issue of consumer protection is moving into the limelight along with the emergent consumer society in the post-reform years.

With the recent efforts to revitalize the country's economy by stimulating consumer spending, the government has taken the initiative to protect consumer interests by promotion consumer rights organisations and sometimes encouraging consumer actions. Malpractices on the part of some enterprises at the expense of consumers have been exposed, including deceptive advertising, trademark violations, and other unethical business practices. In response to these problems, measures have been taken to deal with profi-teering producers and trade people, including the establishment of the China

Consumer Council in December 1984.

Knowledge of consumer attitudes toward marketing in transitional economies is also important for multinational corporations (MNCs). Despite adverse public attitudes at times, many multinationals used a variety of media and techniques to promote their products in developing countries without close scrutiny of consumers' perceptions of such practices, such as in the case of Nestlé's baby formula. In China today, many foreign businesses, including multinationals such as Toyota, Volkswagen, Sony, Hilton Hotels, McDonald's, and most recently Toshiba, have also been implicated in cases where their marketing activities have infringed on consumers' rights. Whether such companies win or lose in court, much more is at stake, including their reputations.

Although consumer attitudes toward various marketing activities have been studied in developed economies such as the USA, Western Europe, and Australia and newly industrialized economies such as Hong Kong, studies of consumerism and consumer attitudes toward marketing in transitional economies are rather limited. As transitional economies such as China and Russia have become in-creasingly attractive consumer markets and consumers have become active in protecting their rights, MNCs and local businesses would benefit from having at their disposal an understanding of consumer attitudes toward marketing. Against this backdrop, more systematic knowledge is needed to shed light on consumer attitudes toward marketing in these markets.

ATTITUDES TOWARD MARKETING IN TRANSITIONAL ECONOMIES

Overall, previous studies have found that consumers in various countries differ in their attitudes toward marketing, and that factors such as consumerism development and demographic variables, income and education for instance, may help to explain such differences. They have also shown that consumer attitudes toward marketing are not uniform across various marketing mix variables. However, the existing knowledge is mainly based on studies of consumers in developed countries such as the USA, Australia or newly industrialized economies such as Hong Kong. Despite the rapid development of marketing practices and surging consumer power in transitional econo-mies, consumer attitudes toward marketing in these countries remain largely unexplored. Therefore, how consumers in transitional economies perceive marketing as compared to their counterparts in other countries warrants investigation.

Reliability

In addition, several methodological and theoretical issues need to be addressed. Although various measures of consumer attitudes toward marketing have been used in previous studies of consumers in advanced economies, it is uncertain whether these research instruments will have the same level of reliability in transitional economies. With a relatively shorter period of exposure to modern marketing practices, consumers in transitional economies may not have the same level of knowledge or understanding of different marketing functions and related issues as their counterparts in advanced economies. Thus, the reliability of previous research instrument needs to be verified in the transitional economy context.

In the existing literature, researchers have used two instruments to measure consumer attitudes toward marketing: one that was developed by Barksdale and Darden , and another that was developed by Gaski and Etzel . The Barksdale and Darden instrument has several subscales that cover consumer attitudes toward the marketing mix variables, consumerism, and government regulations. Although the instrument has been used in other studies, the scale has been shown to have poor reliability in cross-cultural studies. In comparison, the Gaski and Etzel scale, which uses some of the items from the original Barksdale and Darden study, has been adopted and validated in two studies outside the USA. Thus, this study uses the Gaski and Etzel scale and tests its reliability in a transitional economy.

Validity Issues

Previous studies used correlative results among consumer

attitudes, satisfaction with marketing mix variables, and beliefs about business to measure the discriminate validity and convergent validity of their instru-ment. However, given the multiple dimensions of marketing and its components (i.e. marketing mix variables), consumer attitudes toward marketing represent a complex and a higher-order construct. Before such concept can be used for further model building and theory development, its construct validity also needs to be established. Further-more, how consumer attitudes affect their satisfaction has not been explored. In other words, the predictive validity of consumer attitudes toward marketing is not apparent. Thus, it is necessary to examine whether consumer attitudes toward marketing are effective in predicting other consumer variables such as satisfaction in a multivariate setting.

Therefore, this study will explore whether consumer attitudes toward marketing can be used to predict other consumer variables. In this study, we adopt consumer satisfaction with marketing as the dependent variable. Consumer satisfaction has been increasingly viewed as the ultimate goal for businesses and adopted as a measure of the effectiveness of marketing activities. Consumer attitudes toward marketing are their affective evaluations of marketing and its specific functions. Previous studies indicate that consumers attach different levels of importance to the functional areas of marketing, and differ in their beliefs about business. These factors may interact with consumer attitudes toward marketing in affecting consumer satisfaction. Thus, the perceived importance of the marketing mix variables and business beliefs can be used as additional independent variables to test the unique effect of consumer attitudes toward marketing on consumer satisfaction. In the following section, we discuss the relationships among these factors and the research hypotheses.

First, many studies have found that attitudes toward specific products or brands affect consumer satisfaction. Whether consumers' attitudes towards marketing in general affect consumer satisfaction is yet to be determined. While several previous studies indicated that there was a significant correlation between consumer attitudes toward marketing and satisfaction, these authors emphasize whether consumer attitudes toward marketing independently affect consumer satisfaction needs further investigation. Since consumer attitudes are based on their experiences in the marketplace, consumer attitudes toward marketing should have a direct and significant effect on satisfaction. Meanwhile, there are variations in terms of the level of importance that consumers attach to the marketing mix variables.

According to the multi-attribute model of attitude, the weight that consumers attach to a specific attribute of an object often affects their attitude toward that object.

Thus, following the logic of Fishbein and Ajzan's attitude model, consumers' satisfaction with marketing functions also depend on the level of importance that consumers place on a specific marketing mix variable. In other words, it is plausible that the perceived importance of the marketing mix variables moderates the effect of consumer attitudes on satisfaction.

Although brand specific beliefs have been studied intensively, and industry-specific beliefs have been studied occasionally, the effects of consumers' general beliefs about business and marketing have rarely been investigated. Consumer beliefs about business are their global impression of businesses and their beliefs about business philosophies, i.e. whether businesses believe that consumers are always right or they operate on the principle of "Buyers be aware". A number of studies reveal that consumers differ in their beliefs about business. Several studies found that the beliefs of consumers about marketing affected their attitudes toward specific marketing activities.

For instance, Andrews found that although US con-sumers agreed strongly that advertising was essential, they were very critical of its social effects. However, little is known about consumers' overall beliefs about business in transitional economies, and how they might affect consumer attitudes toward marketing. As consumers in transitional economies have had relatively less exposure to modern marketing practices compared to their counterparts in developed economies, their beliefs about business may be different from those in advanced economies and inevitably affects their attitudes toward marketing and their satisfaction as consumers.

Based on Fishbein and Ajzan's attitude model, people's attitudes – their affective evaluation of an object – is based on the cognitive component, i.e. their salient beliefs. Based on their background and experiences, consumers may have positive beliefs about business in general, or negative beliefs and skepticism about business operators. Early research suggested that variations in consumer perceptions of marketing occur as a result of beliefs about business. Thus, consumer beliefs about business may affect consumer satisfaction. Moreover, generalized beliefs may, as moderating variables, may moderate the effect of consumer attitudes on their affective evaluation. Therefore, consumer beliefs about business should influence consumer satis-faction directly, and also indirectly via consumer attitudes towards marketing.

First, we developed a questionnaire that included the measures of consumer attitudes toward marketing mix variables that were developed by Gaski and Etzel. The questionnaire measured consumer attitudes toward each of the marketing mix variables – product, retailing, advertising, and price. Consumers were asked to respond to 28 statements about their sentiments regarding the marketing mix variables, such as "The quality of most products I buy today is as good as can be expected," and "Most advertising is very annoying." A Likert scale was used for measuring consumer responses, ranging from (1) strongly agree to (5) strongly disagree with a point of neutrality in the middle. The Gaski and Etzel instrument also includes measures of consumer satisfaction with each of the marketing mix variables, the perceived importance of the marketing mix variables, and consumer beliefs about business.

The four statements of global impression from the Gaski and Etzel study were used as consumer beliefs about business.

The questionnaire also included various demographic and lifestyle questions. As the consumer revolution has largely been an urban phenomenon in mainland China, studies of Chinese consumers have focused on major urban areas of China. In our study, we conducted a survey in four major cities including Beijing, Hangzhou, Guangzhou, and Xi'an. These cities represent the north, east, south, and west of China. Both authors of the study are bilingual speakers of Chinese and English. The English questionnaire was translated into Chinese by one researcher, and then back translated into English by another to ensure conceptual correspondence. The Chinese version of the questionnaire was used for data collection.

To complete the survey, research assistants were recruited among graduate students who were enrolled at local universities in the four cities. These assistants were trained to conduct personal interviews using the structured questionnaire with residents of these cities. To ensure that samples represent urban consumers in China, multiple sampling methods were used. First, three urban districts were selected from each city, which has about a dozen urban districts. From each district, a neighborhood shopping center was randomly chosen as the interview site. Then, an intercept survey was then conducted at these shopping centers at different times of day and different days during a ten-day period to interview every fifth person until the 200th interview was completed. Finally, 200 usable ques-tionnaires were collected from each of the cities. Several cases from Guangzhou had a significant number of missing values, which resulted in the return of only 197 usable questionnaires from that city.

There were, in total, 391 female and 402 male respondents. In terms of age distribution, 40.2 per cent of the respondents were between 17 and 25 years of age, 24.8 per cent were between 26 and 35, 15.7 per cent were between 36 and 45, 15.9 per cent were between 46 and 66, and 3.4 per cent were 66 or above. Thus, both genders and all age groups are well represented in the sample. Furthermore, the data on education includes all levels from primary school to post-graduate studies, and are coded into two categories: high school education or lower, and college education and higher. Occupation includes a dozen different categories, and is then collapsed into several categories including white-collar professions, blue-collar professions, students, and others. Due to the large number of inter-viewees who were reluctant to give their income information (especially in public), income was excluded from subsequent data analysis. Overall, the sample provides a good representation of urban consumers in mainland China.

First, the reliability of each measure toward the marketing mix variables was assessed by Cronbach's alpha. We performed the same item purification procedure that was used by Gaski and Etzel, Wee and Chan , and Chan *et al*. After purification, these measures demonstrate adequate reliability: 0.678 for product, 0.698 for retailing, 0.753 for advertising, except for price (0.559). As in another study of the Chinese population, these measures are slightly lower than those in the USA and Australia, but still acceptable given the pioneering nature of the study. Further exami-nation of the deleted items in the purification process suggests that those items which deal with the effect of competition on product prices and government regulation of advertising, such as item four and item six for advertising, demonstrate poor item-total correlations, perhaps because consumers in less developed countries are less familiar with these concepts.

To construct the index scores for the overall sentiment and for each marketing mix variable, we followed the method that was used by Gaski and Etzel, Wee and Chan and Chan *et al*: 2 for "strongly agree", 0 for "neutral", and 2 for "strongly disagree", so that the total index score could range from 200 to –200. Negative statements were reversely coded. The overall index score is the sum of the weighted measures of all sub-scales for product, retailing, advertising, and price as in a multi-attribute attitude model. The results suggest that the overall index score for consumer sentiment toward marketing in mainland China is 0.84, and the index score for the marketing mix variables are 1.37 for product, 1.34 for retailing, 0.04 for advertising, and 0.58 for price. It appears that the index scores for Chinese consumers are slightly negative but close to the point of neutrality.

As each scale has an alpha coefficient that is considerably higher than its correlations with other scales, discriminant validity is upheld. In addition, the correlation coefficient between the composite measure (the index) and the global impression (beliefs about business) is 0.393, and the correlations between the index measure and overall consumer satisfaction are 0.643.

These results indicate adequate convergence between the index measure and the others, with all of the correlation coefficients significant at the 0.01 level. Thus, the convergent validity for the instrument is also supported. To test the construct validity of consumer sentiment toward marketing, all three previous studies used exploratory factor analysis. Gaski and Etzel proposed that consumer sentiment toward marketing was a latent factor in a reflective model. Therefore, we adopted confirmatory factory analysis (CFA), which is a more rigorous method of assessing construct validity.

The CFA model includes four latent factors that represent consumer attitudes toward the four marketing mix variables, and treats the overall consumer sentiment as the second-order latent factor. We used the structural equation modeling software AMOS to test the model.

The results indicate that most of the factor loadings are strong. The results also suggest that the confirmatory factor analysis model has an adequate fit of the data, with a goodness of fit index (GFI) of 0.944 and an adjusted GFI of 0.929. Other fitness measures including a÷2 value of 446.93 (p=0.000), RMR of 0.065 and a comparative fit index of 0.821 also indicate a reasonably good fit of the data. Given the complexity of the model, five items per latent factor, and a large heterogeneous sample, these results suggest reasonable goodness of fit for the second-order CFA model and adequate construct validity for consumer sentiment toward marketing.

As for the predictive validity of consumer sentiment, we treated consumer satisfaction as the dependent variable and others as the independent variables, including the perceived importance of the marketing mix variables, beliefs about business, interactions between perceived importance and attitudes, interactions between beliefs about business and attitudes, and the demographic variables. We then performed multiple regressions on consumer satisfaction with each of the marketing mix variables.

The results suggest that positive attitudes toward the marketing mix variables have a significant and strong effect on satisfaction: â=0.210 for product, â=0.531 for retailing, â=0.445 for advertising, and â=0.34 for price, which indicates that each category scale has good predictive validity and provides support for *H1*. While perceived importance has a significantly negative effect on satisfaction with advertising (â=–0.175), it does not affect satisfaction with the other marketing mix variables. Furthermore, the interactions of the importance of the marketing mix variables and consumer sentiment have no significant effects on satisfaction. Thus, the results do not support *H2*.

The results also show that consumer beliefs about business have positive effects on satisfaction with product (â=0.192), retailing (â=0.197), and price (â=0.066), but a negative effect on satisfaction with advertising (â=–0.171), which again suggests that consumers are especially critical of, or disillusioned about, advertising. This is consistent with the findings of previous studies. Furthermore, the interactions of beliefs about business with consumer attitudes have significant negative effects on satisfaction with product (â=–0.115) and advertising (â=–0.171), suggesting that consumers who think positively about businesses and have favorable sentiments toward marketing somehow tend to be less satisfied with product quality and advertising.

Overall, these multivariate analyses suggest that demographic variables have no significant effect on consumer satisfaction. However, the univariate analyses reveal some interesting findings. First, older people tend to dislike advertising (corr=0.13), which is similar to the findings of previous studies. There are also some significant gender differences in their overall sentiment and specific attitudes. For instance, the sentiment of women toward marketing is more positive than that of men (1.45 vs -3.19). Women also report a more favorable attitude toward advertising than do men (0.36 vs -0.03).

Those with college education tend to be less satisfied with retail service than are others (0.83 vs 1.84). As for occupational background, blue-collar workers are more positive about retailing, but less satisfied with advertising than are white-collar workers, students and others. Although the overall consumer sentiment toward marketing does not vary across the four cities, there are some significant regional differences in consumer perceptions of product quality, advertising, and retailing.

Findings and Comparisons

First, the overall consumer sentiment toward marketing in mainland China is largely neutral. Among the category scales, consumers feel slightly positive about retailing, largely neutral about advertising, and slightly negative about product and price. Compared to previous studies of consumers in the USA and Australia, our results suggest that Chinese consumers are less critical of marketing. It is probably true that consumerism and consumer protection in mainland China are at the beginning stage and lag behind advanced economies. Thus, the findings are consistent with the life cycle concept of consumerism development in that consumer attitudes toward marketing tend to be less critical in those countries in which consumerism is a recent phenomenon.

However, although consumer sentiment in mainland China is more negative than in Hong Kong, the index scores of consumers in mainland China are closer to those of Hong Kong consumers. Thus, it is plausible that the consumer sentiment in mainland China is also a reflection of the cultural values of favoring harmony and being non-judg-mental. As for the psychometric quality of the instrument, the results suggest that the Consumer Sentiment Toward Marketing scale has lower reliability than those in previous studies of other countries, especially for price subscale. Meanwhile, the results support the discriminate and convergent validity of the scale. The confirmatory factor analysis of consumer sentiment toward marketing as a second-order latent factor indicates that the model adequately fits the data, and suggests that the index has good construct validity in the context of mainland China.

Moreover, while controlling for a host of other variables and interactions, the findings of multiple regressions indicate that consumer attitudes toward these marketing mix variables significantly affect consumer satisfaction, thus demonstrating strong predictive validity. Furthermore, the results show that consumer beliefs about business play a significant role in affecting the satisfaction with marketing in mainland China. Moreover, there are significant inter-actions between beliefs about business and consumer attitudes, which significantly affect consumer satisfaction, i.e. negatively for product and advertising. These findings suggest that the differences between consumer expectations and experiences play a critical role in consumer satisfaction. In the same vein, it is noteworthy that Chinese consumers place great importance on advertising. However, they are the least satisfied with this marketing function.

These findings are consistent with those of previous studies and pose special challenges for marketers. This is hardly surprising in a transitional economy, given the widespread skepticism about advertising in other countries. As the most visible arm of marketing, advertising is always under scrutiny by consumers. Moreover, consumer atti-tudes toward marketing differ across gender, age, edu-cation, occupational groups and location of residence, revealing significant diversity in the dynamic and big emerging market.

Implications

In transitional economies such as China, the two types of consumerism – increased personal consumption and organized movements to protect the sovereignty of consumers – go hand in hand. After decades of scarcity, continuous economic development has led to flourishing products and brands, and new forms of marketing and promotion. In the meantime, consumers have become increasingly aware of their rights and become more critical and discerning about marketing functions and business behaviours. Our results suggest that consumer attitudes toward marketing and beliefs about business in China are not entirely positive, and that such attitudes and beliefs significantly affect consumers' experiences in the marketplace. Consumers are not quite convinced that marketers have their best interests in mind. Thus, in economies such as China that are becoming increasingly market-driven, businesses still have much room for improvement in terms of both communicating to consumers the benefits of marketing and their integrity as business operators.

These findings should sensitize marketers to consumer attitudes toward marketing and their beliefs about business. When consumers' expectations are not met, they become dissatisfied and frustrated, and may resort to disapproval. Therefore, businesses should tread with greater care when targeting the emerging middle class consumers in transitional economies. They should make realistic claims about their products, and more importantly should be more devoted to fulfilling consumer expectations. Although Chinese consumers are less critical of marketing by comparison, such perceptions may reflect their cultural values rather than a higher level of satisfaction with marketing *per se*. In fact, consumers in transitional economies have begun to follow the footsteps of their counterparts in advanced economies. It is foreseeable that consumer attitudes toward marketing will become more critical in the future, and consumers will be more active in protecting themselves as they become more educated and informed and as the legal infrastructure continues to develop.

Although China is a latecomer to the consumer movement, consumers' rights have steadily taken root in China in the post-reform years, as evidenced by the growing number of consumer organisations. Disgruntled consumers are increasingly willing to stand up for their rights and take action against businesses that they consider to be unscrupulous, including some large multinationals. Recently, Chinese government banned all "direct sales" activities in late 1997 due to the deceptive techniques of the distributors and inevitably hurt companies such as Amway and Avon. As the Chinese government tends to be reactive, and sometimes over-reactive, to such incidents, it is in the best interests of businesses that they become pro-active and join forces in terms of self-regulation. As consumers in transitional economies have been exposed to various forms of marketing, they have become less gullible and more discerning about marketing activities. Consumers increasingly demand higher quality products, better customer services, truthful advertising and promotion, and fair pricing. Rising consumer awareness has prompted MNCs as well as local firms to rethink their approaches to marketing in transitional economies.

For instance, after receiving many complaints about the lack of availability of its parts, Sony decided to establish a customer service center in China. Many others have followed suit. After China's accession to the World Trade Organisation in 2002, competition is expected to intensify. Many leading companies have realized that customer satisfaction is critical and have devoted more effort to managing the interface with consumers. Because the efforts to increase the satisfaction of current customers primarily affect future purchase behaviour, companies need to take long-term perspectives when improving product quality and customer satisfaction. Businesses with high customer satisfaction usually enjoy superior economic returns.

Limitations and Suggestions

First, the findings suggest that the Consumer Senti-ment toward Marketing scale needs to be revised and tested again to improve its reliability in different countries. Second, this study focuses on one transitional economy. Thus, the cross-cultural generalizability of the findings needs to be tested with consumers in markets that are undergoing similar transitions. Simultaneous multi-country studies can help to separate the effects of the level of consumerism development, cultural values, ethical philosophies, beliefs about business, and other market and consumer characteristics, and to identify other sources of cross-cultural differences such as possible response set biases. Whether consumer attitudes toward marketing and beliefs about business change over time is an important research question. In light of the rapid development of various marketing practices, government regulations, and consumerism movements in transitional economies, the evolution of consumer attitudes and beliefs and their implications for marketing management warrant continuous monitoring.

Several broader issues demand attention in future studies. Despite the frequent ethical problems that involve consumers, few have considered the role of consumer perceptions in theories of business and marketing ethics. Thus, the effects of consumer attitudes toward marketing on their behaviour and satisfaction need to be defined in a broader context with a theoretical framework that examines their relationships with other relevant variables. This study examines consumer attitudes toward the four marketing mix variables. Consumer perceptions of many specific marketing practices, such as sales promotions, are virtually unknown in transitional economies. Studies of specific issues, including attitudes toward media and responses to advertising and promotion, would help to improve operational effectiveness in areas such as product positioning and promotional strategies.

In addition to economic development and consumer sophistication, further research needs to investigate whether consumer responses to evaluative questions about marketing are grounded in cultural values and beliefs as well as ethical philosophies. Thus, how cultural differences in individualism and idealism would influence consumers' affective evaluations of marketing provides a fruitful avenue for future research. Likewise, MNCs should consider consumer attitudes toward marketing, beliefs about business, and cultural values when planning marketing strategies in transitional economies.

Understanding the diverse yet fast changing consumer market is an important element for long-term success in transitional economies.

The Consumer Society Begins in China

Over the years we have got used to a significant amount of consumer cynicism about marketing and the motivations that underlie marketing activity. Nevertheless, in developed economies people are, generally speaking, aware of the nature and purpose of marketing and are able to deconstruct marketing messages so as to realize individual benefit. While there remain those who are not content with this *laissez-faire* approach, preferring regularity control, most people see that businesses have the right to communicate with customers and potential customers. For the USA and other developed economies mass advertising through television, radio and newspapers are an accepted part of life - we could not imagine a society without freely under-taken marketing and high levels of consumer awareness of that marketing's purpose.

Furthermore, consumers in these markets are able (most of the time) to protect themselves from misplaced marketing without recourse to regulatory intervention confident that the existence of trading stands rules and other long-standing elements of consumer protection provide sufficient safeguard. For a country like China, slowly emer-ging from a totalitarian environment where there was no advertising and communications were a virtual Govern-ment monopoly, we might expect the situation to be dif-ferent and for consumers to respond differently to com-mercial speech. Chan and Cui comment that the way in which these consumers "perceive marketing and its specific functions remains largely unknown and may be different from their counterparts in advanced economies".

While governments in advanced economies do inter-vene in marketing activity (e.g. through restrictions or bans on advertising certain products), the primary constraints on marketing rest with individual and collective consumer action plus the operation of market forces. Government only intervenes when the nature of the product or activity does not provide this opportunity (e.g. complex financial products such as pensions) or where such intervention accords with some part of that Government's wider social agenda (e.g. restrictions on the sale, promotion or distribution of tobacco products). The indication from Chan and Cui's research is that this balance between governments acting and consumer pressure is struck differently in a transitional economy such as that of China. Consumers are more likely to call for Government action when faced with perceived marketing misdeeds and, as the authors point out "... consumerism is still at the developing stage in transitional economies and consumers are less experienced in protecting their rights and interests".

The likelihood of government intervention in marketing activity - typically to control, constrain or restrict elements of the promotional mix - are more likely in economies where the free (or fairly free) operation of market forces is a fairly new phenomenon. This likelihood must guide the actions and activities of marketers and should place some limits on the choices made in marketing. We should seek to avoid or reduce the use of the kind of activity that we know encourages (in some) a negative reaction. These activities include:

- intrusive selling such as unsolicited doorstep sales activity;
- large scale direct mail and the use of unaddressed doorstep leafleting;
- unrequested outbound telemarketing to non-cus-tomers;
- complex warranty and consumer credit offers;
- sales promotions that encourage stockpiling; and
- advertising masquerading as publicity.

These activities (and others no doubt) are all areas where we have seen calls for legislative intervention in advanced economies. Given the greater likelihood of consumer calls for such intervention in a transitional economy, the chances of regulatory action are greater. Not all of the activities listed above are either unethical or contrary to the principles of free commercial speech but they do represent a risk given the likely consumer response – there's no point in taking the risk.

The Mature Consumer Society

Regardless of the "political" debate about the values of a consumer driven society such as we see in the USA and other advanced economies, these values and, more importantly, the degree of comfort that the individual consumer has with marketing activity, cannot be transferred. Many of the techniques and activities we take for granted will be strange to the typical Chinese consumer unused to choice, personal liberty and economic freedom. It is likely that future generations of consumers in these transitional economies will be more at home with marketing activities and more able to respond personally. In the meantime, the expectation of these consumers will be that the primary role mediating between them and the marketer rests with Government.

It is not a criticism to say that Chinese consumers are less mature in their relationship with marketing and, as a result, less able to assess when what they experience is misleading and exploitative (or just not to their liking). Crucially, the understanding of choice and of consumer power is far less developed. And it is this understanding that gives rise to direct consumer action as opposed to the actions (often heavy-handed) that a government might take ostensibly for the purpose of consumer protection. Marketers in transitional economies such as China need to exercise caution and should exercise the same constraints as they would within a society where individual consumers are aware of their powerful position. We must never assume that less developed economies than our own with less authoritative consumers merit more exploitative marketing activity.

SOCIAL CONTRACTS AND MARKETING ETHICS

The need for normative theory to provide guidance in evaluating ethical issues is particularly pressing in marketing.

There have been many instances of unethical conduct in marketing; indeed, marketing is viewed by some as the worst offender of the business functions. Social contract theory is evolving into one of the major alternatives for approaching business ethics. Although it has received limited attention from marketing scholars to date, its potential for analyzing marketing ethics deserves exploration. In this chapter, our purpose is to show the relevance of social contract theory to marketing, to intro-duce a specific social contract based approach, known as Integrative Social Contracts Theory (ISCT), and to demon-strate ISCT's particular applicability to marketing ethics. Below, we examine the search to date for a normative moral foundation for marketing. We then introduce social contract theory and discuss its pertinence to marketing. Next, we explain ISCT and show in detail how ISCT may be applied to one of the more intractable problems of marketing ethics, that of bribery. Finally, we identify implications for managers and researchers.

Normative Moral Foundation For Marketing

The literature on marketing ethics can be differentiated between descriptive and normative approaches. Descriptive approaches include attempts to describe or model ethical decision making and empirical studies of the ethical attitudes and/or behaviours of different populations, such as marketing researchers or salespeople.

Normative approaches to ethics identify moral principles and methods of moral reasoning that justify judgments of what is right and wrong. It is normative marketing ethics that is concerned with prescribing what managers "ought to do" when faced with an ethical issue. Reviews of the marketing ethics literature show that there have been a substantial number of descriptive contributions, but far fewer normative contributions. The relative scarcity of normative articles reflects the difficulty in making non-controversial, yet definitive, ethical evaluations of marketing decisions and practices, though this is both necessary and important. Consider the sub-stantial physical and financial harm that can result from unethical decisions about product safety, truth in advertising, and fairness in pricing. The evaluation of these decisions as ethical or unethical—by the decision maker(s), by those affected by the decision, by public policymakers, or by researchers—may be better informed by sound theories of normative marketing ethics. The normative marketing ethics literature parallels the pluralistic approaches found in the broader business ethics field. Business ethicists have sought to develop frameworks for applying the classical ethical theories to business dilemmas. This work includes Kantian ethics, virtue, rights, utilita-rianism, justice, and social contract theory.

Each of these frameworks incorporates foundational principles such as impartiality or consent as a basis for moral guidance. Advocates of individual theories argue for their superiority in dealing with at least a defined class of ethical problems, while others take a more ecumenical approach looking for a convergence of judgment among alternative theories. Within the literature on marketing ethics, a creative variety of frameworks and theories have been developed, typically relying upon one or more of the classical theories.

Examples include a diagnostic framework for assessing individual responsibilities of marketing executives for the consequences of their unethical actions; a test that requires marketers to establish that consumers can exercise informed choice; a contingency factor model of ethical behaviour which incorporates an assumption that "marketers develop guidelines and rules for ethical behaviour based on moral philosophy"; a framework presented as a series of questions based on theories developed by Ross, Garrett, and Rawls, and later revised to include additional theories of moral philosophy; a descriptive model of ethical decision making in marketing that assumes most individuals apply both a duty-based and a teleological analysis; and a framework suggested for integrating social responsibility and ethics into the strategic marketing planning process.

Half of the chosen frameworks are pluralistic in that multiple ethical theories are recognized. This may have the consequence of restricting their ability to predict outcomes, because results may vary, even with the same contextual factors, depending on the normative theory chosen by a given moral agent. On the other hand, pluralistic approa-ches recognize a possible tendency for moral agents to either follow a multi-step pluralistic analysis in their own reasoning or to go back and forth between theories depending on the context of the decision required. Typically, the marketing-specific attempts at developing a normative framework have incorporated general summaries of the classical ethical theories, particularly utilitarianism, Kantian or other duty-based approaches, virtue, rights, and justice. Generally, they are agnostic as to the normative theory to be applied among those included within a given pluralistic framework.

The prototypical normative model, Laczniak as revised in Laczniak and Murphy, would apply the following questions in evaluating the ethics of marketing practices:

i. Does the contemplated action violate the law? (legal test).

ii. Is this action contrary to widely accepted moral obligations? (duties test).

iii. Does the proposed action violate any other special obligations that stem from the type of marketing organisation at focus? (special obligations test).

iv. Is the intent of the contemplated action harmful? (motives test).

v. Is it likely that any major damages to people or organisations will result from the contemplated action? (consequences test).

vi. Is there a satisfactory alternative action that produces equal or greater benefits to the parties affected than the proposed action? (utilitarian test).

vii. Does the contemplated action infringe upon property rights, privacy rights, or the inalienable rights of the consumer? (rights test).

viii. Does the proposed action leave another person or group less well off? Is this person or group already a member of a relatively underprivileged class? (justice test).

An affirmative answer to any of the tests is assumed to indicate that the marketer's decision is quite probably unethical and should be reconsidered. Pragmatic considerations constrain the value of this approach. If every type of ethical theory must be satisfied, few marketing decisions would be likely to ever pass muster. Further, the answering of certain questions as yes is likely to produce a no in another context. For example, a duty of justice that contemplates some reasonably equivalent distribution of benefits may consistently conflict with shareholder property rights. Indeed, Laczniak and Murphy acknowledge that there may be conflicting responses to their questions.

Hence, while use of this framework undoubtedly has merit in assisting marketers to reflect on the ethics of their decisions, it is less satisfactory in providing definitive ethical evaluations of specific practices. Approaches in business ethics based upon the classical theories, particularly those relying on Kantian ethics and utilitarianism, have been criticized as being too abstract and general to provide adequate guidance for managers. The problems with utilitarianism are well known. In many cases, utilitarian analysis requires forecasting of unknowable future events (e.g., the percentage of women who would develop medical problems from silicone breast implants). Also, comparing different types of utilities is notoriously difficult. How, for example, should the joy and excitement of riding on a three-wheel all-terrain vehicle be measured against the associated physical dangers?

Finally, the tradeoffs required by the underlying principle of impartiality—such that the utilitarian is indifferent to who is hurt and how—strike many people as counterintuitive. Consider the marketing harmful pesticides banned in the U.S. to less developed countries. A utilitarian might well be comfortable balancing the "costs" of possible deaths overseas caused by the marketing of pesticides banned in the United

States in less developed countries against the "benefits" of jobs retained in the U.S. But it is surely fair to ask whether a tradeoff of lives or physical well being versus income is fully consistent with commonsense morality. Although rule utilitarianism—utilizing predefined rules to deal with repetitive ethical issues—may resolve some of these problems, the inherent complexity of modern business and professional life vastly complicate its use as a realistic guide.

Duty-based (or deontological) approaches avoid some of the problems with utilitarianism by establishing clear duties, often based upon some rational criteria or assumptions concerning the nature of humanity. Even so, in some situations, it may appear that no obvious duties can be invoked or that duties are in conflict. In other cases, the recognition of duties is dependent upon unknowable facts. In many business-related contexts, duty-based theories produce conflicting obligations without any clear-cut method for resolving the conflicts. Thus, a manager acting under a perceived ethical duty to give appropriate consideration to the legitimate claims and interests of stake-holders finds little guidance in resolving competing stake-holder claims. For example, animal rights advocates might demand that a cosmetics company cease all testing on animals while consumer activists demand that the firm use all known effective measures for guaranteeing the safety of its products.

These and similar problems have led Robin and Reidenbach to note that the "grand narratives" of moral philosophy seem inadequate for the rich, complex context of the marketing function. They despair of identifying any unifying general ethical theory and instead argue for the development of a workable, ethical approach specific to marketing. Few of the frameworks reference social contract theory, despite its increasing prominence as a theory in business ethics, and its use elsewhere in the marketing literature. We turn now to explore whether social contract theory might be a useful addition to the frameworks for decision-making in marketing ethics, either as one of the alternatives in a pluralistic approach or as a primary theory in certain contexts. As a first step, we provide a brief introduction to social contract theory and its use in business ethics.

Social Contract Theory

Social contract theory has its origins in the social upheavals of seventeenth and eighteenth century Europe. The decline of feudalism and the rejection of the divine right of kings as a basis for obedience to the state gave rise to a search for a political philosophy legitimizing state authority. Consent theories of political obligation developed, best articulated by the English philosopher John Locke (1632-1704). He argued that "a citizen's obligation to obey the law can be grounded only in that citizen's personal consent to the authority of the law". In Two Treatises of Government, Locke sought to identify a basis for the legitimacy of state authority. His resulting social contract justified the existence of the state and identified the reciprocal obligations of citizen and state.

Subsequently, Locke's ideas informed the American Revolution, the U.S. Declaration of Independence, and the U.S. Constitution. Locke was influenced by Thomas Hobbes, one of the earliest proponents of the social contract. Hobbes' Leviathan argues for the institution of an absolute sovereign as a way to further the peace of the community and thereby promote the preservation and comforts of its citizens. Hobbes identifies a "state of nature", a world without a state, wherein people act to satisfy their desires, principally self-preservation.

He suggests this state of nature would be a "war of every one against every one" and that life would be "solitary, poor, nasty, brutish, and short". Under these conditions, Hobbes argues, people would accept the only logical solution and agree to recognize an absolute sovereign. Similarly, in The Social Contract (1762), Jean-Jacques Rousseau (1712-1778) suggests that pre-social discord may be solved by individuals placing themselves under the direction of a "general will". Accordingly, three elements are common to most social contract theories:

1. Consent of the individual;
2. Agreement among moral agents; and,

3. A device or method whereby an agreement (actual or hypothetical) is obtained.

Social Contract Theory and Business Ethics

Questions about the legitimacy of business decisions are more common today than questions about the legitimacy of the state. Business ethicists are interested in justifications for the exercise of corporate power and the appropriate forms and effects of business decision making. Accordingly, the search for a basis for establishing that the pricing of a life-saving drug is "fair", or that an advertising campaign using fear appeals is "right", has much in com-mon with Locke's search for a basis for obedience to the state. Donaldson has constructed a social contract for business that provides for corporate legitimacy on the basis of the consent of those affected by business; i.e., cor-porations exist only through the cooperation and commit-ment of society.

This suggests an implied agreement between the corporation and society: "If General Motors holds society responsible for providing the condition of its existence, then for what does society hold General Motors responsible? What are the terms of the social contract?" Donaldson's device for agreement (akin to Hobbes' "state of nature") is to imagine a society without the productive organisations being analyzed—a "state of individual production"—and to recognize the problems solved by the introduction of productive organisations.

As an alternative to a state of individual production, ordinary people, economically interested and rational, would consent to have productive organisations. In this way, Donaldson uses social contract theory to establish the moral foundation of the corporation. He argues that "corporations considered as productive organisations exist to enhance the welfare of society through the satisfaction of consumer and worker interests, in a way which relies on exploiting corporations' special advantages and minimizing disadvantages." However, Donaldson does add a caveat.

The inevitable tradeoffs that must be made, especially between the interests of consumers and workers (lower prices or higher wages?), require that the contract must not violate certain minimum standards of justice; while welfare tradeoffs are permissible, organisational acts of injustice are not. Hence, at the minimum, productive organisations must "avoid deception or fraud...show respect for their workers as human beings, and... avoid any practice that systematically worsens the situation of a given group in society".

Some moral philosophers are critical of social contract theory, denying the existence of actual contracts while arguing that hypothetical contracts cannot provide for meaningful consent and agreement. Hume, for example, used the analogy of the press-ganged seaman, asked when at sea to "consent" to service. Anticipating this criticism, Donaldson writes: "There may never have been a pen and ink contract, but remarkably enough, thousands of people have acted as if there were" (his emphasis). However, Kultgen's critique of Donaldson's social contract for business argued that either it must be claimed that the contract is "a mere heuristic device" or that it exists or that it could be made to exist.

Donaldson disputes this assertion; although, in his later work (with Dunfee), he has proposed Integrative Social Contracts Theory as a framework that incorporates actual (micro) social contracts. In sum, Donaldson has established the role of a social contract for business and the likelihood that it would be consented to by individuals. Social contract theory is attracting considerable attention within the business ethics field. A special issue of Business Ethics Quarterly has been devoted to the topic and recent major books on business ethics have featured this approach. Frederick, for example, refers to its "compelling theoretical significance".

Social Contract Theory and Marketing

The particular relevance of social contract theory for marketing ethics lies in part in its shared focus with marketing on exchange. Essentially, under Donaldson's hypothetical social contract, the firm offers advantages to society—its customers and its employees—in exchange for the right to exist and even prosper. While at the same time, the exchange relationship between the firm and its customers is considered to be fundamental to marketing by many theorists. Clearly, the two are conceptually similar. Thus, there is an attractive conceptual congruity to using an exchange-based model of ethics to understand the ethical issues associated with and to provide ethical guidance for a domain based on economic exchange. As important, the shared focus on exchange grants social contract theory a unique advantage in offering prescriptive advice to marketers.

The concept of social contracts has been used both explicitly and implicitly within the general marketing literature. For example, Goolsby and Hunt define social responsibility as relating "to the social contract between businesses and the society in which they operate." Reidenbach and Robin include social contract items within their multidimensional ethics scale (MES). Moreover, various researchers have referred to "norms", an implicit reference to generally understood standards or obligations derived from social contracts. Heide and John define norms as "expectations about behaviour that are at least partially shared by a group of decision makers," and note that "specialized normative structures have been shown to govern individual exchange relationships between firms."

However, while the marketing literature makes use of social contracts or norms within exchange relationships; little attention has been given to their potential use in a normative evaluation of marketing practice. Social contract theory has been used in marketing ethics-related empirical studies. In the context of direct marketing, Culnan used social contract theory to analyze privacy issues associated with consumer awareness of name removal procedures. Robertson and Anderson implicitly used social contract theory when they found that sales managers and salespeople respond differently to the same ethical dilemmas and attribute this to differences in roles, responsibilities, and cultures among the two groups.

We would suggest that the two groups may operate under different social contracts. Robertson and Ross make explicit reference to social contracts when hypothesizing about differences between students and salespeople in responses to ethically related scenarios. They found that salespeople, who better understand the norms operating in a selling situation, are less influenced by situational pressures than are students. Thus, there is some tentative empirical validation of the importance of social contract concepts in the thinking of salespeople.

Given the connections to marketing theory, it remains surprising that the normative marketing ethics frameworks have not made greater use of the concept of social contracts. In considering how social contract based approaches may be more directly relevant to marketing we now describe a specific social contract based approach to business ethics, Integrative Social Contracts Theory.

Integrative Social Contracts Theory Donaldson and Dunfee's Integrative Social Contracts Theory relies upon real, contextual micro social contract norms within an overall framework based upon a classical, hypothetical macro social contract similar to those envisioned by Rawls, Hobbes and Locke. The term "integrative" captures the fact that ISCT encompasses two very different types of social contracts: a hypothetical macro social contract used as a heuristic device, and actual micro social contracts based within living communities. The use of the plural term, "contracts", refers not only to the two types of contracts, but also to the millions of community-based micro social contracts whose norms are important in rendering normative judgments in business ethics.

Hence, ISCT is grounded in the familiar idea of social norms that serve as the foundation for rules of behaviour within communities. Following the classic contractarians, Donaldson and Dunfee envision rational humans seeking to design a binding, though unwritten, agreement establishing the parameters for ethics in economic relationships. In order to justify consent on the part of the contractors, they limit themselves to parsimonious assumptions and a minimalist global social contract. The terms of the contract are based upon the global contractors' rational response to two assumptions. First, the contractors are assumed to be aware of, and concerned about, bounded moral rationality. Bounded moral rationality represents an extension of the well-grounded idea of bounded economic rationality to the moral sphere.

It is assumed that individual moral agents lack the information, time and emotional strength to make perfect judgments consistent with their moral preferences. Thus, a breast implant salesperson who knows she is a committed utilitarian may not be able to apply her preferred theory because she lacks the time and information to determine whether the risks associated with the product may exceed its positive cosmetic and psychological value. The bounded moral rationality assumption also acknowledges that global contractors may not be able to identify and agree to an omnipotent comprehensive moral theory. ISCT assumes that the individual contractors would wish to retain the right to select their own values to the maximum extent possible and that they would "desire to participate in economic communities that reflect their personal and cultural values." In so doing, the contractors would be recognizing bounded moral rationality insofar as it limits the ability of moral theorists to design a moral calculus applicable to all decision contexts for all of diverse humanity.

The second parsimonious assumption is that the global contractors would, in response to bounded moral rationality, recognize the need for a community-based moral fabric as a necessary condition for both the generation of wealth and for the maintenance of an environment conducive to a good and productive life. Without this moral fabric, which is the purpose of the global convention, there is the threat of social denigration into Hobbes' "war of every one against every one". In response to these core assumptions, Donaldson and Dunfee hypothesize that the global contractors would agree to the creation of a binding macrosocial contract. Donaldson and Dunfee argue that this global macrosocial contract is the only rational solution to the need for a moral fabric in the face of bounded moral rationality. Because it is assumed to be logically compelling, all rational humans are assumed to consent to its terms, which are spelled out below.

Moral Free Space and Protected Informed Consent

The first two terms of the macro social contract are:

1. Local economic communities may specify ethical norms for their members through micro social contracts (i.e., the "moral free space" term). 2. Norm-generating micro social contracts must be grounded in informed consent buttressed by rights of exit and voice (i.e., the "protected informed consent" term). 1 Communities are the core focus of the macro social contract. A community is defined in ISCT as "a self-defined, self-circumscribed group of people who interact in the context of shared tasks, values, or goals and who are capable of establishing norms of ethical behaviour for themselves." Corporations, subsidiaries, even departments or informal units within an organisation, along with partnerships, professional groups, trade associations, and nation states may all be ISCT communities in the context of a given ethical decision.

In focusing on communities, ISCT recognizes that norm-governed group activity is a critical component of economic life. The idea of moral free space is consistent with the contractors' desire to keep their options open. It also recognizes that communities are entitled to have differing norms. The parameters of ethical behaviour in advertising may vary between Japan, France and the United States; for example, comparison advertising is not con-sidered acceptable in Japan while it is in the United States.

Acting within their own moral free space, each of these communities may generate indigenous "authentic" ethical norms. A norm is defined as authentic when it is supported by the attitudes and behaviour of a substantial majority of the members of a community. Proxies such as professional codes and standards may be used to point toward potential authentic norms under ISCT. But whenever there is evidence that most members of the community hold a different view, then the proxy does not represent an authentic norm. For example, the ethics code of the Professional Marketing Research Society of Canada specifies that "good practice" requires that interviewers indicate to the respondent "a reasonably accurate estimate of the duration of the interview."

Yet, a survey of Canadian marketing researchers including PMRS members, by Laroche, McGown and Rainville, suggests that providing respondents with accurate estimates of the length of research interviews may not be an authentic norm. Seventy- two per cent of their sample agreed that misleading respondents about the duration of an interview was a common industry practice, 76% had confronted the practice and 86% of these respondents had done it themselves. The ultimate, definitive source of norms lies in the attitudes and behaviours of the members of the relevant communities. Thus, the authentic norm of this sample of the Canadian marketing research community appears to be that misleading respondents as to interview duration is acceptable.

A major impact of ISCT is to establish that authentic norms are obligatory for dissenting members of communities. The obligation stems from the consent given when one acts as a member of a community, perhaps by accepting the benefits of the community environment. However, ISCT imposes some additional requirements on the operation of the community. The community must respect the right of members to exit from group membership. Thus, a dissenting member of a community who is quite distressed about a particular authentic norm may elect to leave the community. An employee may, and generally should, leave a corporation whose values are significantly at odds with the employee's important personal values. Similarly, we emphasize that an individual should have the opportunity to exercise voice within the community. This is consistent with much of the organisational justice literature emphasizing procedural justice.

Often, some form of voice (e.g., the right to a "hearing" to present one's side of the case) is critical in perceptions that a firm has acted justly. Individuals desire the right to influence the development and evolution of norms, and, perhaps most importantly, to be able to influence changes in norms they find objectionable. In sum, so long as the requirements of community recognition of voice and exit are met, and the attitudes and behaviour of a substantial majority of the members of a community support a given norm, it qualifies as an authentic norm. Hypernorms and Legitimacy thus far, the only mechanism that would protect a dissenting individual from having an ethical obligation to comply with a distasteful norm is the right to leave the community or to try to change the norm. Beyond that it appears as though the "is" has become the "ought".

To avoid excessive relativism, recognizing that communities do indeed develop authentic norms supporting racial and gender discrimination and other problematic practices, it is assumed in ISCT that the original contractors would wish to recognize a thin set of universal principles that would constrain the relativism of community moral free space. Accordingly, the third term of the macro social contract states: 3. In order to be obligatory, a micro social contract norm must be compatible with hypernorms (i.e., the "hypernorms" term). Under ISCT, a hypernorm is a norm by which authentic norms are tested.

The term "legitimate" is used to describe an authentic norm that has passed the hypernorm test. Hypernorms are defined as "principles so fundamental to human existence that ... we would expect them to be reflected in a convergence of religious, philosophical, and cultural beliefs". As expressed by Walzer, they would be a "set of standards to which all societies can be held—negative injunctions, most likely, rules against murder, deceit, torture, oppression, and tyranny." This is a high standard for a set of universal principles and presumably the number and scope of such standards would be, as Walzer suggests, rather thin.

This is appropriate when one considers the dominant role of hypernorms and their effect of constraining choice within local communities by overriding any and all inconsistent norms or standards. An overly thick set of hypernorms could constrain diversity across cultures by imposing a straightjacket of suffocating morality. Advocates of diversity in morality are rightly concerned about the threat of a professional or educational elite defining and enforcing a thick set of moral preferences on individuals based upon some stylized conception of the good. An obvious question is how does one ascertain the existence of particular hypernorms? Donaldson and Dunfee describe the efforts of anthropologists, political scientists, and philosophers, among others, who are searching for a con-vergence of beliefs and values at the global level.

Scholars from many cultures and academic disciplines are asking similar questions concerning what humans commonly believe. An appropriate starting point would be an attempt to identify the extent of convergence among the convergence scholars. In support of the claim for the existence of hypernorms, one can point to studies finding similar methods of moral reasoning across cultures, and agreement concerning certain core principles across large samples of managers. The evidence from the many studies which seek to compare the attitudes and behaviours of managers from two or three cultures is mixed, but may be interpreted in a manner consistent with the concept of hypernorms. Although these studies show divergence of views on certain issues, such as software copying, they tend to show agreement concerning more fundamental concepts such as the value of trust. Further, it is not critical to the existence of hypernorms to show substantial agreement on a single form of expression. Walzer argues that "minimalism" (his term for what Donaldson and Dunfee call hypernorms) "is not foundational: it is not the case that different groups of people discover that they are all committed to the same set of ultimate values."

Instead, minimalism "consists in principles and rules that are reiterated in different times and places, and that are seen to be similar even though they are expressed in different idioms and reflect different histories and different versions of the world". Can examples be provided? Frederick (1991) studied six intergovernmental compacts (including the OECD Guidelines for Multinational Enterprises, the Helsinki Final Act, and the ILO Tripartite Declaration of Principles Concerning Multinational Enter-prises) to identify principles common to the set. Similarly, one could look to the statements of global organisations as potential sources of hypernorms. The Principles for Business developed by the Caux Round Table (which meets annually in Caux, Switzerland), is a prime example; as is the document "Towards a Global Ethic," produced by the Council for a Parliament of the World's Religions. From these we can pull some samples, that seem at least to the authors to be intuitively correct as examples of hypernorms.

Here are three candidates:

i. Firms should adopt adequate health and safety standards for employees and grant employees the right to know about job-related health hazards;
ii. You should not lie; speak and act truthfully;
iii. Businesses (should be expected to) honor their obligations in a spirit of honesty and fairness.

Hypernorms thus bound the moral free space of communities. If, for example, a hypernorm prohibiting bribery can be sustained, then any authentic norm recognizing bribery among, say, a community of corrupt government officials in Russia, is not legitimate ipso facto. However, hypernorms do not provide a complete bounding of the moral free space of communities. The issue may still arise of conflict between two or more norms that are legitimate.

Priority Rules for Conflicting Norms

The final term of the macro social contract is: In the case of conflicts among norms satisfying terms 1-3, priority must be established through the application of rules consistent with the spirit of the overall macro social contract (i.e., the "priority rules" term). Multiple legitimate norms applicable to the same ethical judgment may conflict. This may happen when a transaction crosses two distinctly different communities, often the case in marketing and global business. For example, a European firm doing busi-ness in Beijing must decide whether it will follow the local practice of "Guanxi". A Chinese official wants his sôn hired for a job at a U.S. plant. The action, acceptable in China, violates norms of fairness in the U.S. Here, both norms are recognized as authentic, and both may be considered legitimate, because neither violates a hypernorm.

To resolve such problems, ISCT specifies a loose set of six priority rules derived from the basic assumptions and terms of the macro social contract and influenced by concepts underlying principles of international conflicts of law and dispute resolution. They are as follows:

i. Transactions solely within a single community, which do not have significant adverse effects on other humans or communities, should be governed by the host community's norms;

ii. Community norms for resolving priority should be applied, so long as they do not have significant adverse effects on other humans or communities;

iii The more extensive the community that is the source of the norm, the greater the priority which should be given to the norm;

iv. Norms essential to the maintenance of the economic environment in which the transaction occurs should have priority over norms potentially damaging to that environment;

v. Where multiple conflicting norms are involved, patterns of consistency among the alternative norms provide a basis for prioritization;

vi. Well-defined norms should ordinarily have priority over more general, less precise norms. Some of the more challenging issues of marketing ethics involve conflicting legitimate norms.

The marketing research community, for example, may believe that some "soft" deception of respondents is acceptable to obtain results which further the goals of marketing research and contribute to the general economic welfare. The broader social community may have an opposite norm, thinking that full disclosure of who is behind research or its purposes is necessary to justify the respondent's participation. Thus, the research community is accepting of a utilitarian justification while the broader social community is concerned about dignity and a right to consent. Both norms may pass the hypernorm and exit/voice tests so that both are legitimate. Under ISCT, the priority rules are to be applied as a set, not in isolation. For a given dilemma, several might be involved.

The rules aren't given priority themselves in the writings about ISCT to date; they are presumably to be loosely weighed and applied without a strict calculus of relative value. In this case, the fourth rule, norms essential to the transaction environment, would support the soft deception. But the third, fifth, and (possibly) the second rule, may appear to support the norms of the broader social community, requiring disclosure to the participant. In the next section, we examine the issue of commercial bribery using ISCT. We summarize conventional arguments regarding its moral status and show how ISCT often provides important insights in judging marketing decisions that could involve bribery.

ISCT and Commercial Bribery Marketing Ethics and the Issue of Bribery Noonan's (1984) chronological account of bribery as a moral concept traces its origins back to 3,000 B.C. Despite its condemnation, bribery has persisted as a corrupt practice in human affairs. Nonetheless, Noonan foresees a time when bribery, like slavery, will become obsolete, at least in its central form of the exchange of payment for official action. This would be good news for business and, especially, for marketers. Bribery typically tops the list of practices that U.S. business executives would most like to see eliminated in their industry; accordingly, it is prominently featured in most corporate codes of conduct. Chonko and Hunt's survey of

AMA members found that marketing managers identified bribery as the most difficult ethical issue they faced. Trevino and Nelson observe that it is the "most frequent source of anxiety for American business persons operating abroad."

With the increasing importance of global marketing, the U.S. government, lobbied by business, has stepped up efforts to secure the prohibition of transnational bribery. The prototypical problem areas with global bribery involve the marketing function: promotional expenses such as travel and entertainment for purchasing agents, hiring of self-described marketing agents, customs payments in a channel of distribution, exchanges of gifts and entertainment during the negotiation process, and so on. Clearly, commercial bribery is one of the most important ethical issues in marketing. Bribery has been studied empirically in marketing, but little attention has been given to a normative evaluation.

On the other hand, the ethics of bribery has been thoroughly examined in the broader fields of business and applied ethics. We rely on these analyses to define the concept of bribery and to provide the conventional moral arguments against bribery as well as justifications advanced in its favor. We then show how ISCT can be applied to bribery. Bribery is a particularly appropriate issue for exploring the implications of social contract based analysis, especially bribery in a global context.

During the 1980s and early 1990s, Honda dealers paid over $15 million directly to Honda executives in order to get extra allotments of popular Honda and Acura models that typically sold at a premium to the manufacturer's sticker price. Gifts included shopping sprees in Hong Kong, cash and checks for children's college tuition. Two dozen Honda dealers and executives were indicted, including senior vice-presidents and regional managers. Two were convicted in court trials and 20 pled guilty. At the trial of the two convicted officials, the defense claimed that the bribery was an accepted practice at American Honda and that it was a way to keep salaries below the industry norm. Stanley Cardiges, the senior vice-president in charge of sales, was the main benefactor of the bribery, receiving over $5 million during a ten-year period when his salary was $125,000. Prosecutors called the case the largest commercial bribery case in U.S. history. Subsequently, 1,800 dealers sued I a class action alleging that they were punished if they failed to pay exorbitant bribes. Honda ultimately settled the case for $330 million.

In 1990, Young & Rubicam (Y&R) pled guilty to conspiring to violate the Foreign Corrupt Practices Act (FCPA) and paid a fine of $500,000. The charges resulted from claims that Y&R had made payments to Arnold Foote, a Jamaican business executive, who used the money to bribe the Jamaican Minister of Tourism, Eric Abrahams, in order to win an advertising account for Jamaican tourism. The resulting contract produced the award-winning advertising campaign "Make it Jamaica, Again" featuring the song "Come Back to Jamaica."

In bringing the indictment the U.S. attorney stated: "I'm not sitting here damning Young & Rubicam as a horrible, corrupt organisation. Throughout, there were a lot of very honest people connected with this." Bribery Defined Bribery must be defined carefully to avoid ambiguity, both in determining its moral status and in identifying whether a given action constitutes a bribe. Bribery occurs where one person (the briber) provides an inducement to another person (the bribee) that is intended to be in exchange for the bribee doing, or not doing, something that would favor the briber and be contrary to the bribee's positional duty.

Much analysis of bribery focuses on violations of duty by public officials, including activities outside the com-mercial sphere, such as payments to sway judges in criminal cases. Yet, it is apparent from the above definitions that bribery may occur within private-sector commercial tran-sactions, as in the Honda example. Private-sector com-mercial bribery, as generally defined in U.S. legal statutes, consists of "conferring a benefit on an employee, agent, or fiduciary with intent to influence the recipient's conduct in his principal's affairs". In a principal-agent analysis, the bribee violates the trust of his or her principal and becomes the agent of another in exchange for payment. Accordingly, D'Andrade has referred to bribery as the "alienation of agency". The Moral Status of Bribery: Deontological and Consequentialist Approaches Normative evaluation of bribery could draw on multiple theories of moral philo-sophy. Fritzsche and Shaw (1988) use theories of justice. However, the major works on bribery in applied ethics are largely deontological or consequentialist. This is not surprising; indeed, because of their importance, extant frameworks in marketing ethics also rely heavily on these theories.

A Deontological Approach

From a deontological perspective, bribery is wrong when it involves an intentional violation of a binding moral duty. In such a case, both the briber and the bribee may have engaged in an unethical act. The action of offering a bribe may be immoral because one should not entice others to do what is morally wrong, among other reasons. The bribee's moral duty stems from a special obligation that comes with the position that he or she holds: acceptance of a bribe conflicts with the bribee's binding obligations to a principal and thus would be a violation of a contract or a breach of promise.

Where the agent is a public official, a broader obligation to the public may be involved. Abrahams' actions in the Y&R case violated his duties as a government minister, as well as broader obligations of public trust to the citizens of Jamaica. In private-sector bribery, such as the Honda case, while bribees typically are in violation of duties to their employers, it is less clear that any broader duty exists. The Honda executives had obligations that derived from their employment contracts and their basic job requirements to allocate new cars in a certain manner. They accepted personal inducements to act inconsistently with that duty. D'Andrade extends this analysis to suggest that many employees of private businesses have a quasi-official status, similar to that of public officials.

A Consequentialist Approach

Bribery may be judged unethical from a conse-quentialist

perspective when it produces overall bad conse-quences. Direct or micro-environmental effects may include the following. Bribery may lead to a suboptimal purchase decision by the organisation on whose behalf the bribee ostensibly acts. The bribing organisation may need to falsify its accounts to hide the payment, thereby defrauding stockholders. In its purpose of obtaining an unfair advantage for one supplier, bribery harms that supplier's competitors. In the Y&R case, it may be presumed that competing agencies were unfairly disadvantaged if they did not engage in bribery. Bribery may contribute to the corruption of the moral character of the bribee, which may lead to future harmful actions. In contrast, direct good consequences of bribery may also be identified—particularly by marketing decision-makers—including saving jobs, enhancing share-holder wealth, and maintaining an ability to pay creditors.

Indirect or macro-environmental effects of bribery can include economic inefficiencies. Public sector bribery is a form of rent-seeking by business that can lead to inefficient allocations of resources, including the diversion of time and resources away from the production of useful goods and services or the implementation of monopolistic pricing practices. One effect of corrupt senior government officials is their tendency to favor public-sector spending that provides more opportunity for bribery, such as infra-structure and defense projects, rather than education or healthcare. Both public-and private-sector bribery distorts the market mechanism; the secrecy of bribery means that price information is less meaningful, again leading to allocation inefficiencies. More broadly, there may be diminished trust in the economic system. Other indirect consequences include the wider social harm of corruption. Nichols (1997) refers to its corrosive effect on the social structure, including the diminished happiness of the citizenry, reduced credibility and viability of the government, increased lawlessness, and even the potential for public disgust supportive of revolution.

Problems with these Approaches

In the abstract, at least, bribery appears to be generally unethical when analyzed from deontological and consequentialist perspectives. However, the application of these approaches to specific cases of bribery often requires complex judgments and extensive fact-finding. We must also consider the possibility that some justifications for bribery may carry moral weight. From the deontological perspective, bribery is only prima facie wrong. This means that there may be considerations that override the duties violated under bribery; it is not a categorical rule.

Consider the manager who, in violation of company policy, made a payment years ago to a South African official not to enforce the rules of apartheid. Moreover, a briber may have overriding duties—such as to protect the welfare of other employees—when deciding whether to pay a bribe. Or one may have duties to oneself or one's family when coerced, physically or economically, into making a payment. In addition, there may be problems associated with how duty-based approaches are applied. For instance, it may be difficult to identify the duties that an agent owes to his or her principal. It is often suggested that customs agents do not violate a duty when they take small payments to perform their duties because these payments are seen as an expected part of their compensation (though the right to accept payments is generally not expressly specified and there are often questions as to whether the right indeed exists and the scope of permissible payments).

A similar argument was advanced to justify bribery in the Honda case, with low executives' salaries offered in justification. The payments were claimed to be part of the intended compensation scheme. Moreover, there may be conflicting duties. While some argue there is a duty not to bribe a public official, others argue for a counter-duty to shareholders requiring bribery of public officials when that appears to be the most profitable long-run business decision. Applying consequentialist theories to specific instances of bribery also can be difficult. The forecasting required to assess probable consequences may be beyond the capacity of both marketing managers and business ethicists. How, for example, should Y&R executives have weighed the negative effects of their bribery on competitors as compared to its positive effects on their own firm and even, perhaps, on the nation of Jamaica, if one assumes that they believed they could develop the best advertising campaign?

Business ethicists have suggested similar arguments. Green (1991) has developed an explicitly consequentialist framework which would allow payments of bribes by smaller firms who otherwise might incur large harms if the inducement were not provided. Pastin and Hooker (1988) employed a consequentialist analysis as part of their attack on the FCPA. Perceived positive effects of bribery, at least from the vantage point of the briber, may lead to its attempted justification. For instance, it may be argued that payment of a bribe may retain jobs, save a substantial capital investment, or open up an important market. Thus it could be claimed that paying the bribe would generate significant positive returns to shareholders.

Moreover, consider the direct negative effects of bribery listed earlier and how a potential briber might discount them. The bribee may have long ago passed the point where the briber is causing him or her any further moral harm. Falsifying accounts may be fraud against shareholders, but, if offset by a significant increase in shareholder wealth, this could be seen as no more than a minor reporting peccadillo. The bribe may serve to guarantee that the bribee chooses the "best" supplier for the organisation for which he or she acts. Finally, doing harm to competitors may be seen as business as usual or, at most, one negative consequence in an otherwise entirely positive set of consequences. Although we are unlikely to ever know, Y&R executives may well have engaged in some of this reasoning in deciding to allow Foote to bribe Abrahams.

In sum, under a consequentialist analysis, the ethical evaluation amounts to balancing numerous potential costs and benefits from the perspective of their impact on those affected by the payment. Such judgements are plagued by seemingly intractable problems of forecasting and incommensurability. We examine the role of ISCT in responding to these and other concerns below. First, how-ever, we provide a social contract based analysis of bribery. The Moral Status of Bribery under Social Contract Approa-ches As our earlier review of social contract theory would indicate, an evaluation of bribery from a basic social contract perspective would judge it unethical when it is shown to constitute a fundamental violation of the social contract between business and society. Philips lends support to this analysis, suggesting that the moral obligations of the bribee stem from a social contract model of organisations: "By accepting a position in an organisation... one tacitly agrees to abide by the rules of that organisation.

To be bribed is to violate that agreement... and is, therefore, prima facie wrong." Hence a basic social contract analysis suggests that bribery is often unethical, at least in the abstract. ISCT, as a particular formulation of social contract theory, allows that claim to be made much more strongly in relation to specific instances of bribery. Consider how consequentialist and deontological theories might be applied to the Honda example. Some Honda dealers might well have concluded that bribery was a competitive necessity and that, if practiced by all dealers, would not result in bad (direct) consequences; conceivably, they might argue that there would only be good consequences. Further, they might well have had difficulty identifying a violation of duty by the bribees, if the practice were widespread and seemingly condoned by Honda. ISCT suggests a different and potentially more compelling analysis.

Bribery would be morally permissible under ISCT if all of the following conditions hold. First, the acceptability of bribery is an authentic norm of the communities involved; that is, a norm held by a majority of community members. Second, the norms of all relevant communities have been considered. Third, the acceptability of bribery is a legitimate norm; that is, it does not violate a hypernorm. Fourth, and finally, any conflict among communities' norms is resolved by the priority rules in favor of the communities sustaining the acceptability of bribery. Below, we analyze the Honda and Y&R cases following this procedure. In the Honda case, it is possible that the acceptability of bribery as a means of allocating new cars was an authentic norm of the Honda marketing managers and a subset of the dealers. The bribing dealers and the marketing managers accepting the bribes may have thought that the system was not adequately rewarding them, especially given Honda's marketing success, and that they were entitled to adopt a mutually beneficial system providing extra compensation. However, not all dealers shared this perspective. In a suit filed against Honda, a former Acura dealer in New Hampshire claimed that because he didn't cooperate, he couldn't obtain the cars he needed and was forced to sell his dealership. In the class action, 1,800 dealers sued charging that the bribery racket was under the direction of top company executives. If these protesting dealers represent a majority of dealers, the acceptability of bribery was not an authentic norm among the entire community of Honda dealers. Hence, bribery in the Honda case is not morally permissible under the first condition. If they are not a majority, or if the dealers are treated as multiple communities, then non-bribing dealers must at least be treated as a relevant community in the analysis. In seeking to identify authentic ethical norms, it is essential to consider all potentially relevant communities.

Hence, when communities having pro-bribery authentic norms are identified, it is important to take into account other relevant communities that might have anti-bribery norms. In the Y&R case, there is solid evidence that the broader political community in Jamaica condemned the practice of bribery. The fact that the payment was kept secret would appear to indicate that the participants were aware of a contrary norm in the broader community. The strong negative reactions in both the United States and Jamaica when the payments were disclosed constitute further support for the existence of an anti-bribery norm in those communities. Further, the broader communities are the ones that bear the negative costs of the practice and would rationally be expected to hold an anti-bribery norm.

Once all relevant communities and authentic norms have been identified, it becomes necessary to determine that the norms do not violate a hypernorm and are therefore legitimate. We believe that the practice in the Y&R case, which involved a coarse selling of public assets for private gain, does violate a hypernorm. Bribery is condemned in some form throughout the world, as Nichols makes clear: Corruption and bribery cannot be claimed as accepted phenomena in any culture. These acts are condemned by each of the major moral and religious codes. They are criminalized by every country. And they are universally despised, particularly by those who endure corrupt governments. This claim supports the idea of a convergence of opinion and wisdom to the effect that coarse public sector bribery is condemned by a hypernorm. The concept of a hypernorm is central to the application of ISCT. It serves as a constraint on the moral free space of communities while at the same time providing a source of guidance for ethicists and business decision-makers. The small set of hypernorms believed to exist as part of the assumptions of the macro social contract is universally applicable to all cultures and business functions. In that sense, there are not marketing hypernorms or U.S. hypernorms, per se. But there may be hypernorms that are especially relevant to a particular business function, such as marketing. Accordingly, one possible hypernorm is that the bribery of officials who exchange significant public sector assets for substantial personal gain is wrong.

An anti-bribery hypernorm is supported by the condemnation of bribery in explicit terms by texts of Buddhism, Christianity, Confucianism, Hinduism, Islam, Judaism, and Sikhism; Adam Smith and Mao Ts Tung have also condemned bribery. Coarse public-sector bribery is legally prohibited in every country, even those considered the most corrupt. Indeed, a multi-cultural team explicitly applying ISCT has identified such a hypernorm. A case might also be made that the coarser forms of private-sector bribery violate a hypernorm, even though this does not involve the violation of public trust that occurs when the bribee is a public official. There is, after all, a growing consensus across many world communities that bribery is wrong and that significant efforts should be taken to limit its practice, prompting new initiatives by multilateral organisations, such the Organisation for Economic Co-operation and Development.

The implications for the two examples are as follows. The coarse public-sector bribery found in the Y&R case violates a hypernorm, and thus could be evaluated on this basis alone as unethical under ISCT. The application of an anti-bribery hypernorm is more problematic in the Honda case because public sector officials were not involved. However, putting aside the possibility of a private-sector anti-bribery hypernorm, this case may still be problematic because it is not necessary to rely solely on hypernorms to determine whether the payments were ethical. We turn to the priority rules to resolve the conflict between the possible authentic norms that supported the payments and other norms that opposed the practice. The priority rules are used to resolve conflicts in norms between communities.

The third and fourth priority rules might be used to show that bribery in Honda would not be permissible under ISCT. The third priority rule determines priority based on the relative size of the communities. It would favor the non-bribing dealers if they represent a larger group, because greater priority is given to the norms of more extensive communities. The fourth priority rule determines priority on the basis of whether a norm is indispensable to the transaction environment. It would also appear to favor the non-bribing dealers, because an anti-bribery norm is arguably essential to their economic environment and would thus have priority over a norm favoring bribery that if widely adopted, could harm that environment.

ISCT and Justifications Advanced for Bribery In a survey of over 2,000 U.S. business executives, Longenecker,

McKinney, and Moore asked respondents whether they considered the following scenario "personally acceptable":

A company paid a $350,000 "consulting" fee to an official of a foreign country. In return, the official promised assistance in obtaining a contract, which should produce a $10 million profit for the contracting company. Assuming that the official would act in violation of a positional duty, we have a clear illustration of bribery and an illegal act under the FCPA. However, less than half of the survey respondents condemned the payment perhaps because they believed that the payment could be justified. We now examine some of the popular justifications for making payments. It is often claimed that "certain payments should not be counted as bribes, or that, even though they are bribes, they are still acceptable, generally as the lesser of two evils".

Some payoffs may be defended as coerced by physical or severe economic extortion. Payments also may be justified as mere "grease payments", legitimate third party commissions, or gifts. Justifications for bribery may also be based on arguments about cultural differences in transnational bribery or on claims of greater harm resulting from failure to pay the bribe. ISCT helps clarify these justifications through an emphasis on understanding community norms.

Extortion as Justification

Extortion payments are made under duress. Payment is demanded by the bribee, with the threat of serious harm for nonpayment. Nichols defines extortion as "using the power of an official's office to extract payments." Corporate agents as well as government officials may practice extortion. In the U.S., a buyer for the retailer, J. C. Penney Co., was prosecuted for taking up to $1.5 million from vendors. One vendor claimed that the buyer was engaging in extortion and sued Penney, charging that payment was a matter of survival: "If I had not paid him and he pulled the line as he had threatened, I'd have gone out of business". This vendor explained that he could not report the buyer to the company because he was the Buyer of the Year and highly-regarded by Penney.

Acting as an extortionist is always morally problematic. Giving in to genuine extortion may also be problematic. Philips (1984) observes that it is morally wrong to pay off extortionists in some cases. Under U.S. law, evidence of duress is admissible to establish the nature of the intent involved in the payment. D'Andrade also suggests that extortion payments are excusable under some circumstances, noting that "we just do not expect moral heroism." Turow concludes that "bribery can be justified only if the bribe-giver is truly without alternatives." An ISCT-based analysis of bribery focuses on community norms to determine when extortion demands should be resisted or, contrariwise, when they may be given into. While we may not expect moral heroism of marketers, there may be a legitimate expectation on the part of society of a certain amount of "moral courage", a willingness to face down evil and accept some self-sacrifice.

However, the extent to which we might expect moral heroism by marketers will vary across communities reflecting differing norms about how to face extortion. For example, in a situation where corruption is negligible, strongly prosecuted, and rarely associated with threats of physical harm, there may be an increased expectation that marketers will not bow to extortion. Accordingly, acceding to extortion in many markets in the U.S. may be less morally justifiable than under circumstances often found in, say, Nigeria or Russia. Grease Payments and Legitimate Commissions. A firm may make small payments to induce public officials to carry out their official and nondiscretionary duties, often referred to as a "facilitating" or "grease" payment.

Although the action may have been carried out more expeditiously, it does not confer a substantial advantage on the party making the payment. Similarly, a firm may provide bona fide compensation to a middleman to promote or demonstrate its products and services. Both types of payment may be legal under the FCPA. The Act expressly recognizes that there may be small payments made to obtain permits or licenses to do business, to get mail or phone service, to process visas or to get cargo loaded (particularly for perishable products). But judgment is required.

What types of payments can be justified as facilitating payments? Or what happens when the marketing intermediary (or joint venture partner) uses part of the "commission" to pay a large bribe to a public official as in the Y&R case? Sometimes, it is argued that it is difficult to know where the payment is actually going and thus whether it is legitimate.

The law seeks to determine whether there is an awareness of a high probability of the existence of a prohibited circumstance. Principles such as "willful blindness" and "conscious disregard" are used to prohibit a firm from purposely establishing opaque information channels to be able to deny knowledge of wrongdoing. While in some circumstances it may be difficult to account for the size or recipients of such payments, purposeful ignorance is not a permissible justification for bribery. The ethical issue of when a payment may be proper runs parallel to this legal approach. The critical distinction is the nature of the official function purchased and whether it involves a violation of duty by the official. However, companies often overlook this rather fine distinction.

For instance, when Gulf Oil Corporation was attempting to expand its distribution in Italy it made off-the-book payments to government officials to secure the permits it needed to open new service stations. Gulf officials characterized these payments as "tipping". Thus, an ISCT-based analysis recognizes that the social contract in some communities defines these payments as acceptable bribery or perhaps not even as bribery at all. The firm is responsible for knowing the relevant norms in the specific community in question and, more importantly, in the broader communities influenced by the decision. Such knowledge would allow firms to respond appropriately and avoid mistakes such as Gulf's.

Gift Giving and Entertainment Relationships constitute an important foundation for business. This fundamental fact is recognized explicitly in the marketing function through relationship marketing and selling. In many cultures, norms pertaining to proper behaviour among individuals in all walks of life often specify the giving of gifts and the providing of entertainment in appropriate circumstances. However, bribes can also take the form of gifts and entertainment. The U.S. has a long tradition of gifts and entertainment in business relationships. A large industry exists encompassing well known practices such as parties in corporate boxes at sports stadiums, special golf outings, and meals at fancy restaurants. Yet, in spite of what appears to be a strongly entrenched practice, there is some evidence of a counter-trend. American businesses seem increasingly to be questioning the role of gifts and entertainment in conducting business.

From an ISCT perspective, the norms of gift-giving and entertainment in U.S. business are changing. General Motors, for example, recently introduced a policy that forbids its employees from accepting free meals, hockey tickets, golf outings or most other gifts from vendors. Vendors complained that the new policy restricted the scope for building the social relationships necessary for good business relationships. GM's concern, however, is that their gifts and entertainment were tantamount to bribery. Those who provide such largess are on the horns of a dilemma. If they believe that hosting buyers to corporate boxes makes no difference in the buyer's behaviour, as is sometimes claimed, then how can they justify the expenditures to their shareholders? If they are spending the money and getting nothing in return, the shareholders would appear to have a legitimate complaint that corporate assets are being squan-dered.

If, on the other hand, gifts and entertainment are in exchange for preferential treatment, then providing them may be considered an act of bribery. Priest's advice is to "build strong business relationships but don't be corrupted by them." If the practice is consistent with background norms that provide the ground-rules, as it were, for proper gift giving in business transactions, then the practice may well be acceptable under ISCT. The norms specify the boundaries for acceptable social lubrication while also providing markers concerning what is excessive and out of bounds. The norms vary in their details over time and among industries. Perhaps in recognition of this pheno-menon, many companies have policies that appear vague on accepting gifts because they ask employees to simply "exercise good judgment." This may be interpreted as instructing employees to rely upon their knowledge of industry norms and practices. Other companies have strict, often monetary, limits on what may be received. While such policies may reduce the appearance of bribery, they may also be at odds with well-understood norms of acceptable behaviour. When this occurs, the overly restrictive norms are not likely to be well received by either vendors or their own employees. Gift giving and entertainment, particularly in the context of business-to-business exchanges, may be formally analyzed using ISCT. Consider the trend whereby companies increasingly are sending out "no presents" letters during the December holidays. Absent evidence of close personal friendship, gifts (and entertainment) in excess of industry norms are indicative of bribery. These letters specify com-pany policy concerning what its employees may receive as gifts and ask that suppliers observe these rules.

This can result in a classic conflicts-of-norms situation. One firm, an aggressive marketer, uses gifts and entertainment to build relationships. The firm sending the letter, on the other hand, seeks to limit the pernicious effect gifts may have on its purchasing agents. While duties might otherwise be unclear and consequences difficult to parse out, ISCT approaches the conflict by directing the corporate policymaker to identify organisational, industry and national norms pertaining to gift giving (these norms will often be well known or easy to identify). Under ISCT, if the firm sending the "no presents" letters is acting in a manner consistent with industry and national norms (and thus the letter refers to a legitimate, authentic norm), it should dominate the norms of the selling firm. Under the priority rules the "no presents" norm is essential to the transaction environment, is consistent with other com-munity norms, and represents that organisation's pre-ference concerning conflicts of norms.

Acceptability of Bribery in Some Cultures Many cultures accept and encourage the presence of certain forms of gift giving in business and personal relationships. On the other hand, societies always face a concern that their economic systems be able to generate wealth and allocate resources efficiently, a goal that may be compromised by corrupt behaviour. A plausible community response is to develop norms that specify the boundaries of acceptable behaviour. This may help account for highly ritual gift-giving practices in many cultures. Background norms provide guidance as to the timing and amount of gifts and the context in which they may be given and accepted. Those who act outside of these norms do so at their peril. Fadiman offers a rich description of how tradition plays an important role in business in non-Western cultures. He describes how he misunderstood requests for Chai and Zawadi— which can be Swahili terms for "bribe"—when conducting busi-ness in East Africa.

He turned down his prospective business partner's request for cash and a radio, only later to discover that they were intended for a feast in his honor that, in keeping with tradition, would have been an introduction to his partner's social and business contacts. Building on this anecdote, Fadiman explains how in more communal societies there are often obligations of protection and assistance that extend beyond the nuclear family to an inner circle of "comrades and kin." In these societies, there is a preference for business relationships with people in the inner circle who are known and trusted. Accordingly, there are various traditional ways by which such relationships are developed, including the future favor and gift giving. Fadiman explains, "any individual under obligation to another has entered a relationship in which the first favor must be repaid in the future." This on-going process builds trust and is different from Western approaches: "Western interest lies in doing business; non-Western, in forming bonds so that business can begin.

Westerners seek to discharge obligations; non-Westerners, to create them". Gift giving is one way of creating future obligation. In some cultures, Fadiman suggests, gifts that would be viewed as unacceptable bribes in other cultures are still seen as merely gifts. Accordingly, he advises Western businesspeople to first understand the local context and then look for legal, ethical, and culturally appropriate ways to meet the local partner's expectations. For instance, non monetary responses or public donations might be possible that meet the business partner's desire for local recognition and to assist the community, as well as consolidating the relationship. As an example, Fadiman refers to Coca-Cola in Egypt, noting that "to sell cola, Coke did not bribe ministers, it planted trees."

But why not bribe if, apparently, it is culturally acceptable? Various writers agree that bribery is not unethical if it is an accepted practice in the culture where it takes place. Longenecker, McKinney, and Moore, after noting that for some people "the international setting modifies the ethical character of bribery," reported that many of their respondents justified bribery with the adage, "When in Rome do as the Romans do." At issue, then, is the acceptability of bribery within different cultures. A justification often offered for bribery in foreign markets is that standards are different and, implicitly, lower. However, this claim is made notwithstanding the prevalence of bribery within the U.S. and other Western countries (in the 1997 rankings of the prevalence of corruption by Transparency International, a highly regarded non-governmental organisation, the U.S. ranked 16th, France 20th, and Italy 30th, where lower numbers mean less corruption). Moreover, while noting that in some societies there is not necessarily a violation of duties when an official shows favoritism to friends and kinsmen, Philips warns of the risk of "bribery in ethnic dress."

It has also been suggested that Western business people too readily presume a requirement for bribery, especially when frustrated by red tape and inefficient government practices. Indeed, as noted in The Economist (1988), perhaps it's LDCs that are brought down by MNCs, not the other way round. ISCT provides a framework specifically set up to resolve the ethical issues arising between communities. According to our earlier analysis, bribery in a foreign country would be morally permissible under ISCT if its effects are limited largely to the community in which it is acceptable (assuming bribery does not violate a hypernorm). Thus, arguments in favor of bribery in certain culturally defined contexts may be interpreted in a manner consistent with ISCT. But it would be very rare that such a situation would hold. In practice, there would typically be some affected communities for which the acceptance of bribery is not an authentic norm. Of course, in any specific situation, this may be subject to empirical verification. What ISCT does in this instance is to prompt the marketer to identify all relevant communities.

At least where managers have good knowledge of the countries and cultures where they ope-rate, empirical research should not be necessary. If, as D'Andrade suggests, there is always a third party to bribery, we might argue that it is never sufficient to consider only the norms of the immediate participants in bribery. As in our analysis of the Y&R case, we must instead look to the broader communities within which bribery occurs. ISCT's insistence on attention to the relevant communities and their norms, and its priority rules that favor larger or more extensive communities, can be generally expected to lead to the identification of overriding anti-bribery norms.

Competitive Disadvantage as a Justification for Bribery

Bribery has been justified as an unfortunate necessity, given that a likely outcome is the loss of business to a bribe-paying competitor. The justification often is tied to a consequentialist analysis with the briber arguing that payment preserves jobs, increases profits and produces future business opportunities. It may also be akin to the extortion argument, as the bribee's threat of lost business may be seen as a form of economic coercion. In that context, the justification offered under a deontological analysis would be that the briber lacked intent due to the over-coming of free will by the economic threat.

The consequentialist argument has been implicitly recognized in the broad claim that U.S. companies are at a competitive disadvantage because of their inability to make payments due to the FCPA. However, evidence for this is mixed. The moral justification for a payment due to competitive disadvantage must depend in part upon the extent of the harm threatened. Competitive disadvantage is likely to be less significant when it pertains to a threat to future business prospects in contrast to a direct threat to existing and substantial capital investment. Whether competitors are likely to make payments to obtain the business should also be a factor.

In the Penney case, discussed earlier, prosecutors discovered that other vendors had rejected requests for payment and not suffered, contrary to the extortion claim. In the Honda case, there is evidence of harm resulting to dealers who chose not to make payoffs. Competitive disadvantage is less likely to justify bribery under ISCT. Only if authentic ethical norms support such payments, and even then, no hypernorms are violated, can ISCT be used to support such a payment. Further, there may be contrary norms in other communities, which would also not allow the briber to use competitive disadvantage as an argument in support of payments.

Implications of ISCT for Marketing Ethics

A social contract perspective on marketing ethics, especially within the framework provided by ISCT, would appear to offer considerable insight on the issue of bribery, going beyond that provided by extant approaches. In this section, we illustrate ISCT's broader potential and consider its implications for managers and researchers by examining it in relation to other normative frameworks and noting its particular applicability to marketing. We then conclude this section by identifying opportunities that ISCT provides to researchers in marketing ethics and by showing how marketing research techniques may facilitate application of ISCT.

ISCT Compared to Extant Normative Framework

We first look at how ISCT supplements, complements or otherwise informs the existing models of marketing ethics. What are the general merits of an ISCT-based analysis, relative to extant approaches?

1. ISCT provides normative legitimization for the relevance of community and professional norms.

1. Relativism is the bete noir of moral philosophy. Within the field of business ethics it is attacked as illogical and self defeating: relativism "represents an admission that our human reason can no longer be useful . . . that we must engage in . . . deception, physical coercion, even war, rather than try to do the admittedly difficult job of resolving conflicting moral viewpoints". In spite of this, some theorists of marketing ethics have explicitly or implicitly advocated a form of relativism as an effective approach to problems of marketing ethics. Fear of being branded a relativist may result in the downplaying of the role of community, organisational and professional norms. Yet, as recognized in most of the descriptive approaches to marketing ethics, background norms are important in making normative judgments about marketing practices. ISCT invokes the use of a traditional, accepted philosophical methodology (social contracts) to legitimate giving significant weight to authentic norms of marketing ethics. The ultimate impact of ISCT is to provide a middle ground in which marketing norms may be given weight, yet are checked by hyper-norms and the occasional priority of other communities.
2. ISCT provides a formal definition for authentic norms and relevant communities that are often important components in marketing ethics frameworks. Many of the extant marketing ethics frameworks are designed to explain individual decision making. They are thus subject to the individuals' own preferences as to the choice of moral reasoning and the recognition of others' interests. This would seem to allow for an egoist to make successful

use of the model. One response to a concern about potential egoism is to recognize a leavening role for social norms. Thompson recognizes them as a source of cultural meanings, Mascarenhas as the source of standards for fault or accountability, and Hunt & Vitell as a source of duties. Sparks and Hunt identify awareness of norms as an influence on ethical sensitivity. ISCT extends this recognition by specifying the sources of norms and the processes by which norms are to be identified for normative analysis.

3. ISCT encourages decision-makers to consider the norms of all relevant communities, and thus ensures a broad consideration of stakeholder interests. In addition to the eight tests in their framework for ethical reasoning, Laczniak and Murphy add stakeholders, recognizing that "weighing the concerns of multiple stakeholder groups... becomes the essence of appropriate ethical decision-making [and] 'the root of the complexity of such decision-making." ISCT, in its emphasis on the norms of relevant communities, provides a systematic method to encourage decision-makers to make sure that they have considered all possible communities that may have a significant interest in a decision. Sparks and Hunt found that ethical sensitivity, which involves the ability to recognize and ascribe importance to an ethical issue, is learned. Their results indicate that ethical sensitivity of marketing researchers may be influenced more by organisational norms than by professional norms. They suggest that this may be due in part to the youth of the marketing research profession and its less systematic structures and activities compared to professions such as law, medi-cine and accounting. ISCT's emphasis on looking for relevant norms in broader communities may enhance ethical sensitivity on the part of marketing researchers.
4. ISCT acknowledges the role of a thin set of universal standards that can serve to limit the excessive relativism of some frameworks. The concept of a hypernorm is

central to the application of ISCT. It serves as a constraint on the moral free space of communities while at the same time providing a source of guidance for ethicists and business decision-makers.

5. ISCT provides a means for dealing with cross-cultural issues. With the possible exception of Thompson, the marketing ethics frameworks do not explicitly deal with the problem of cross-cultural application, including their use by someone more familiar with Eastern philo-sophies who may not be inclined to apply Western deontological or teleological thinking.

The moral free space recognized in ISCT is open to cultural and philosophical diversity. Under many of the marketing ethics frameworks, divergent answers may be obtained when the framework is invoked by, on the one hand, a manager in the United States and, on the other, a manager in Japan. These frameworks and models are generally silent concerning how such divergence is to be handled.

ISCT'S Particular Applicability to Marketing

The advantages of ISCT relative to extant approaches are applicable to its use throughout business ethics. However, we would suggest that ISCT is especially appli-cable when the marketer's activity is spanning multiple communities with conflicting norms; particularly, for instance, in international marketing, relationship marketing, and personal selling and sales management. This leads to the first of our reasons why ISCT is particularly applicable to marketing.

1. The role of the marketing manager as a boundary spanner; operating at the interface between the corpo-ration and its customers, competitors, and channel members. As a boundary spanner, the marketer is subject to the norms of numerous communities, including the marketer's firm, the marketer's depart-ment, the industry or marketplace, the individual customers, and the channel. Thus, ISCT's explicit recognition of numerous micro-social contracts and the communities that spawn them, provides a

framework for understanding the ethical pressures on the marketer and for providing guidance to marketing managers.

2. The theoretical congruence of ISCT as a framework for examining exchange relationships. We noted earlier that the exchange concept is fundamental to marketing and to social contract theory and thus that contractarian approaches appear particularly appropriate for ethical reasoning in marketing. ISCT sharpens these advant-ages by bringing clearer focus to the ethical ambiguities associated with exchange. Exchange occurs between parties who are each simultaneously members of multiple communities. Each party draws the norms that guide his or her beliefs, attitudes, and behaviours from a relevant set of communities. Moreover, the exchange transaction itself occurs in an environment which itself is often a community, each of which has developed norms that may significantly affect the exchange process (consider, for example, the global diamond business, sometimes nested within more general communities). Simply put, the exchange transaction cannot be fully understood without reference to the communities and norms in which it is embedded.
3. The potential for ISCT to integrate the normative and empirical streams of research in the marketing ethics literature. To date, in marketing as in many other domains, the two streams have followed separate courses with little or no overlap. In ISCT, the conflict between the "is" of empirical research and the "ought" of normative research may be bridged. Theoretically, ISCT requires both the normative and the descriptive to function adequately; thus, it defines a significant role for each. Practically, ISCT's willingness to consider any authentic, legitimate norm as binding on the com-munity and its insistence on the existence of numerous micro-social contracts that are community based offer considerable scope for the "is" of descriptive research. Yet its insistence on the existence of hypernorms and priority rules for dealing with conflicting authentic, legitimate norms offers a true normative

foundation with considerable scope for continuing conceptual development.

4. Social contract theory is all the more relevant given the development of relationship marketing. This important concept, with its emphasis on fostering on-going, tightly linked relationships between buyers and sellers, implicitly acknowledges the role of shared values. Clear recognition of buyer and seller expecta-tions concerning the other's behaviour will influence successful interactions and become reflected in norms that essentially frame their relationship. Perhaps more importantly, tightly linked marketing relationships may themselves become communities, with their own norms. A foundational principle of relational marketing is trust. Norms based in informal social contracts are critical to the development of trust in exchange relationships. Social norms provide a more flexible and enduring fabric for relationships than do other alternative fibers, such as litigation or government regulation. ISCT provides a framework for under-standing and potentially resolving the ethical issues that arise in this context.
5. Managerial attractiveness - we believe that ISCT will be found to be intellectually comfortable for many educated, reflective marketing practitioners.

The limitations of a strict use of utilitarianism or any one of the other basic models have probably led to the focus by marketing ethics researchers on composite models as they have sought realistic, pragmatic approaches. The basic notions of ISCT—community specific, authentic norms that are acceptable if they fit with a thin set of hypernorms and do not conflict with norms of other significant communities — would seem to provide a latitude for professionalism coupled with realistic checks and balances that should be appealing to marketing managers.

Implications for Researchers

Given the foregoing implications, we believe that ISCT provides marketing researchers with greater scope for making normative contributions to the marketing ethics literature by evaluating some of the more troubling ethical issues in marketing, such as: privacy obligations in the cross-marketing of financial services; conflicting goals in the marketing of for-profit health care; inter-segment differences in the acceptable level of product safety (especially across different country markets); conflicts of interest in personal selling; the acceptability of puffery in advertising; and fairness in pricing. Below, we show how empirical research may be critical to an ISCT-based analysis of some of these issues. We then conclude this section by identifying directions for further research that may advance ISCT. Marketing Research Techniques May Facilitate the Application of ISCT. ISCT relies on actual community norms.

This attribute imposes a prerequisite for the success-ful application of ISCT, accurate information as to com-munity norms or adequate proxies from which to infer those norms. A number of marketing research techniques, particularly those associated with ascertaining an individual's brand or store loyalty, can be applied to this problem. Broadly, these divide into three classes of techniques: 1) direct inquiry, for example, techniques based on Fishbein and Ajzen; 2) indirect inquiry, for example, conjoint analysis-based techniques; or, 3) measurement of behaviour.

The first type is subject to self-presentation issues, making the latter two classes more attractive (though both are more complicated to administer). In particular, some conjoint analysis based techniques have the distinct advantage of being derived from preferences for complete scenarios rather than being directly elicited. As such, they are less susceptible to biases of both self-presentation and self- deception. And for deeper probing of community norms and the basis for those norms, other techniques, such as focus groups, might make a real contribution. Thus, well-established marketing research techniques are available to assist with the identification of authentic norms within defined communities. This suggests a different approach to marketing ethics research, an approach that would be norm- focused rather than issue-focused. Studies could be conducted of the authenticity and legitimacy among norms espoused by marketing communities.

For example, is there substantial agreement among salespeople in particular industries that denigration of a competitor's product is acceptable conduct? Yet one of the challenging issues in applying ISCT is defining the boundaries of a community. Market segmentation techni-ques such as cluster or discriminate analysis and dimen-sional reduction techniques can be used to ascertain com-munity membership and the parameters that actually define membership. More qualitative methodologies such as those associated with sub-cultural and reference group determination could also prove useful. Thus, in a sense, there is a symbiotic connection between ISCT and marketing. ISCT provides a useful ethical framework for marketing, but marketing provides the empirical techniques necessary to utilize ISCT at its best.

Research to Advance ISCT

Research on the more difficult ethical issues in mar-keting, possibly augmented by the application of marketing research techniques, represents one set of directions for future research. In addition, there is scope to further develop ISCT. First, in relation to hypernorms: Clearly, the application of ISCT would benefit from a more definitive set of hypernorms. This is no small task. A starting point might be to identify hypernorms that are especially relevant to particular business functions, such as marketing. Below, we suggest possible marketing-relevant hypernorms in the hopes that others will extend, and where necessary, modify our list. We base our suggestions on the assumption that they reflect a sufficient convergence of thought and opinion to satisfy the definition of hypernorm used in ISCT.

- Human beings should be treated with dignity and respect in all marketing transactions.
- Promises should be kept.
- Deception of any sort in marketing transactions or marketing research is wrong unless a substantial

justification convincing to the membership of all rele-vant communities is possible.

- Property rights including intellectual property, consis-tent with widespread views of the nature of property, should be respected.
- Bribery of officials who exchange substantial public sector assets for personal gain is wrong.

Norms represent a second area of research that could advance ISCT. More specifically, what are the antecedents of authentic and legitimate norms in a community? How transferable are norms? How easy is it for firms or profes-sional associations to impose norms on new members? In this chapter we have explored the very real potential that social contract theory in general and ISCT in particular has for the field of marketing ethics. We see them as complementing and strengthening the existing frameworks and constructs for marketing ethics.

To recapitulate, ISCT has a number of significant theoretical advantages. First, it provides a core set of principles—hypernorms—which may be used to specify the line of the moral minimum that no marketing practitioner should ever pass over. Second, it explicitly recognizes differences across communities and the conflict that differing community-based norms engender and develops a process for resolving that conflict. Third, it offers a process for determining the appropriateness—that is the authen-ticity and the legitimacy—of a community-based norm.

Finally, ISCT provides a legitimating theoretical foundation for much of the emphasis on norms, attitudes, beliefs and cultural meanings in the field of marketing ethics. We have suggested a symbiotic relationship between ISCT and marketing. ISCT complements frameworks for ethical decision making in marketing and provides greater clarity concerning judgments about some of the difficult issues in marketing ethics, such as bribery. At the same time, marketing research, perhaps more than any other field, offers techniques that can allow ISCT to be effectively and efficiently applied.

3

The Consumer and the Manufacturer

It is not too much to say that in general the manufacturer wants to produce the article that the woman wants to buy. In many cases the reason he does not accomplish it is due to the fact that he does not divide his expenditures wisely. He neglects to pay the price for the highest grade skill in designing and he markets his product too quickly. The importance of developing a specific design cannot be overestimated. No machine on the market, of any type, is one hundred per cent perfect and none on the market should, therefore, be taken as a standard to be met by the new manufacturer. It is a patchwork, only, that is obtained by one common method used to obtain a newly designed machine. Namely, the manufacturer purchases every type of machine, already marketed to perform a given work, and adapts one part from one machine, another part from a second machine and perhaps still another part from a third machine. Such a design must always be a compromise, and it is seldom possible to obtain the original working efficiency of the several parts in the new machine because of the necessary compromises.

A second point that the manufacturer is apt to overlook is the importance of including the most minute of details in his general high standard of manufacture. For instance, he elects to use copper for a water container, but forgets to provide that every bolt and rivet and screw, no matter how small, shall be of a rust-resisting metal. The small part capable of rusting is as much an eyesore to the purchaser and in certain conditions can do as great damage as though the manufacturer had not spent the major sum to insure his rust-resisting container. And a third point: sometimes a manufacturer neglects to make certain of a perfection of detail in the factory that will produce one hundred per cent of uniformity in his product. Thus vacuum cleaner manufacturers, merely by installing equipment that would measure for them, under actual conditions of service, the correct air displacement of the particular machine tested, could eliminate any possibility of lack of uniformity in their product.

Further, it would take no more time for the inspection than is at present accorded to the routine reading of current consumption. Yet up to this time we know of no vacuum cleaner factory that has installed this comparatively simple and inexpensive equipment. When attempting to market a product to women, factory faults are of far greater importance than when marketing a product for the use of men. The latter understand the difficulties of factory production and accept the occasional defective product as a routine. They expect it to be credited. They expect prompt correction on the part of the manufacturer or dealer, and, once adjusted, with them the matter usually ends.

Not so with the average woman purchaser. First of all, and last of all, she remembers that something was the matter with the machine for which she paid her money. Oftentimes only the most drastic and unusual service on the part of the manufacturer will take away the sting that was left in her mind by the original transaction. In club, church, or in confidential chat at home, somewhere she leaves the impression that there is still something the matter or she would not have gotten a poor machine. The advertising value, therefore, of a uniformity of product cannot be overestimated. No amount of costly after-service will compensate for the lack of it.

A manufacturer sometimes fails to satisfy the woman consumer because he is attempting to satisfy a dealer's demand for "flashy" rather than practical selling points and, therefore, loses sight of the value to him of a perfect functioning of his device. Exclusive points of design that can be used for a spectacular demonstration have been up to this time perhaps the strongest of selling aids; but manufacturers and dealers alike are beginning to realize that they have an element of danger. Thus, the confetti test for vacuum cleaners was an unfortunate misuse of the machine. It has never convinced the woman purchaser that it would accomplish the more trying task of removing "grimed-in" soil, even while it fascinated her as a spectator and even while she left as a purchaser. She doubted her own machine because of the unconvincing test.

It was only a short time ago that in one of the trade papers dealing with household equipment there appeared an editorial endorsement, and an exceedingly strong one at that, of a certain dealer display which had attracted great crowds on both sidewalk and street before the dealer's window. The crowd had been drawn by the display of a number of different washing machines grouped around a central machine which was absorbing the "limelight." It had a swinging wringer and the wringer was revolving at so rapid a rate it became plain that any woman who stepped in the way of that particular type of wringer was doomed to a severe blow if not a fall. The idea of the dealer in using such a display was of the "stop-look-listen" variety, and he obtained all he could desire of this variety of interest. But he had not safeguarded the interest of _any_ washing machine in his window. For women have a certain reluctance toward machinery in motion and he failed to reckon with them as the purchasers of his washing machines. Would she buy one in order to use the swinging wringer as an obvious menace to herself and to her household? No.

In selecting an Iron, the woman looks for:

1. A weight of household iron that is around six pounds.
2. A general design that is easy to handle, of good balance and with comfortable large handle grip.
3. A thin sheet metal hood; weight in hood decreases ironing efficiency.

4. A correct relation between the weight of the storage heat mass above the heating element, and the weight of the sole plate beneath the heating element. Upon this relation depends good ironing results.

(If heating element should be inset in sole plate with one-fourth inch margin, a direct heat connection between the two masses of metal could be secured at a consequent reduction of heat loss.)

5. Cord connections to slip in and out easily.
6. Switch in plug connection or on cord.
7. Plug connection so heat insulated as to prevent conduction of heat, and overheating of cord at connections.

Undoubtedly if there was a prospective woman purchaser in that group in front of the window she left to become one of the hundreds of women who still are asking themselves the question "is a washing machine safe?"

It is not difficult to see how quickly this particular kind of demonstration becomes a boomerang to the manufacturer. It is as true of every type of spectacular appeal. The time has surely come to discontinue all such practices and to sell appliances: because they will do the work more quickly, more easily, or more cheaply, because they are so built that they will prove durable, and therefore, a satisfactory investment; and finally, because they are the only logical solution of comfortable, well-ordered present day family life.

It has been amply proved that women are not especially interested in fine points of design unless that interest is implanted by competitive statements of the salesmen. They are not especially interested in form or color or detail, but they are supremely interested in dealer assurance that the machine is solidly built; that it will accomplish the work; and that its purchase will save them money, time or labor, perhaps all three. Let the appliance itself impress them with the strength of the materials used, the cleanness of its design and the perfection of work performed, and the sale is made.

Cost is Considered

The question of cost considered only from the woman's standpoint of expenditure is more difficult to discuss. In the case of small equipment priced under or around five dollars it is easy to make large sales upon the time or labor-saving qualities the devices may have. But repeat sales are affected by the quality of construction and materials used. In all higher priced equipment the question of strength and quality seems uppermost in her mind, but a difference in price between two makes or two models of same manu-facture, often results in the sale of the higher priced, because she has enjoyed the opportunity of discrimination. There seems to be no question that the woman purchaser is willing to pay any added sum required to make construction better or convenience greater—always provided that the salesman convinces her she is obtaining the quality she is paying for.

In selecting a Vacuum Cleaner, the woman looks for:

- A design that will prove efficient at low upkeep cost over a period of time.
- If motor driven brush type, there must be correct relation between air suction power and brush sweeping action.
- If air type, a narrow floor nozzle so designed as to clean by small amount of air at high velocity.
- As light a construction as is consistent with quality.
- If air and brush (geared to wheels) type, a broader nozzle with inset brush is permissible provided care is exercised in design to prevent air leakage. This type cleans by a larger volume of air with correspondingly lower velocity.
- Durable construction, aluminum or steel casings, an assembly that secures tight joints and seams that won't leak air.
- Easy operation—weight of appliance not so important if weight is easily handled.
- Convenient switch; handle designed long enough for comfortable operation at woman's height.

- Bag, double seamed; strong, tight connections; easily emptied; durable material, preferably of cotton flannel type.
- Winding posts for cord to be strong and conveniently placed.
- Convenience in connecting attachments.
- Elimination of noise, in so far as this is possible.

Instead, then, of attempting merely to learn the dealer's demand for selling points, put part of your effort into learning the demands of the user of the machine. Consumer suggestion or demands are apt to come only after a period of use. Obvious ones are sometimes reported by the dealer, but very often they never come to the manufacturer through the reports of the trade in time to be of service. It took a period of years for the dealer to realize the importance of enclosed moving parts. It finally came to him through the reaction developed by women using the machines.

In the same way the manufacture and marketing of both gas and electric ranges, which has been uniformly efficient, has overlooked one very important detail. The broiler grids are often so placed that the steak is an inch and a half away from the flame instead of one-half inch. With such a broiler, perfect broiling is impossible. Again a kitchen cabinet may be made of high grade materials but the hardware proves too light to stand the constant closing and opening. Such a kitchen cabinet is handicapped in any neighborhood because constant use makes the minor annoyance a cumulative one, which reacts directly upon the manufacturer's product.

The vacuum cleaner that is easily sold on the dealer's floor because it looks big and imposing oftentimes discloses its poor efficiency only after from four to six months of use. This is due to the fact that from time immemorial women have ordained a period devoted to housecleaning twice a year. And it is at this crucial time that they discover if the routine care of rugs and carpets by their vacuum cleaner has accomplished a work satisfactory to them. This conclusion is well borne out by a conversation we had with a large dealer in vacuum cleaners from the west coast. He freely told us of handling two vacuum cleaners, one a comparatively inexpensive and absolutely inefficient machine (as we had proved by test), the other a more expen-sive and a thoroughly efficient machine.

He claimed that the first proved only a feeder for the second, since when the woman, after a longer or shorter period of use, realized that the first machine would not do the work, she returned to buy the more expensive and better machine. And the average time was six months. Now this dealer could have selected a machine no higher in price than his less expensive model which would have done good work and thoroughly satisfied the user. We leave you to draw your own conclusions as to the fate of the manu-facturer's product in the first place, and the dealer's selling methods in the second place.

In selecting a Washing Machine, the woman looks for:

- Compact, trim appearance with all machine parts covered.
- Plain outlines.
- Swinging wringer with safety release.
- Pump attached to machine to rapidly drain off water when drain connection is not practical.
- Metal tub exterior painted (easy to keep clean).
- A waterproof finish on a wood tub.
- Switch control of motor, clutch control of tub and wringer.
- Height that will obviate stooping.
- Design to insure efficiency.
- Motor and switch insulation.
- Materials and workmanship that insure durability.
- A water outlet that allows rapid running off of water.
- Threaded outlet to allow for connection.
- All handles and levers to be easy to grasp and to turn by wet hands.
- Tub body slightly off the level to allow for draining.

It is easy to sell a refrigerator that has a slightly appear-ance, that is equipped with a sanitary seamless lining and that is marked with a price that spells to the woman good workmanship. But it is only actual use in storing food that develops the fact that the insulation is of sufficient quantity and is assembled with high grade construction, or that cheap material and workmanship have been substituted. The service that can be obtained from the appliance after it is marketed is of the utmost importance for the manufac-turer to learn. It is peculiarly impossible to sell and "forget" any product sold to women.

Undoubtedly a phase of manufacturing that acutely interests the average manufacturer deals with the selection of the materials that are to be used in the construction of his product. Too often the person who selects these materials fails to take into account the fact that women are almost fanatically intolerant of two things, rust and discoloration. It may be but one bolt that can rust, but women under our observation have utterly condemned a washing machine for which they paid from $125 to $165 because of this one bolt alone. We have heard them further condemn a machine because of the difficulty of keeping it polished.

It is not purpose, we are convinced, but it must be carelessness on the part of that manufacturer who allows the use of a rusting screw here or a bolt there when the rest of the equipment is safeguarded against such conditions. In one specific instance a single part of a machine intended to be used in connection with water was made up of five different metals. Each one of these metals had its own different reaction towards hard water in the presence of soap. That this manufacturer had intended no slight toward his product was indicated by the fact that the largest section of this part was constructed of the most expensive material. He probably fully believed that he had made that particular part of rustproof material but it was the selection of defective small parts that offset any advantage due to his use of fine materials for the major part of the machine. Because a great deal of household equipment that is of interest to women must be used as a water container, the effect of water of varying degrees of hardness upon the several metals is of interest. Most metals have some electrolytic action. There are throughout the country water supplies of every known degree of hardness. There are water supplies whose hardness can be corrected and there are supplies of the type known as "permanent" hardness. In actual practice the salts in these hard waters react with soap of any variety to form a sticky gray precipitate. This precipitate is increased in quantity in direct proportion to the activity of the metal. Therefore, the material selected for the tub and cylinder of a washing machine, for the container of the dishwashing machine, or for the tea kettle that demands constant contact with water should be given the careful attention that its importance demands.

In selecting a Refrigerator, the woman looks for:

1. Seamless lining.
2. Compartment beneath ice high enough to hold quart milk bottles.
3. Generous insulation.
4. A selection of wood and treatment of it that will prevent warping.
5. Heavy hardware.
6. Positive-closing, lever locks.
7. Plain unpanelled trim—high leg base.
8. Dull, rather than highly finished wood.
9. Easily accessible drain.
10. Adjustable shelves.

A universal metal that can withstand any and all attacks of these several waters is difficult if not impossible to locate. In our judgment there is no perfect metal. Copper comes the nearest to it and yet copper must be tinned, and there is some slight consumer reaction against its use, in large containers, because they claim copper must be scoured in order to be slightly. However, enamel paint on the outside of such a container, leaving only a fair sized name-plate to be burnished, would overcome this objection. Galvanized iron, zinc, nickel, all have a disadvantage of inducing electrolytic action (producing whitish precipitate) and that should be taken into account in your selection of metals. In sections save those in which waters are of the "permanent hard" variety, this disadvantage can be overcome by including directions that the machine should not be scoured.

Flush with rinsing water only. With such care, the whitish deposit acts as a film over the metal, and, once the latter is completely covered, reduces the precipitation. But in the presence of extremely hard waters, the quantity is so great that the precipitate snows a tendency to deposit on the linen itself, instead of being thrown solely to the sides of tub, cylinder, or suction cup. Once this does get on the fabric, it has all the sticky characteristics of chewing gum. Bronze or brass rather than steel or iron should be used for any bearings that come in contact with water. Only thus can you fully safeguard against rust.

Little Things that Often Prove Great

Safety demands that every equipment involving an electric motor be so fully insulated from the machine frame by waterproof fittings and insulated shaft couplings, etc., that a maximum of safety can be assured. It is indeed remarkable that this is not more often cared for in the original design. In one short period, at least three machines were forced into the disapproval group in the Department of Household Engineering of Good Housekeeping Institute with such lack of insulation as one of the causes.

It is thus clear that consumer needs, in this great classification of merchandise (household appliances) as reflected by consumer attitude is often ill-defined and extremely difficult for the manufacturer to interpret. Therefore, as a recognition of this condition, the basic purpose running throughout all of the testing work at Good Housekeeping Institute is to test every device so as to duplicate the conditions under which the device will be used by the ultimate consumer, be she intelligent or unintelligent.

It has furthermore been the Institute's special province to express to each manufacturer the trend of consumer demand as seen, not only through the Institute's use of appliances, but through the thousands of consumers who report their experiences. It is an interesting and surprising fact that mechanical tests develop data which often interpret the results obtained under practical usage of the equipment, and the results obtained under the practical usage quite as often define the value of the mechanical data. Any effort a manufacturer may make to develop these two angles of testing will more than offset any money cost that may be added to the factory overhead.

Complete testing of this character will also save ultimate consumer reactions against the completed manufactured product. It is not enough, as so many manufacturers have done; to place the appliance in a variety of homes and take the consequent "say-so."

It must be remembered that it is only possible to compare an appliance when you have something to compare it with, and that something must be an appliance designed to do similar work. How many instances are there where manufacturers allow their products to go out without comparative information of this kind, just because such information is so extremely difficult to get? To all interested in or concerned with this great industry, there is one thing to be remembered above all else—study and test not only the mechanical construction and perfection of your product but know from every conceivable angle what the user or consumer is going to demand of it. If this be done, and done thoroughly, and exhaustively, you will build the appliance of the best materials obtainable, because it must wear well; of the most efficient design, because it must operate smoothly; and you cannot fail to so build it that it will do its work completely and well because you will have the measure of these values within the experience of your own investigation.

The results of this care in manufacture will promptly be reflected when marketing your product in at least three ways,—first, increase of sales and repeat sales; second, a lowered overhead cost for servicing, repairing, and replacing defective machines, and third, a fairer and lower price to the consumer because it is based on the cost of her machine only since she is not burdened with a share of her neighbor's repairs in your "overhead." There is perhaps no household device operated by electricity that is more complicated in its oiling system than the old-fashioned sewing machine and yet the manufacturer managed to train the housewife to ninety per cent efficiency in caring for the machine. Therefore, well defined and specified places for oiling should be provided for, and decalcomaniac or otherwise permanent directions placed on all enclosed gearings, in order that the user may continually have before her the correct places marked for oiling. It is not enough to supply a circular of directions: she loses it promptly as has been proved over and over again. All important service directions must be permanent.

The Present and the Future

It is largely because there has not been a consumer demand that was well defined that we find few equipments designed with attention to the proper working heights. Moreover, we are convinced that it is a decidedly difficult question to settle. However, it is possible to group most exertions that women must practice into two classes: those that involve upper arm muscles, as work at a sink, range, washtub, or washing machine, etc., and secondly, exertions that involve the muscles of the forearm, as the mixing, stirring, and beating involved in cookery processes. In the first case any variations in a woman's height makes com-paratively little difference. A range of heights from five feet to six feet would be served equally well by a similar height of equipment. This makes it possible to lay down the rule that sinks should be designed and plumbers should provide for piping them at a height of thirty-five inches from the bottom of the sink to the floor. Ranges should be thirty-four inches in height to the working top, and both washing machines and tubs should be thirty-eight inches to their rims. This enables all work to be done with straight unstrained back. Where the forearm muscle is involved, however, it becomes a far more delicate question.

The distance between work-table top and elbow must be the control on designing. For that reason it is not possible to establish a constant and ideal height for kitchen cabinets and working table surfaces, although in general most of these have been from one to two inches too low. "Adjustable in height" seems to be the only answer to this phase of the problem. Some one, sometime, will undoubtedly design a well made table (we have already seen one of poor construction) that will have strong, as well as adjustable leg support. Some one, sometime, will build a good refrigerator (as we have seen a poor one) constructed with the sanitary, high leg-base of the present day office desk.

It will obviate stooping and it will enable one to get the refrigerator pan without groping provided there can be no drain. It will further allow for a refrigerator pan large enough to prevent the common accident of overflowing. Again, sometime, we believe the manufacturer of kitchen cabinets will see a picture of kitchens built with four, straight, clean walls and completely equipped with the pantry on one wall, consisting of kitchen cabinet and side units for storage cabinets, each one of these side cabinets to be only fourteen inches deep. The time will come—it is almost here—when the demand from women for the high sink we have already indicated is going to be strong enough so that the Plumber's standards for cutting pipe will be changed to meet her demand. It is difficult to realize, but it is nevertheless true, that every woman who wishes a properly placed sink in her kitchen or pantry has to over-come the inertia of the plumber not only because of his conservative unwillingness to do this unusual task, but because he is put to the extra expense and trouble of getting "specials" in pipe length, due to the fact that the plumbing trade, as yet, has not recognized an at least partially developed consumer demand.

CONSUMER RIGHTS AND RESPONSIBILITIES

These rights were conceptualized in the developed world's consumer context where consumers are wealthy and completely dependent on the market to fulfill their needs.

These rights had to be redefined keeping in mind the realities of a developing country like India. Consequently, two very important rights were added viz.:

- The Right to Basic Needs and
- The right to a healthy and sustained environment.

These two rights are very closely linked with the realities of developing countries where environment plays a very important role as a resource and support-structure for the people. In a country like India, a large section of the population looks for food security, assured safe water supply, shelter, education and health services. Most consumers relate very little to imported goods stacked in supermarkets or for choice among latest models of cars, as is the case in the developed wȏrld. For India's 1 billion popu-lation, food security and a safe environment are more pressing needs than any other consumer options and rights. The developing country natural resources also serve as a resource base for the developed world's industrial output.

Right to Basic Needs

Access to food, water and shelter are the basis of any consumer's life. Without these fundamental amenities, life cannot exist. In September 2001, India's stock of food grains were around 60 million tonnes, yet one third of the Indian population lives below the poverty line and consumers often go hungry or remain severely malnourished, leading to poor health. The recent starvation deaths in Orissa are a case in point. A very crucial objective of the conceptualisation and existence of consumer rights is to ensure that consumers have an assured food supply, safe and permanent dwellings, basic amenities of life like sanitation and potable water, and power supply.

Urbanisation is seen as a mark of development but for rural migrant population, living conditions in cities is very poor. The population of cities is growing rapidly in India and after 1988, the percentage of urban poor has been more than that of the rural poor. Around 20 to 25 per cent of the urban households live in slums, make-shift colonies or refugee settlements due to non-availability of affordable and decent habitat in urban areas. According to some esti-mates, in urban areas alone, there is a housing shortage of 17 million units. This has led to a habitat crisis in Indian cities. In rural India, the situation is equally bad, with a large part of the population still living in make-shift dwellings and hutment. With non-permanent housing comes lack of sanitation facilities and other amenities like running water and electricity supply. Due to burgeoning population, most people do not have access to dry toilets in rural and urban areas.

Food Security for Consumers

The recent deaths of poor people in Orissa due to starvation in August 2001 have indicated that food security is still a myth of a section of the Indian consumers. To solve this food scarcity problem, the Government of India mooted the PDS (Public Distribution System) to help reach food grain to the masses at subsidized rates through government-run 'Fair Price Shops'.

There are about 4.5 lakh Fair Price Shops all over India of which 3.05 are in rural areas and 0.94 in urban areas. On an average there is 1 PDS shop for every 2000 consumers. Yet, many parts of India still suffer from food shortages. Poor distribution and under-utilisation of food grains has led to artificially-created food scarcities in the country.

Presently, there are 60 million tonnes of food grain in terms of buffer stock in Indian godowns. This food grain is rotting due to unutilisation and improper storage facilities. The need of the hour is to channelise this stock towards needy consumers and offer them 'food for work' programmes, which will not only give them employment but also money.

Besides making sure that there is enough food accessible to consumers at all times, nutrition is another area which the health of children and the vulnerable sections of population is at stake. This is an area where consumers can take responsibility for ensuring that quality is added to their basic food supply.

Right to Safe Environment

For urban consumers, environment means parks, gardens, and deteriorating air and water quality. Most urban areas are bereft of any wildlife and people are unaware of the biodiversity around them. On the other hand, rural consumers rely on their environment for fulfillment of their basic needs. The need for environmental conservation is seen as a necessary defence against deteriorating quality of life world-wide. We are all victims of contaminated food and water supply, pesticide-ridden food, adulterated milk and choking exhaust fumes emitting from vehicles. According to a World Bank report, India is being pushed back due to its high environmental costs. We lose around Rs. 24,500 crores every year in terms of air and water pollution alone. If you live in a city, you must have experienced air and water pollution at some point of time. Children often fall ill due to polluted environments, it leads to increased health costs and discomfort for consumers.

Valuable resources and man-days are lost due to polluted environment and living conditions. Consumers need to understand that only a safe environment can ensure the fulfillment of their consumer rights. If we look closely at our immediate surroundings and our consumption patterns, we would find that we, ourselves, are responsible for causing environmental pollution to a certain extent.

For instance, our monthly purchases include various kinds of washing detergents, toilet cleaning acids and chemicals like Harpic or Sanifresh, and a lot of non-biode-gradable packaging for pre-packed food products. This leads to environmental problems like water and soil pollution, and waste disposal problems. It also shows that our consum-ption patterns are closely linked with the state of the environment and that environmental damage is mostly a result of irresponsible consumer behaviour.

International Standards for Safeguarding Right

Consumers International (a nodal agency of consumer organisations from all over the world) has made certain guidelines for ensuring consumers' right to safe environment. Consumers should be protected from environmental pollution by:

- Promoting the use of products which are environ-mentally sustainable.
- Encouraging recycling.
- Requiring environmentally dangerous products to carry appropriate warnings and instructions for safe use and disposal.

Promote the use of non-toxic products by:

- Raising consumer awareness of alternatives to toxic products.
- Establishing procedures to ensure that products banned overseas do not enter national markets.
- Ensure that the social impacts of pollution are minimised.
- Promote ethical, socially and environmentally respon-sible practices by producers and suppliers of goods and services.

Rural consumers are invariably closer to their environment than urban consumers. Their livelihoods and way of life depend on the environment around them. Their firewood and sources of energy come from trees, manure for fields comes from livestock, water is procured either from underground water supply or from rivers, the crops heavily depend on annual rainfall, even pesticides for safeguarding of crops and storage also come from trees like neem. In short, the rural life revolves around natural resources. For them, this dependence on the environment is complete and they have a stake in its preservation, whether it is for building their houses, fodder for their cattle, etc.

Right to Safety

Consumer right to safety is as vast in its purview as the market reach itself. It applies to all possible consumption patterns and to all goods and services. In the context of the new market economy and rapid technological advances affecting the market, the right to safety has become a pre-requisite quality in all products and services. For e.g. some Indian products carry the ISI mark, which is a symbol of satisfactory quality of a product? Similarly, the FPO and AGMARK symbolise standard quality of food products. The market has for long made consumers believe that by consuming packaged food or mineral water, consumers can safeguard their health. This notion has been proved wrong time and again due to rampant food adulteration in market products. Right to food safety is an important consumer right since it directly affects the health and quality of life of consumers.

Earlier, the interpretation of the right to safety was limited to electronic products and other such products. Now, its definition has expanded a lot to include safety aspects of new technologies like GM food, food labelling, chemical ingredients in food products etc. In today's scenario of globalisation, consumers have no control over where the products or commodities they use, come from. For instance, the chocolates or syrups we consume, may be manufactured in countries as far as the U.S. or Australia. Consumers in India would have no control over or knowledge of the manufacturing practices of those countries and will have to rely completely on import regulations of the Indian government and food labelling. This makes the consumer right to safety a very important and critical issue for consumers.

GM Food - Safe or No

Earlier, right to safety meant that a consumer should be protected from health risks of using electronic products like irons, plugs, or other such things. Technological changes have however widened the ambit of this consumer right. The right to safety has now expanded in purview to include GM food. GM food can be Food safety should ensure that consumer has no short-term or long-term ad-verse health effects due to consumption of GM food. Genetically Modified organisms can be defined as 'organisms produced as a result of

Biotechnolo-gical changes or genetic engineering'.

GM technology is suspect because making changes in the genetic code alters the entire sequence of the material and that might lead to unintended development of many undesirable traits. For e.g. A virus while in contact with a gene resistant plant may acquire the genetic material (disease resistant quality) and may become even more dangerous. If any such virus becomes virulent, it may destroy desirable plant species and create serious imbalance in the given eco-system. Also, if a consumer eats GM food products, s/he may develop resistance to anti-biotics or allergies in certain cases. Safety of natural food products is also a problem of growing concern since due to increased chemical inputs in farms, our food supply is being contaminated with pesticides and chemicals. This poses a grave danger to consumer health. For non-vegetarians, the problem is even more serious since food animals are being fed antibiotics to fight diseases among animals and boost their growth. This can have serious repercussions on consumer health.

Right to Information

Right to information means the right to be given the facts needed to make an informed choice or decision about factors like quality, quantity, potency, purity standards and price of product or service. The right to information now goes beyond avoiding deception and protection against misleading advertising, improper labelling and other practices. For e.g. when you buy a product or utilise a service, you should be informed about a) how to consume a product b) the adverse health effects of its consumption c) Whether the ingredients used are environment- friendly or not etc .Due to the ever increasing influence of the market and the ever changing scene with price wars and hard-sell techniques, the consumer's right to information becomes even more important. The right to information means much more than simple disclosure of the product's weight or price.

A consumer has the right to know how the product has been prepared, whether it has been tested or animals or not, if environmentally-sound techniques and resources have been used in its production processes, what kinds of chemicals are used into its manufacturing and what could be their impact on consumer health. Clearly, a consumer has to consider a lot of factors before s/he buys a product. Ideally, a consumer should have knowledge of the entire 'cradle to grave' journey of the product to determine whether its safe and beneficial for use or no. The 'cradle to grave journey' refers to the processes a product goes through- from the time of it being made out of raw material, the processes of its molding into its final shape, trans-portation, labour, ingredients used, to the form in which it ends up on market shelves.

It is only when a consumer is aware of the history of the product that he can make informed choices. An example of this is the GM food controversy. GM food is promoted as the answer to world's hunger and malnutrition but its safety for consumers and the environment is yet to be proved. Despite strong lobbying by pro-GM groups and the market, consumers in Europe have campaigned effectively against the entry of GM food into their food chain and markets. There are information and publicity campaigns that have made consumers rally behind a common consumer stand against GM food. As a result, the governments and the European Union have placed strict restrictions on the trial uses of GM technology in the market or in agriculture.

Recently, it has come to light that most cosmetics like lipsticks, kajal and mascara are tested on animals in laboratories to see whether they have any adverse effects on them or no. There was also a controversy about how Nike shoe company was using sweat labour in South Asian countries, paying its workers abysmally low wages for manufacturing shoes. Similarly, there was a 'McLibel' case against McDonald's alleging that Mc Donald's generated a lot of unwanted waste due to its excessive packaging and harmed the environment.

The advertising techniques of many products, directly targeting and featuring children have also been questioned. Many .parents don't even know that their children are being targeted by market surveyors to determine their consumption habits by collecting data through surveys, interviews and by offering free samples of products. It is not just the consumers who use information gathering or disseminating techniques and tools to protect their consumer rights. Information dissemination is also used very extensively by advertisers and the market to get their message across to the consumer. Tools and agencies of information like news-papers, print media, television and the Internet are utilised by marketing of consumer products and services. This has made advertising a multi-million dollar industry in India and also world-wide.

Right to Choice

Different interests can interpret the right to choice in different ways. For the developed world consumers, right to choice translates into more and a variety of products to choose from. For e.g. American consumers can choose from 25,000 super market items, 200 kinds of cereals, and read 11,092 magazines. This kind of choice often gives consumers a sense of well-being and safety and encourages them to believe that abundance leads to good living. The market also perpetuates this line of thought by advertising and promotion gimmicks. The right to choice has a very different definition in developing countries. For a population dependent on the environment for livelihood, the right to choice and other consumer rights need a shift in focus. The focus needs to be on choice of good practices like organic farming and conservation of natural heritage. In cities, people should be able to choose cleaner and safer ways of transportation over polluting ones. Similarly, healthy and fresh food should be chosen over junk food. The right to choose must essentially be a con-sumer's right to choose a safe and healthy product of good quality over an unsafe or defective product. This can give a consumer immense leverage not just to choose products that are safe but also to influence the practices adopted my the market.

Misinterpretation of choice by market forces has systematically weakened the consumer's position vis-à-vis the market. The market has exploited this situation by interpreting the right to confuse and exploit the consumer. The consumer has been made to believe that more varieties of the same product on the market shelves give him or her the right to choose what s/he wants. In reality, more varieties of the same product just encourages false advertising claims and give the consumer a false sense of choice. Various kinds of shampoos, soaps, and other cosmetics differ merely in colour, smell and brand image. Each one of them claims one-upmanship over the other but gives the consumer very little value for money or a better quality product.

Ever since trade liberalisation in India started taking place, the consumer world has been witnessing increased availability of exotic fruits, vegetables and imported food items. These days, one can buy imported apples that cost Rs. 200 a kilo and syrups, jams, sauces, drinks that are manufactured overseas. However, neither the market nor the consumers pay any attention to the over-consumption of resources as a result and its environmental impact. When products are manufactured in distant lands, they have to be packaged and preserved in a special way to last longer. A lot of resources go into its packaging and transportation. All these facts and their impact are often not made known to consumers and they end up harming the environment and paying an exorbitant price for their consumption choices.

Right to Be Heard

The right to be heard means that consumers should be allowed to voice their opinions and grievances at appro-priate fora. For e.g. if you have been cheated in the market place or deprived of the right quality of service, your complaint should be heard and given due attention by the authorities. Consumers should also have a right to voice their opinion when rules and regulations pertaining to them are being formulated, like the recent amendments in the Consumer

Protection Act. The right to be heard holds special significance in the Indian context because Indian consumers are largely unaware of their rights and passively accept their violation. Even when they have legal recourse, they prefer not to use it for fear of getting embroiled in legal complexities. To allay consumer fears and to allow them to express their views and grievances, consumer forums have been in existence in India for a long time. Consumers have been approaching these forums and consumer NGOs regarding their problems and complaints.

Right to Redress

Competition is the by-product of the market economy. Everyday, manufacturers are discovering newer ways of cheating and duping consumers. Unscrupulous market practices are finding their way into consumer homes, violating consumer rights and jeopardising their safety. It is to protect consumer interests that consumers have been given the right to obtain redress. In India, we have a redress machinery called Consumer Courts constituted under the Consumer Protection Act (1986), functioning at national state and district levels.

But it has not been made complete use of under due to lack of awareness of basic consumer rights among consu-mers themselves. While in the developed world, right to redress is perhaps the most commonly exercised consumer right, in developing countries, consumers are still wary of getting involved in legal redress system. There are consumer courts in India where any consumer can lodge a case if s/he thinks he or she has been cheated. The details of how to lodge a complaint have been explained elsewhere in the manual.

Right to Consumer Education

Consumer education empowers consumers to exercise their consumer rights. It is perhaps the single most powerful tool that can take consumers from their present disadvan-tageous position to one of strength in the marketplace. Consumer education is dynamic, participatory and is mostly acquired by hands-on and practical experience. For instance, a woman who makes purchase decisions for the household and does the actual buying in the marketplace would be more educated about market conditions and 'best buys' than a person who educates himself about the market with the help of newspapers or television. Also, today, it is not just the market or products that a consumer needs to educate himself about but s/he also needs to know about company profile, government policies and introduction of new technology.

Market influences have grown so much that not just wholesale and retail sellers but even medical practitioners are falling prey to their pressures. The pharmaceutical industry is one such example. India, with its 1 billion population and largely uneducated consumers, is a very lucrative market for this industry. The pharmaceutical industry, to boost its sales, offers free samples of medicines, freebies, and even free luxury holidays to physicians to influence them to use their brands and give them preference over other brand names. There have been many instances when drugs banned in countries like US, have been prescribed to Indian consumers and are readily available as over-the-counter drugs. It is a sad example of gross violation of consumer trust by medical practitioners.

This situation is rampant not just in rural areas but also among educated urban consumers. The reason why the market, in connivance with physicians, is able to exploit consumers is that Indian consumers are not aware of the prevailing situation and do not keep themselves abreast with latest developments taking place around them. Consumer education can play a crucial role in protecting consumers against such dangers. In the Indian context, sustainability and traditional knowledge can play a vital role in empowering consumers but consumers are unable to connect to their knowledge base. Consumer education can rejoin the broken link and make traditional knowledge accessible to consumers again. Some sources of consumer education are past experiences of consumers, information dissemination by government agencies and NGOs, classroom teaching by teachers and informal lessons by parents.

CONSUMER RESPONSIBILITY

While we all like to know about our rights and exercise them, we hardly ever accord the same importance and urgency to our consumer responsibilities. Consumer rights and responsibilities are intertwined together and without sharing consumer responsibility, consumers will find it very difficult to enjoy their rights on a long-term basis.

Consumers need to tread cautiously in the market place. While buying a product, ask yourself these questions:

- Do you really need this product?
- For how long would you like to use it? Will it last as long as you would like it to?
- What are the health fallout of that product? If it is a food product, does it give you any health benefits? Check the labelling of the product to see the nutritional chart of the product.

You can also empower yourself by knowing the law. For e.g., did you know that ISI mark on bottled mineral water has been made mandatory by the government and now labelling of non-vegetarian ingredient in food products will also mandatory for the industry? Consumer responsi-bility can play a very important role in not only checking the market but also in restricting unnecessary consumption. It is not the sole responsibility of the market or of the government to provide consumers with detailed information. A consumer, on his part, must make every effort to inform himself of the product or service.

For example, if a consumer consumes a health product, he must make efforts to inform himself beforehand about its possible side-effects, and must also exercise caution regarding his eating habits, diet and physical exercise, to take full advantage of the product. Consumer responsibility is based on ethics and rationale. There are no definitive set of consumer responsibilities and a consumer must exercise restraint in consumption to consume responsibly.

For example, conservation of the environment cannot be forced upon consumers but a consumer must make a conscious effort to reduce consumption, choose environment-friendly alternatives and conserve energy. Consumer responsibility needs to be shouldered by different consumer segments. Every segment has its own special consumer profile and consumption patterns. These patterns define the kind of consumer responsibility that a segment must discharge.

Responsibility Towards Safe Waste Disposal

Most often we consume without sparing any thought for what's going to be left behind as waste. More and more percentage of waste generated in urban areas today consists of non-biodegradable waste. Urban consumers are making use of plastic, paper and cardboard packaging, disposables batteries, plastic throw-away pens, use and throw nappies ,empty cans etc are becoming a common feature of an urban dustbin. India's urban population is around 300 million. By 2011, the total quantity of solid waste generated in urban areas is expected to cross 56 million tonnes, creating a waste management crisis for urban India. Consumers need to become accountable for their consumption patterns and their serious environmental and economic implications. The 4 Rs. of consumption are not just a consumer's prerogative but also his consumer responsibility.

RESPONSIBILITY TO ENDORSE SAFER PRODUCTS

Eco-friendliness is an important criterion in judging a product's feasibility. It is a way of assessing how much damage a product has caused to the environment. 'Eco-mark' is one way of knowing which products conform to environmental standards and are more envrionment-friendly than others. Ecolabelling is a methodology practised by many countries in the world, including India. The Indian government has formulated a scheme whereby some categories of products are awarded the 'Ecomark' if they conform to certain standards set by the Ministry of Environment and Forests. Unfortunately, in India, the scheme has not taken off due to consumer apathy and lack of response. The market has manipulated this situation to lobby with the government to make ecolabelling a voluntary scheme, which will allow manufacturers to disclose and cover information at will.

Consumer Bonding

The consumer movement needs active participation of consumers to lobby with the government, pressure the market to deliver better quality, and to support consumer rights campaigns. Empowerment of consumers by NGOs and public campaigns is a two-way process and without continuing consumer support, no campaign can flourish.

YOUNG CONSUMERS AND CONSUMER RESPONSIBILITY

Children, teenagers and youth constitute a very impor-tant consumer segment for the market. Their consumption habits are unique and their purchase decisions are based on popular trends, brand image, use of new technology, flavour of food products, and style. The market also realises that young consumers have a propensity to consumer junk food and prefer them over traditional forms of food. This characteristic is exploited by the market by associating convenience and a brand image with junk food like colas, pizzas, and fast-food joints. There are three major brands of toothpaste in India, viz. Colgate, Pepsodent and Close Up. All three of them compete with each other to capture maximum market share.

In order to achieve this, they not only target children as consumers but also feature them in their advertisements to attract other young consumers. Colgate, for e.g., targets young children in the age group of 5 to 12 and offers free cartoon booklets along with toothpastes. Pepsodent vies for the same consumer segment and depicts some children relishing snacks, confectionery and sweets, while others are scolded by their mothers for having done the same thing. This advertisement makes children believe that consumers who use Pepsodent are immune to any tooth decay because of the superior quality of the product.

This claim is unauthenticated and attempts to mislead children. Close Up, on the other hand, does not perceive children as its target audience. Instead, it targets teenagers and the youth. It creates a brand image of confidence and popularity for young consumers between the age group of 16-30. Its advertisements constantly feature successful friendships and romances between Close-Up users. Millions of rupees are spent on advertising a product which costs as little as Rs. 30 and is considered ordinary by most consumers. From pushing toothpaste on neem sticks to advertising in the Kumbh mela, the market can go to any extent to boost its sales. After a point, the sales tend to stagnate. This negative development is offset by constantly repackaging the present product and introducing new products. For instance, Colgate has a number of brands in the market, like Colgate Total, Colgate Dental Cream, Cibaca, Colgate Gel and Colgate Herbal.

Junk Food and Young Consumers

Young consumers are special targets of the junk-food industry. The market knows that fast food is addictive and once young people get used to having their fat, salts and sugar rich food, they will become their consumers for life. Also, young consumers have the indirect purchasing power of their parents, which makes them a very lucrative consumer segment. Thus it does not come as a surprise that the market spends huge sums of money at advertising campaigns alone. Some of their marketing figures are as follows:

- $ 2 billion is roughly spent on advertising to young consumers every year.
- The children's direct influence in parental purchases was estimated to be around $ 188 billion dollars in 1997, up from $132 billion in 1990, $50 billion in 1984 and $20 billion in the mid-70s.
- The market for children aged 4 to 12 years alone rakes in some $ 30 billion annually.

- The junk food sector attaches images and perception of fun, enjoyment and prestige with their products and eating outlets. They also use popular film stars and sports personalities to strike an instant rapport with young consumers.
- Young consumers should consume in moderation and buy a product on the basis of its quality and merit and not because of the brand image. Students also need to see beyond the veil of advertising, brand pushing and market influences, to identify their real needs.
- The environmental impact of consumption must be considered before buying a product. A young con-sumer must consider what kind of waste is going to be left behind after s/he has consumed goods or services. For example, in school and college canteens, drinking cold-drinks in plastic cups, using disposable plates and mineral water bottles, has become very com-mon and also a fashion statement. Students no longer bring home-cooked food or lunch boxes to schools. This has not only created a. shift towards unhealthy food but also added to the waste management problem.
- Environment conservation and safe waste management is a prime consumer responsibility. We should be responsible for the garbage we create as a result of our consumption habits.

  Young consumers can actively contribute to safe disposal of waste by minimised generation of non-biodegradable waste and by participating and initiating activities like vermicomposting and segregation of waste.
- Paper is a very important consumable in every student's life. Everyday tonnes of paper are used in schools and colleges by students, teachers and office workers alike. Students can initiate a paper-recycling campaign and also learn how to make recycled paper themselves.
- Students must also acquaint themselves with energy consumption patterns like water usage and electricity consumption.

  They should sensitize themselves to the transportation

sources they use in everyday life, re-cycling of second-hand books in the library and the air-pollution causing use of firecrackers during festivals like Diwali. In the state of Delhi, young consumer parti-cipation in anti-cracker programme is a perfect example of community participation and student initiative, when students shunned fire-crackers and were able to bring down pollution levels dramatically in the city during Diwali.

- Schools are learning grounds, not just for education but also for practical life skills. Students can be introduced to the concept of 'polluters pay' by teaching them paper recycling, conservation of electricity, and recycling of water.

  Also, leadership qualities can be instilled in students by allowing them to monitor activities like garbage disposal, paper recycling, and rain water harvesting.

WOMEN CONSUMERS

Women consumers not only constitute 50% of the total consumer population but also make 80% of all purchase decisions. They are being specifically targeted by the market because of their growing purchasing power and their 'working-woman' status. Now, women have the dual role of family-makers and work professionals to play. As a result, they have less time, increased pressures and are slowly being de-linked from their traditional knowledge bank.

The market takes advantage of this situation by offering to women instant services and products, like fast-food, 'two-minute' snacks, and refrigerators and washing machines with supposedly better technologies. Women consumers have the responsibility of choosing products that are not just convenient but also safe to use and eco-friendly. They must evaluate the nutrition content of food products before buying them and weight their quality with traditional foods that are less-expensive, have better nutritional scores and consume less resources like packaging and transportation.

4

Consumer Protection Act

The issues relating to consumer welfare affects the entire 1986 million people since everyone is a consumer in one way or the other. Ensuring consumer welfare is the responsibility of the government. Accepting this, policies have been framed and the Consumer Protection Act, 1986, was introduced. A separate Department of Consumer Affairs was also created in the Central and State Governments to exclusively focus on ensuring the rights of consumers as enshrined in the Act. This Act has been regarded as the most progressive, comprehensive and unique piece of legislation. In the last international conference on consumer protection held in Malaysia in 1997, the Indian Consumer Protection Act was described as one "which has set in motion a revolution in the fields of consumer rights, the parallel of which has not been seen anywhere else in the world."

The special feature of this Act is to provide speedy and inexpensive redressal to the grievance of the consumer and provide him relief of a specific nature and award compensation wherever appropriate. The aim of the Act is also to ensure the rights of the consumer, viz. the right of choice, safety, information, redressal, public hearing and consumer education. The Act defines the consumer as one who purchases goods and services for his/her use. The user of such goods and service with the permission of the buyer is also a consumer. However, a person is not a consumer if he purchases goods and services for resale purpose. The most important feature of the Act is the provision for setting up a three-tier quasi-judicial machinery popularly known as "consumer courts" at national, state and district levels. The apex court, National Commission functions in Delhi. Every State Government has a State Commission. The third tier is in each district and is called district forum.

As on January 1999, there are 543 district forum. All these courts have handled nearly 13 lakh cases of which about 10 lakhs cases have been disposed of. The disposal of 77 per cent of the cases is not a mean achievement. However, it should be noted that only 27 per cent of the total cases have been disposed of within the prescribed period of 90 days or 150 days (where testing is required). This fact really causes concern for the Government and the consumers in general. The National Commission has identified the reasons for the slow disposal and have come out with suggestions for amending the Act with a view to improving the disposal rate within the time limit prescribed in the Act. The Government has been contemplating a number of amendments to the Act and these amendments will be brought out in the next session of Parliament. The consumer movement in India is as old as trade and commerce. In Kautilya's *Arthashastra*, there are references to the concept of consumer protection against exploitation by the trade and industry, short weighment and measures, adulteration and punishment for these offences.

However, there was no organised and systematic movement actually safeguarding the interests of the consumers. Prior to independence, the main laws under which the consumer interests were considered were the Indian Penal Code, Agricultural Production, Grading and Marketing Act, 1937, Drugs and Cosmetics Act, 1940. Even though different parts of India exhibited different levels of awareness, in general, the level of awareness was pretty low. An average Indian consumer is noted for his patience and tolerance. Perhaps because of these two traditional traits and due to the influence of the Mahabharata, the Ramayana and the *Bhagavad*

Gita, he considers the receipt of defective goods and services as an act of fate or unfavourable planetary position in his horoscope.

When a new television or refrigerator purchased by him turns out to be defective from day one, he takes it reticently, blaming it on his fate or as the consequence of the wrongs committed by him in his previous birth. Very often he is exploited, put to avoidable inconveniences and suffers financial loss. It is rather paradoxical that the customer is advertised as the "king" by the seller and service provider, but in actual practice treated as a slave or servant. Goods are purchased by him along with the label "Items once sold by us will never be received back under any circumstances whatsoever." This unethical, illegal and unilateral declaration has to be viewed in the light of the practice in developed countries where the seller declares, "In case you are not fully satisfied with our product, you can bring the same to us within a month for either replace-ment or return of your money."

This will clearly indicate the level of consumer consciousness. However, things are changing - slowly but steadily - and the momentum has increased considerably since the establishment of consumer courts and due to the efforts of a number of consumer organisations and the media. The next millennium will witness a high degree of consumer awareness and the concepts of "comparative costs", "consumer preference/ resistance/ abstinence" and "consumer choice" will become vital aspects of the economy. An analysis of the data from the consumer courts in different States shows that there is a direct relationship between literacy and consumer awareness. Statistics relating to Kerala and Bihar will justify this. The question to be considered is what can the Government do to improve the position?

The Government wears three hats to deal with cases of three different categories. The first one is dealing with the ministries and departments of government. Recently, the Standing Committee of Parliament on Health said Government hospitals should be brought under the purview of the Consumer Court. To this, we had pointed out the latest ruling of the Supreme Court which lays down that the Consumer Protection Act will apply only when the consumer pays for the goods and services and on this count the government hospital, where the services are not charged on the consumer, will not come under the Act. For such cases the government has developed the concept of "Citizen's Charter". All government departments dealing with the public are to publish a "Citizen's Charter" clearly indicating the services offered and the procedure to be followed. All the information has to be made available in a single window. This programme is in its incipient stage and has a long way to go to achieve the desired levels of consumer satisfaction.

The general reaction of the consumer to this is - what happens if what is stated in the Citizen Charter is not adhered to? Unless and until this is clarified, the responsibility fixed and those held accountable are dealt with, the purpose will not be achieved. The second area is where the services/ utilities are provided and charged either by the government department or the agencies under its control. At present, a number of regulatory authorities have been constituted and the country is entering a new regime of "regulatory economies" in the services sector. It is heartening to note that the regulatory bodies like the Telecom Regulatory Authority of India (TRAI) have given importance to the interests of consumers and this has been publicly declared as one of the main objectives. In the field of telecom, power, transport and water supply, the consumers today are going through a number of problems not knowing how to get their grievances redressed.

The number of cases relating to these sectors is increasing in the consumer courts. It must be possible for the government to take steps to see that the areas of grievances are identified and remedial steps taken through proper systematisation of procedure and working style. There are a number of areas where the procedure has to be made simple and consumer-friendly. For example, when it was felt that the quality of bottled water purchased by the consumer has to be ensured by fixing standards, it came out that even though it is necessary and desirable, under the existing laws it cannot be done. The Ministry of Law pointed out and rightly so, that water is not "food" as per the provisions in the Food Adulteration Act.

The process of getting statutory notification in the interest of the consumer in this case, where all concerned are agreeable, is likely to take 12 to 18 months. In such a situation the only answer is to prevail upon the manufacturers to go for voluntary ISI (Indian Standards Institution) certification. This method is working in the case of bottled water, thanks to the cooperation of producers and the clear preference expressed by the active consumer groups. Similarly in the area of "investor protection" in spite of several steps taken by the regulatory authorities such as the Reserve Bank of India and the Securities and Exchange Board of India, the case of exploitation of con-sumers is increasing. This is an area of grave concern and requires concerted action by the regulators, government and the consumer organisations.

We must find a way out to save the consumers from the unscrupulous functioning of Non-banking finance companies. The third category is the protection of consumers from the private sector dealing with goods and services. It is not to be construed that the entire business sector is keen on exploiting the consumers. These are established business firms which really care for consumer satisfaction, their own reputation and goodwill. Voluntary bodies like the Fair Business Practices Forum are functioning effectively and are quick in removing the grievances of the consumers. These can go a long way in reducing the number of cases in the consumer courts. If the Government is to take a proactive role in increasing consumer awareness, encourage consumer education, training and research and administer the infrastructural need of the consumer courts - then it should have enough funds. It is not easy to get adequate budget allocations for obvious reasons.

The best way appears to be to work out methods by which the Central Consumer Welfare Fund is augmented and a similar fund is set up at State level also. It is gratifying to note that action has been initiated in this direction and there is every reason to hope that the future will be better. The consumer has to be aware of his rights and play a key role. The success of "consumerism" is a strong function of consumer awareness and the assistance the movement gets from the government. The consumer movement got a boost and moral support from the late U.S. President John F. Kennedy in the historic declaration in Congress on March 15, 1962, declaring four basic consumer rights (choice, infor-mation, safety and the right to be heard). Subsequently, March 15 every year is celebrated as World Consumer Rights Day. However this annual ritual observation does not appear to have produced the desired results. A sub-continent like India with regional imbalances and diversity of languages, requires not one but several Ralph Nadars.

A recent survey has revealed that a number of consumers in the urban as well as rural areas are not very much aware of the consumer movement and the rights of the consumers. It is in this context that it is considered relevant to quote the objectives adopted by the General Assembly of United Nations in 1985. The U.N. guidelines for consumer protection are meant to achieve the following objectives:

- To assist countries in achieving or maintaining ade-quate protection for their population as consumers,
- To facilitate production and distribution patterns responsive to the needs and desires of consumers,
- To encourage high levels of ethical conduct for those engaged in the production and distribution of goods and services to consumers,
- To assist countries in curbing abusive business practices by all enterprises at the national and international levels which adversely affect consumers,
- To facilitate the development of independent consumer groups,
- To further international cooperation in the field of consumer protection,

- To encourage the development of market conditions which provide consumers with greater choice at lower prices.

It is interesting to note that in spite of U.N. recognition, encouragement from the developed countries and the pro-active role played by the Government, the consumer in India still does not get his due. It is time that he wakes up and realizes his rights. Even the great Hanuman required someone older and wiser to remind him of his potential strength. It will be useful if voluntary consumer organi-sations take up this role and make way for the realization of the objectives of the U.N. guidelines and the Consumer Protection Act. In the next millennium, every consumer in his own interest has to realize his role and importance in the right perspective. Each citizen in a democracy derives his power at the time of elections and exercises it through the ballot.

In a competitive economic environment the consumer has to exercise his choice either in favour of or against the goods and services. His choice is going to be vital and final. He should realize his importance and prepare himself to exercise his rights with responsibility. It is very often stated "Customer is sovereign and consumer is the King." If that is really so, why do we have the Consumer Protection Act? Why is there a need for protecting the King? Should it not be rightly called "Consumer Sovereignty Act"? It is for the consumers to decide. After all the dictum in democracy is, the citizens get a government they deserve. Similarly the consumers in society get a position in the market depending upon what they do or do not do. It is agreed on all hands that "consumer empowerment" in India has a long way to go. This is the right time to act. Let us prepare for the next millennium and usher in a new era of "Consumerism". When we cross the winter, spring cannot be far behind.

CONSUMERISM IN THE GLOBALIZED WORLD

It would be in fitness of the fact to recall the greatest of Arab historians, Ibn Khaldun saying: "That in civilization there is a limit that cannot be overstepped. When prosperity and luxury come to a people, they are followed by excessive consumption and extravagance, with which the human soul itself is undermined, both in its worldly well-being and in its spiritual life", particularly in context of globalization liberalization and consumerism in India.

This is what happening in India under the auspices of MNCs and trade policies of developed countries which are supposedly formulated to devour the third world consumer kingdom. Indians have a particular tendency to imitate what western nation states do but in context of consumer rights and responsibility we turned out as losers even in this art of ours. It was in1900 AD that the American consumer league was found in the USA, but we could not enact consumer protection law even after 40 years (1947-1986) of independence, though, in Kautilya's *Arthashastra*, there are references to the concept of consumer protection against exploitation by the trade and industry, short weighment and measures, adulteration, and punishment for these offences.

Consumers are now participants in a global market, and possibly in a cyber market. Law can only protect them (or us-we are all consumers) through rules which are essentially national, and which can only be enforced within national frameworks. Most of those rules have been enacted through a democratic political process. If the rules are useless in practice, people may question the usefulness of democracy and nation states. Consumer protection laws enable the correction of market failures and the redress of inequalities of information and power. Recent cases indicate that consumer protection laws, for a number of reasons, will be of little practical use to protect consumers in the global economy and in cyberspace. That raises the question of whether democratic politics can ever be used to bring countervailing force against those who abuse their position in the global market or the cyber market. If so, what other national laws will be rendered useless: labor laws, environ-mental laws, other laws that result from an often vigorous political process? What functions remain for democratic politics?

Fighting for the consumer interests has been there since the time of Adam, but in the beginning it was restricted to self satisfaction due to absence of mutual belief and societal needs. The ups and downs of various cultures saw changes in the face of consumer revolution over a period of time. Relevant changes and due arrival of multi class welfare state from end of the last century, led the beginning of the present consumer movement. In India, the consumer movement found a clear conception during the freedom movement of the 40's when Gandhi established the lead. Father of nation - Mahatma Gandhi has been defined as the greatest consumer advocate the world had ever seen. His various pronouncement in the consumer interests were even applauded by Ralph Nader, who himself has been considered the greatest consumer activist of USA in recent times. Gandhi's concern for the consumer is reflected in the following dictum: "a customer is the most important visitor on our premises. He is not dependent on us. We are dependent on him. He is not an interruption in our work he the purpose of it. We are not doing him a favour by serving him. He is doing us a favour by giving us an oppor-tunity to serve him."

1949 saw the first consumer organisation in India established by a gandhian R.P.Dalvai in madras. Since then the consumer movement in India started taking shape and by assumed the role of pressure group, with few mass membership organisations. It was in 1962, on 15th march, when John F. Kennedy the US president speaking to the US congress, declared four consumer rights and the movement in the USA took root. Subsequently, various countries passed consumer interests laws of different kinds.15th march, 1962 is the day in the history of consumer rights.

On this day Kennedy said: "it is the consumer's right to safety, information, and choice and hearing." On 9 April, 1985, the General Assembly of the United Nations unanimously adopted a set of general guidelines for consumer protection. The 1984 and the 1986 amendment in the monopolies & restrictive trade practice act 1969 and the 1986 consumer protection act in India formed the basis and fillip to consumer movement through legal measures in our country.

GLOBALIZATION, LIBERALISATION AND CONSUMERISM

Positive Implications

The process of development coupled with increasing liberalization and globalization across the country has enabled consumers to appreciate their increasingly important role in society and governance. Though it is said it to be 'self reliant' but in present scenario it seems unfeasible to tag along the same in this day and age the world has transformed into 'global village' not only due to the advancement of trade and commerce but more due to technological advancement. Therefore liberalization is inevitable for a nation-state disposed to develop itself. It is very difficult for any nation to produce everything to satisfy its customer citizens, so the process of globalization and free trade is serving a noble cause for all the probable con-sumers by satisfying their otherwise unaddressed desires. Globalization is almost inevitable but mostly desired at the same time from the consumer's point of view. In fact it enforces consumer's 'right to choice', as envisaged by UNO in its guidelines for consumer welfare, in more sensible manner by exposing him to varieties of availabilities.

Negative Implications

Noam Chomsky, one of the world's noted intellectuals, describes globalization thus: "Insinuation of extension of transnational corporate tyranny...Their first interest is profit— but much broader than that it is to construct an audience of a particular type ...addicted to a certain lifestyle with artificial wants, an audience atomized, separated from one another, fragmented enough so that they don't enter the political arena and disturb the powerful." This, is what all about existing Indian consumer, who is now heading opposite to its own philosophy of consumerism when we compare and contrast it with that of the Gandhiji's which says that "while there is enough on earth for every man's need there is not enough for everyone's greed and that poverty is really the other face of the problem of possessive-ness. "It is the consumerist mode of thinking." Being the consumer of environment and nature today's punter of the third world is really underprivileged of his very deep-seated, fundamental and natural right in the newly evolved monstrous paradigm of globalization in which human well-being is equated with material con-sumption regardless of the impact of unregulated economic growth on social ties and the environment. 6% of the world's population in America is usurping 40% of the earth's non-renewable fossil fuel resources and non-fuel mining alone produces 1300 million tonnes of garbage annually. If everyone in the world were to enjoy the American standard of consumption, it has been estimated that three planets Earth would be needed.

In the World Economic Forum 1999 meet, Nobel lau-reate and UNDP Goodwill Ambassador, Nadine Gordimer, condemned the process of globalization for increasing consumption unprecedentedly, jeopardizing truly human prospects: "While those of us who have been the generations of big consumers need to consume less, for more than one billion of the world's poorest people increased consumption is a matter of life and death and a basic want—the right to freedom from want." She asserted that consumption is necessary for human development "when it enlarges the capabilities of and improves people's lives without adversely affecting the lives of others." This is how globalization turns out fatal for present and probable consumers as well as for national entities also.

Law and Globalize World

The presence of an international or transnational ele-ment is likely to make the application of political will, trans-lated into law, extremely difficult. International law does not operate directly on human behaviour, or the behaviour of corporations; the effective actors in international law are nation-states. Rights and remedies acquired under the law of one nation may be recognized and enforced in another nation, but this is not guaranteed. To obtain redress of grievances may be difficult and technically complex quite apart from the practical difficulties of language, location of parties, and finding a party with sufficient assets to justify initiating enforcement procedures.

Even where nation-states have the political will to unify or harmonize their legal rules, there may be difficulties in securing an expression of the policy which produces the same effects. However, the crucial factor in achieving any political solution to the control of anti-social behaviour lies in the effective application of legal rules by entities sufficiently capable of asserting sanctions to affect their efficacy. If netizens can remove themselves from the scope of national laws, nation states may defeat the political process and it is not sufficiently clear what sanctions they may impose to assure compliance with rules they may themselves promulgate. Since 1960, most developed coun-tries with common law legal systems, the nations of Europe and most recently of Asia have enacted significant consumer protection legislation (For example, Japan, Korea and Taiwan have all recently introduced product liability legislation which is based on the 1985 Product Liability Directive of the European Communities).

Such laws are national, and operate only within the geographical limits of the enacting jurisdiction, except where conflict of laws rules permit them to be applied as part of the law of some other country. Attempts to apply such existing laws to activities outside the geographical boundaries of the enacting state might prove ineffective. Examples include marketing and sale of goods or services (including financial services) online through the Internet or satellite TV by suppliers who are in remote areas, often beyond the reach of legal process. If it is impossible to locate production, marketing, distribution and trade in goods and services in a defined physical and juristic locality, no legal control is possible.

Consumer Protection Laws in the Global World

Consumers have sought protection through legislation because the general laws and market forces have failed to provide it. Many consumer protection laws either relate to the terms and conditions of contracts that consumers make with suppliers for the supply of goods and services, or to conduct intended to encourage the making of such contracts (marketing, packaging, advertising and provision of information). Previous laws, especially the law of contracts, assumed that the parties to contracts are legally equal in terms of power and information. In substance, in real markets, almost invariably consumers have markedly less power and information than suppliers.

The law deems the action of a consumer in buying a commodity to be the making of a contract - in theory a free, consensual act. In practice, the legal consequences are attributed to the action by the law without any consideration of what the consumer actually knows or wants. The common law of contracts simply cannot afford consumers the protection they probably would seek if they were rational, fully informed, and equal in economic power to the supplier. Because contract law offers an inadequate basis for an equitable legal transaction, it must be modified by legislation in order to afford greater protection to consumers than they can negotiate individually for themselves.

Problem of Legislative Jurisdiction and its Ways Out

Both public and private international law restricts the power of nation states to provide legal sanctions and re-medies. United States anti-trust law provides a good example of Globalization being challenged in its earliest stages. The year, 1892, saw the passage of Anti Trust Laws which made the nascent Industries of the Big Business Era account-able to the people and the Government of the day. Recently, Bill Gates was brought to the book for Anti Trust violations, which turned out to be a big theme for the U S economy in the first tenure of George Bush.

How law, politics and practicalities intersect in ways that destroy international goodwill. Attempts by any single nation to proscribe activities beyond its physical boundaries by people who are neither residents nor citizens are likely to create the problem of legislative jurisdiction. When this happens, a state may enforce its extraterritorial laws within its own boundaries, but other states will steadfastly, block any attempt to enforce those laws within their own terri-tories. A preferable solution seems to be bilateral or multi-lateral international agreements under which governments concur that each will make criminal, under its domestic laws, the conduct which all desire to prohibit. This process is sometimes called "unification" or "harmonization" of law. If any activities in the Networld are to be made criminal, even though this process seems cumbersome, it may be the only acceptable means available. There are problems of securing agreement of uniform laws.

Consumer Protection Act 1986 (COPRA)

The Consumer Protection Act, 1986 (68 of 1986) is a milestone in the history of socio-economic legislation in the country. It is one of the most progressive and compre-hensive piece of legislations enacted for the protection of consumers. It was enacted after in-depth study of consumer protection laws in a number of countries and in consultation with representatives of consumers, trade and industry and extensive discussions within the Government.

The main objective of the act is to provide for the better protection of consumers. Unlike existing laws which are punitive or preventive in nature, the provisions of this Act are compensatory in nature.

The act is intended to provide simple, speedy and inexpensive redressal to the consumers' grievances, and relief of a specific nature and award of compensation wherever appropriate to the consumer. The act has been amended in 1993 both to extend its coverage and scope and to enhance the powers of the redressal machinery. It confers upon consumers eight rights i.e.: basic needs, safety, information, choice, representation, redress, consumer education, healthy environment. It provides remedies to the aggrieved customer in form Replace, Remove, Refund, Redress.

Merits of COPRA:

- Simplicity, straightforwardness and inexpensiveness.
- Swift disposal of disputes.
- Comprehensible to layman.
- Easily accessible.
- Consumer welfare oriented.

Loopholes in COPRA:

- Devoid of practibility- legal technicalities which need lawyers to deal with.
- Irregular functioning of consumer council.
- Constrained powers of judges' i.e. magisterial powers (though enhanced by the amendment of 2003 but not yet implemented).
- No austere provision to dishearten proxy litigation.

Suggestions and Annotations:

- It is extremely imperative to encourage volunteers, who are gallant, audacious and forthright, concerned in consumer protection movements.
- Organisations, NGOs, institutions and agencies allied to consumer movements should hearten administrative advocacy in settling consumer disputes so the hitch of case pendency and delay in case disposal can be avoided.
- Govt. should come up with varieties of plans to esta-blish and manage laboratories, equipped with latest available international standard technologies, for testing samples of consumer goods with a view to determining their quality, purity and relative merit.
- Government should enter into treaties with various countries in order to ensure extra territorial operation of the act.
- Government should be pro active towards the cunning policies of MNCs to exploit the consumer.
- A heavy sum should be taken from the multination

companies in the form of security money at the time of their establishment and incorporation.

- Most of the Indian consumers know only COPRA but they are not aware about other laws and statutes which protect their right so along with the dissemination of COPRA consumer should be made aware about the existence of other laws i.e. MRTP, Essential Commodities Act 1955, Bureau of Indian Standard Act 1986 etc.
- Government should make efforts to create a consensus for 'global consumer policy.'
- Judicial activism should be increased in consumer related issues also and parental role should be played by the Supreme Court for consumer redressal agencies.
- Administrative advocacy should be encouraged in order to reduce the burden of consumer redressal agencies.
- Indian consumer suffers from lack of political willing-ness to enforce consumer rights emphatically. V.R. Krishna Iyer, former Chief Justice of India, expresses himself more stridently:" The country's greatest enemy is GATT and the pro-MNC politics...leading to de-colonization of India...Their capacity to corrupt, terrorize, propagandize, destabilize, colonies and subvert...has been the disaster of our country and of many others. And who invites them into our hallowed Bharat? The greats who have taken the oath of office under the secular socialist constitution and worship Gandhi as the Father of the Nation.

CONSUMER RESPONSIBILITY

Strange as it may seem, most consumers do not know that the law is on their side. It is for the consumers to enforce the provisions of law by vitalizing enforcement. The machinery is available. It has to be use effectively. Marilyn Ferguson writes in The Aquarian Conspiracy, "Countries like ours are full of people who have all the material comforts they desire, yet lead lives of quiet (and at times noisy) desperation, understanding nothing but the fact that there is a hole inside them and that however much food and drink they pour into it. Therefore, being aware about rights a consumer should also understand his responsibilities for procuring the better outcomes.

The globalization of markets makes it very difficult for the laws of nation states to control the excesses of businesses operating outside of their physically defined territories. Computer mediated communication networks afford new opportunities for transnational marketing that may ignore the restrictions afforded by national consumer protection laws. How then could consumers be protected in this new virtual marketplace? A few possibilities are suggested, but none really offers promise of the level of protection which consumers receive under national laws.

- First, the most obvious step would be for nations to seek bilateral treaties that establish reciprocal arrangements for enforcing consumer protection laws between nation-states that have similar laws.
- Secondly, the most effective means, but most difficult to accomplish would be an international agreement concerning the rights of consumers online, similar to the international agreements governing transnational postal services and telecommunications.
- Thirdly, the World Trade Organisation might determine that consumer fraud online constituted a threat to the viability of international trade. As sanctions may be imposed upon non-conforming nation-states.
- Fourthly, individual nation-states may enforce their own consumer protection laws unilaterally by inhibiting the travel of offending parties foreclosing entry into their territories.
- Fifthly, Information Service Providers and Internet Access Providers may themselves unite to establish industry norms for appropriate behaviour in offering consumer transactions over their systems.
- Sixthly, major commercial interests that choose to offer products online may establish industry organisations that purport to guarantee an optimum level of consumer protection for purchasers of their products.

We believe the more guidelines are required because there are always two sides of a coin, each instance of Consumer affairs could be easily termed as another 'Consumer mistreatment' .By the time market forces have time to operate, far too many consumers are dead, maimed, or impoverished. Within a nation-state, national laws may prevent some of this harm, but once national boundaries are crossed, their effectiveness is limited, and consumers can hope for very limited protection, If online trade proliferates and consumer fraud becomes a major problem, nation-states and commercial interests that provide online access are fairly restricted in the action they may take to curb unacceptable and deleterious practices. Certainly if consumers perceive online commerce as a hazardous place to make purchases, they will not choose this alternative, and a major opportunity for electronic commerce may be forfeited. Consequently, there is strong motivation for reputable business to observe high commercial standards of behaviour.

Global capitalism has developed a planetary consumer culture based upon exploitation and exclusion. In the West, the current economic system is capitalism which is based upon private ownership, which opposes a socialist economy with its state or community ownership. Consumerism has grown with capitalism, and can be seen as providing an excuse, reason or driving force for capitalism, allowing the masses to benefit through their individual consumption whilst capitalists profit.

Consumerism is becoming increasingly important. Recently spreading into areas of life which in the past have been controlled by the state instead of private companies (education and health, for example), people have more choice and so can be identified through their consumption. We've moved from a work-based to a consumer-based society in which people are identified more through their consumption and less so by their occupation and general citizenship. This consumer-based society incorporates its own culture, one with many widely different and contrasting principles to the work and citizen culture it is replacing.

Capitalism and consumerism have become global as capitalists look for new markets to sell their goods and individuals are tempted by the rewards and benefits of consumption. The third principle aspect of capitalist production, according to Karl Marx, is "[t]he creation of a world market". It is in a truly world market that profits can be maximised, and McDonaldization, Americanization and Westernization are processes which homogenize aspects of this world market. The result is the development of a single planetary consumer culture rather than numerous consumer cultures or a mixture of cultures, some based upon consumption and some not. Companies aim to maxi-mise profits, whilst consumers act as individuals, searching for the lowest price and best quality. Neither are urged to pursue issues of social responsibility, to tackle the problems of the divisions that consumption creates.

The government and communities have historically been responsible for societal problems, however globali-zation acts to redistribute power from governments and communities to their people as individuals, through processes of democratization of technology, finance and information. This essay will tackle the nature of consumer culture, exploring the ways and reasons in which it may be considered to be exploitative and exclusive, both directly and indirectly. It will explore the benefits and costs of consumption, contrasting this with alternatives. Discussion will be channelled through seven loosely defined themes: resources, living standards, empowerment, labour, environ-ment, ways of life and community.

Consumption requires money which is not equally distributed throughout a capitalist society. Resources are not unlimited, and part of a currency's purpose is to act as a rationing device, ensuring that resources are not overused. As such, consumption does not give full choice to all, but only those who can afford. But a question arises as to whether divisions are necessary for all or just the rich. That is, does consumerism allow the rich to protect their wealth through a devisive system, or is it a system which allocates resources in a fair or necessary way. Miles looks at many ways in which consumption creates an illusion of choice for all, something which is necessary to ensure that the poor do not feel cheated by the system. He notes that "consumerism cannot be all things to all men and women. Rather, it protects those with resources from those without."

Whilst advocating the view that the rich will try to protect their resources, the word 'cannot' leads to the understanding that Miles believes that an equitable non-exclusive system of distribution cannot be achieved through consumerism. However, part of Miles argument is tenuous and short-sighted. He states that the "Internet... [is] clearly beyond the means of the majority of people... [and is] largely the preserve of the privileged who can access it through business or education". Written.in 1998 at the dawn of the Internet revolution, Miles' statement was partially true, but he was unaware of the network's exponential growth throughout a wider and wider cross-section of society. Today it is possible to go on the Internet in an Internet cafe for £1/hour, or buy an Internet PC for under £300, clearly placing it within the reach of the majority of people, rather than beyond it as Miles suggests.

Admittedly there will still be some who cannot afford, at least for more than a few hours, but as prices continue to fall year by year it gradually becomes possible for the whole of society to make advantage of it. By the year 2005 it will be possible to buy a computer for under £100 which will be better than any computer sold in 1998. This fall in price and increase in power is fuelled by consumption and would not be possible in a communist economy at such immense speed. The Internet and PCs in general is just one example of the gradual spread of at-first exclusive products infiltrating to society as a whole. Other notable examples include TVs, telephones, cars, fridges, dishwashers, ovens, microwaves - or more generally, technology. Whilst non-technological products also spread, they generally do so at slower rates as their costs historically have decreased less over time. But recent rationalization of organisations which increase efficiencies, together with globalization, now enable almost all goods and services to be provided at cheaper prices, and hence are available to a wider number of potential consumers.

Recent critics have cast doubt upon the benefits of consumerism. "Many writers doubt that the consumer society results in the empowering of consumers and argue that it simply divides the rich from the poor". It is true that consumption does divide the rich from the poor. But communism, an alternative to consumer-capitalism, creates no choice or empowerment, except for the ruling body. History also shows that past attempts at communism have resulted in stagnation and ruin.

When Marx wrote that "[t]he ultimate cause of all real crises is always the poverty and restricted consumption of the masses" it was during the industrialist period before the latest stage of rapid globalization. Perhaps he failed to fully grasp the full reach of consumer-capitalism in later years. Although the trickle-down effect has not been as great as was hoped, the 'masses' have benefited from consumption in increases in living standards. The rich-poor divide has widened, but the poor are now less poor.

Friedman discusses how the end of the Cold War (and the end of communism and barriers to trade) has led to greater democracy. Specifically he deals with the 'democratization of information' through empowering technological innovations such as the TV and Internet. Whilst the Internet itself was largely the invention of the US government, the systems which it requires to run (fast PCs, network equipment, cables, satellite) have been developed predominately by private companies whose profits - obtained through consumer purchases - have been injected into fueling research and innovation. Rather than people now has access to restricted information, or only a few exclusive members of society having access, an incredible amount of information is now easily and readily available to everyone with a PC and modem.

Consumption has particularly empowered women, who in the past have been excluded from many activities due to patriarchy. Marginalised groups are also catered for through niche markets which are particularly possible through the Internet as it is global in scope. Ritzer's work on McDonaldization looks at how consumer culture can be exploitative to domestic workers and the local society as a whole. "[r]ational systems are dehumanizing" (2000: 124), he tells us, arguing that companies treat workers as disposal commodities rather than accepting their human qualities. Almost anyone can get a job at McDonald's (suggesting an inclusive nature to consumerism) however the jobs which are given are sub-standard, offer low wages and little enjoyment.

But whilst rationalized companies like McDonald's may exploit their workers, enhanced through the effectual banning of trade unions, the company and its associated consumer culture are not based primarily on exploitation. Instead, the process of McDonaldization is based upon efficiency, reliability, predictability and control. Exploitation is an unintentional by-product of these primary goals. Capitals ultimately have few options but to seek profit before everything else. If there is nothing (for example legislation or pressure groups) to force Company A from using exploitative practices, then it would be commercial suicide not to, as Company B would do it instead, and could lead to the demise of Company A. Capitalism is increasingly competitive, especially since the prevalence of globalization and the ability to move capital quicker and easier across further distances.

The Consumer Association now acts solely for consumers and not for those who may be exploited through consumption. That is, in reviews in their magazine 'Which?' they discuss the advantages of products to a consumer - features, price, quality - but do not mention anything about possible sweatshop work, environmental degradation and other forms of exploitation required to produce it. In 1999 the Fair Labour Association (FLA) was founded as it was realised that if companies and consumer groups do not look after the needs of the exploited, some other body has to. The FLA is "an independent monitoring system that holds its participating companies accountable for the conditions under which their products are produced". The goal of the FLA is to "advance fair, decent and humane working conditions (ibid) and does so through enabling brands to be differentiated through the use of an FLA label on products that adhere to the standards of the International Labor Association (ILO).

It is hard to argue that McDonald's and similar companies' consumer culture is based upon exclusion. Its products are cheap enough to be purchased by everyone in society. But the recent McLibel case brings aspects of McDonald's exploitation of consumers to light. "[T]he judge ruled that McDonald's exploits children, deceptively claims its food is nutritious, and poses a risk to the health of its long-term customers." Companies such as McDonalds spend millions in marketing and PR in an attempt to improve their corporate image to consumers. However, as this example also illustrates, often the money is spent in a deceptive or inaccurate manner. Multinationalmonitor.org named and shamed Shell Oil as one of 'The 10 Worst Corporations Of 2002' "for continuing business as usual as one of the world's leading environmental violators – while marketing itself as a socially and environmentally responsible company. "

McDonalds and Shell are by no means the exception, and closer to the rule in this way. Ben & Jerry's and The Body Shop are two companies usually associated with high moral and ethical standards, however are condemned by Ritzer as not being as ethical as they claim. In a fictional novel, Elton make an amusing jibe at con-sumption's ultimate goal: "Consumer confidence is actually considered a measure of a country's relative economic strength... Consumption is synonymous with 'growth' and growth is good... Judged by the logic of world economics, the death of the planet will be the zenith of human achievement, because if consumption is always good, then to consume a whole planet must be the best thing of all". Of course nobody would advocate the destruction of the planet, but Elton does illustrate the point that current levels of consumption may not be sustainable, and that there is little room for maneuver because of limited choice in a global economy, described as 'Golden Straightjacket'.

Consumerism has become global and may be seen as exploiting religions and alternative ways of life. The militant Islamic fundamentalists of al-Qaeda argue that consumer-capitalism and its associated Christian history is obtrusive to their way-of-life and must be stopped. Consumerism makes alternative ways of living harder as people are tempted by the benefits of consumption. However the important question is whether these people are then exploited or empowered by consumerism. Edwards sees three key themes behind consumption, of which one is that "despite its expansion, consumer society remains *socially divisive*,... constructing new forms of stratification according to income, credit status and physical access" (2000: 188, italics mine). Edwards also suggests that "advertising and marketing tend to work to perpetuate, recreate and even add caveats and divisions to an already socially divisive situation". Consumption may increase material quality of living, but here the argument is that in dong so it also increases societal problems associated with divisiveness.

When most people shop, the criteria for consuming usually comes down to a compromise between price and quality, little ethical consideration appears to occur. There are various explanations for why this may be. Perhaps consumers don't care about exploitation - they are selfish; perhaps they do care but have no choice, as all company's products have similar ethical problems; perhaps they do care and some products are more ethical than others, but information isn't readily available to document this; or they do care, but feel constrained themselves (by time or money, for example) and so must consider their own needs first; or maybe they're simply not aware that exploitation exists, or are unable to make the link between their own consumption and the processes required to get a product to market. Of course, these possibilities can also work concurrently within an individual consumer, or change from one consumption to the next, or one day to the next.

Bauman argues that often the fifth possibility above is prevalent as "consumers rarely catch a glimpse of the other side [those affected by their consumption]... If they ever visit the 'Third World', it is for safaris and massage parlours, not for its sweatshops". The consumers here are distancing themselves and their consumption from the sweatshops which result. Whilst they may care about the quality of life for the workers if they thought about it long enough, they don't necessarily want to care - after all, it may take away much of the enjoyment gained from consumption if the full truth I known to them. Bauman also sees various ways in which moral offensiveness is obfuscated by various walls (predominately protecting the capitalist) through the route of production, and masks (predominately protecting the consumer) which products wear at the point of con-sumption. "Walls seldom appear as walls; instead, they are thought of as commodity prices, profit margins, capital exports, taxation levels. One cannot desire poverty for others without feeling morally contemptible; but one can desire lower taxes."

Consumer culture has been discussed as either protecting the rich or allocating resources fairly or necessarily. It has been seen to increase living standards for all whilst accentuating a divide between the rich an poor. Whist it empowers it also divides. Through technology it promises a sustainable way-of-life, although currently exploits the environment in unsustainable ways. It tempts people away from alternative ways-of-living, but does so in an exploi-tative manner. It is based upon individual selfishness and not communal goals. To conclude, it is evident that global capitalism has developed a planetary consumer culture and that that culture both excludes and exploits. However, consumer culture is not 'based' upon exploitation and exclusion. Instead, it is based upon progress and the continual rise of living standards. It is an unfortunate consequence that this occurs in an exploitative and exclusive way, but it is not an intended goal.

5

Consumer Protection and Competition Policy

CONSUMER PROTECTION

Promotion of consumer welfare is the common goal of consumer protection and competition policy. At the root of both consumer protection and competition policy is the recognition of an unequal relationship between consumers and producers. Protection of consumers is accomplished by setting minimum quality specifications and safety standards for both goods and services and establishing mechanisms to redress their grievances. The objective of competition is met by ensuring that there are sufficient numbers of producers so that no producer can attain a position of dominance. If the nature of the industry is such that dominance in terms of market share cannot be avoided, it seeks to ensure that there is no abuse on account of this dominance. Competition policy also seeks to forestall other forms of market failure, such as formation of cartels, leading to collusive pricing, division of markets and joint decisions to reduce supply. Mergers and acquisitions also need to be regulated as they reduce competition.

Consumer Protection Policy

The consumer movement in India is as old as trade and commerce. In Kautilya's *Arthashastra*, there are references to the concept of consumer protection against exploitation by the trade and retailer with respect to quality, short weight, measurement and adulteration of goods. Yet until the late 1970s, there was no systematic movement in the country for safeguarding the interest of consumers. But now it is widely acknowledged that the level of consumer awareness and protection is a true indicator of development of the country and progressiveness of civil society. The main reason for this is the rapidly increasing variety of goods and services which modern technology has made available. In addition, the growing size and complexity of production and distribution systems, the high level of sophistication in marketing and selling practices and in advertising and other forms of promotion, mass marketing methods and consumers' increased mobility resulting in reduction of personal interaction between buyers and sellers, have contributed to the increased need for consumer protection.

Protection of consumer rights in modern times dates back to 1962.On 15 March 1962, the Consumer Bill of Rights was proclaimed by the United States President in a message to the Congress. The message proclaimed: (i) the right to choice, (ii) the right to information, (iii) the right to safety, and (iv) the right to be heard. Subsequently, the right to consumer education, the right to a healthy environment and the right to basic needs (food, clothing, and shelter) were added by Consumer International. In India, 24 December is celebrated as National Consumer Rights Day as the Consumer Protection Act, 1986 was enacted on that day. 15 March is observed as World Consumer Rights Day since 1983, when International Organisation of Consumer Unions declared it so.

In India, 15 March was also adopted as the National Consumers Day and has been observed since then. Another significant day in the history of world consumer movement is 9 April 1985, when the General Assembly of the United Nations adopted a set of guidelines for consumer protection and the Secretary General of the United Nations was authorized to persuade member countries to adopt these guidelines through policy changes or law. These guidelines constituted a comprehensive policy framework outlining what governments need to do to promote consumer protection in the following areas:

- physical safety,
- protection and promotion of consumer economic interests,
- standards for safety and quality of consumer goods and services,
- measures enabling consumers to obtain redressal,
- measures relating to specific areas (food, water, and pharmaceuticals) and
- consumer education and information programme.

These guidelines provided an internationally recognized set of basic objectives, particularly for governments of developing countries, enabling them to identify the priorities and structure of their consumer protection policy and legislation. Subsequently, the guidelines were expanded to include 'sustainable consumption' which was an important subject in the changed social, political and economic scenario. The importance of 'sustainable consumption' is aptly highlighted in Mahatma Gandhi's words, 'the rich must live more simply so that the poor may simply live'. Sustainable development is crucially dependent on sustainable consumption. Article 21 of the Constitution requires the State, inter alia, to protect life, which must be construed as including the right to a healthy and safe environment. A healthy and safe environment is inalienably linked with sustainability and promotion of sustainable consumption. The concern in the Indian Constitution for protection and promotion of an individual's rights, and for the dignity and welfare of the citizen makes it imperative to provide for the welfare of the individual as a consumer, a client and a customer.

The rights under the Consumer Protection Act, 1986 flow from the rights enshrined in Articles 14 to 19 of the Constitution of India. The RTI, 2005 which has opened up governance processes of our country to the common public also has far-reaching implications for consumer protection. The consumer protection policy creates an environment whereby the clients, customers, and consumers receive satisfaction from the delivery of goods and services needed by them. Good governance requires efficiency, effectiveness, ethics, equality, economy, transparency, accountability, empowerment, rationality, impartiality and participation of citizens. The concern of consumer protection is to ensure fair trade practices; quality of goods and efficient services with information to the consumer with regard to quality, quantity, potency, composition and price for their choice of purchase. Thus, proper and effective implementation of consumer protection law promotes good governance.

Education is the most powerful tool for the progress of the country and is a social and political necessity. Education helps an individual—as a consumer—in making rational choices and protects him from trade and business-related exploitation. But more is needed for the effective functioning of the national market to create an increased level of awareness of consumer rights, and for this consumers have to be educated about rights and responsibilities through concerted publicity and awareness campaigns. In the awareness campaigns, special emphasis needs to be given to vulnerable groups such as women and children, students, farmers and rural families and the working class. The report of the study on the Consumer Protection Act commissioned by the Comptroller and Auditor General (C & AG) of India and conducted in July- August 2005, brought out that 66% of consumers were not aware of consumer rights and 82% were not even aware of the Consumer Protection Act. In rural areas, only 13% of the population had heard of the Consumer Protection Act.

Standards, which are the essential building block for quality, play a key role in consumer protection. Standards could be on technical requirements (specifications), standard terminology (glossary of terms), good practices (codes of practice) or test methods or management system standards.

Developed countries generally rely on manage-ment system standards like ISO 9001 (Quality Management System), ISO 14001 (Environmental Management Systems) and hazard analysis and critical control points (HACCP) as an indicator of the ability of an organisation to meet quality needs and address environmental concerns. These stan-dards are set generally by governmental or inter-governmental bodies but there are some private initiatives as well, which are widely used such as OHSAS 18000 (Occu-pational Health and Safety), SA 8000 (Social Accountability) and WRAP (Worldwide Responsible Apparel Production).

Setting standards is not enough for assuring the consumer of quality. For this, governments need to establish the full quality infrastructure, embracing standardization, conformity assessment and enforcement. The constituents of quality infrastructure are:

- Standardization
- Standard development
- Standard information
- Metrology
- Quality assurance/conformity assessment
- Testing
- Inspection
- Product certification
- Management Systems Certification
- Regulation and enforcement
- Accreditation

CONSUMER PROTECTION IN INDIA

The Consumer Protection Act was enacted in 1986 based on United Nations guidelines with the objective of pro-viding better protection of consumers' interests. The Act provides for effective safeguards to consumers against various types of exploitations and unfair dealings, relying on mainly compensatory rather than a punitive or preventive approach. The Act applies to all goods and services unless specifically exempted, and covers the private, public, and cooperative sectors and provides for speedy and in expensive adjudication. The rights provided under the Act are:

- The right to be protected against marketing of goods and services which are hazardous to life and property.
- The right to be informed about the quality, quantity, potency, purity, standard and price of goods and services, as the case may be, to protect the consumer against unfair trade practices.
- The right to be assured of access to a variety of goods and services at competitive prices.
- The right to seek redressal against unfair or restrictive trade practices or unscrupulous exploitation of consumers.
- The right to consumer education.

Under the Consumer Protection Act,1986 a three-tier, simple, quasi-judicial machinery has been established at the national, State, and district levels for hearing cases raised by consumers. The Act had been amended in 1991 and again in 1993. A comprehensive amendment was last made in 2002 for making the Act effective, functional and purposeful. The amended Act, inter alia, provides for the attachment and subsequent sale of the property of a person not complying with an order. Although implementation of the Consumer Protection Act can be viewed as a success, there are still serious shortfalls in achieving consumer welfare because of the deficiencies in quality infrastructure in the country.

First, there is a regulatory deficit in many products and services which impact on the health, safety and environment of the consumers and mandatory standards have not been prescribed for such products as electrical and electronic goods, IT and telecom equipment, industrial and fire safety equipment and toys. There is a multiplicity of regulatory/ standardization/conformity assessment bodies and proliferation of certification and inspection bodies. At present, the Quality Council of India (QCI) is the main accreditation body for conformity assessment bodies taking up product or system certification or for inspection bodies, and the National Accreditation Board for Laboratories performs the same function for laboratories. However, there is no compulsion on the conformity assessment bodies, inspection bodies or laboratories to obtain accreditation, thus creating a lack of certainty about the existence of quality products, systems, inspections and laboratories.

Laboratory infrastructure is weak in terms of international norms. Quality professionals lack the skills to guide quality improvement efforts in industry. There is apathy among businesses towards standardization in general, and lack of awareness among them about the impact of stan-dards on quality, competitiveness, and profitability.

There is absence of consumer demand for quality goods and services primarily because of lack of awareness among them regarding quality issues. In short, there is absence of a quality culture in the country. At a time when tariff barriers are falling worldwide as a result of multilateral trade negotiations and in the context of Foreign Trade Agreements (FTAs), and technical barriers to trade have become more significant as determinants of trade flows, urgent action has become necessary to correct the situation in the country as described above. If the quality of Indian products and their conformity with international standards is to be accomplished by Indian producers, the impulse must be generated from within the country. Nothing can have a more powerful impact on the producers than the demand for quality products by quality-conscious domestic consumers.

ESTABLISHMENT OF NATIONAL QUALITY AND STANDARDIZATION AUTHORITY

As of today, the Bureau of Indian Standards (BIS), set up under the BIS Act, 1986 functions as the National Standards Body. Apart from the BIS, there are other organisations which are formulating specifications for their own internal use. In some areas, regulators are also prescribing the standards to be observed by the industry concerned. There is need to have a mechanism for the dclaration of a harmonized Indian standard in different areas. For this purpose, the establishment of a National Quality and Standardization Authority through appropriate legal framework to ensure uniformity of approach for setting of standards and ensuring regulation of conformity assess-ment, is necessary. The framework should provide for set-ting voluntary standards in all areas of economic and social activities, and mandatory regulations in areas that impact on health, safety, and the environment.

A national system of conformity assessment and com-pliance should be established to bring in complete synergy in standardization, conformity assessment and enforcement. In sectors critical to health and safety like food or drugs, infrastructure upgradation should be supported for MSE sectors to attain national/international standards/regulations like GMP/ Good Hygienic Practiçe (GHP)/HACCP.A National Regulatory System Database should be developed. More specifically, the following are the measures that need to be undertaken:

i. Strengthening Regulations

Some of the priority elements that should be considered by the concerned ministries or their agencies (Regulatory Bodies) for strengthening the regulation are:

- Mandatory standards for products which impact on health and safety of the consumer and on the environment such as electrical appliances, electronic, IT and telecom products, medical devices, industrial safety and fire safety equipment, helmets, plastic and other material used for food packaging.
- GHP/GMP/HACCP being made mandatory as a rule under the PFA Rules/ Integrated Food Law for the food industry and for hotels and restaurants.
- Mandatory national standards for compliance by all water agencies—rural or urban.
- Introduction of law for product liability provisions including punitive damages as a deterrent for sub - standard goods.
- Laying down residue limits for contaminants for raw materials as well as food products.
- Mandatory compliance with Good Agricultural Practices

or Good Animal Husbandry Practices (GAHP) by commercial farms.

ii. Extending Voluntary Standards into the Services Sectors

For consumer protection, voluntary standards should be extended to the area of services, in particular, medical and hospital services, financing and investor services provided by non-banking financial companies, real estate services, e-commerce, and so on.

iii. National Standards System

The Bureau of Indian Standards (BIS) may be made the national standards body and repository of all voluntary national standards. Wherever voluntary standards are being formulated by other standards development organisations which are recognized as national (like Indian Roads Congress or Agmark), these may be published as national standards by BIS while these bodies continue to make these standards.

iv. Policy on Conformity Assessment

The policy should be laid down for the government recognizing only one National Accreditation Body for conformity assessment for each area of activity. All conformity assessment bodies should be required to obtain accreditation either from national or international accreditation bodies within a reasonable period. As a general rule, functions of regulation, standardization and conformity assessment should be performed separately. Similarly, there is need to enlarge consumer choice in the matter of certification. Appropriate mechanism would need to be evolved for this purpose.

Setting up of National Consumer Protection Authority

There is need to deal effectively with deceptive practices, including misleading advertisements. Besides, there would be a gap in legislation to be caused by the proposed winding up of the Monopolies and Restrictive Trade Practice Commission (MRTPC) with respect to unfair trade practices. The gap can be filled in by establishing a National Consumer Protection Authority through enactment of a National Consumer Protection Authority Act.

Enhancing Consumer Awareness

There is necessity for continuing consumer awareness campaigns on a large scale to sensitize the population on basic aspects such as Maximum Retail Price (MRP), Gold Hall Marking, Indian Standard Institute (ISI) mark on products, and expiry dates. As and when voluntary standards are extended into the services sector or regulations are imposed for mandatory compliance with standards for reasons of health, safety or environment, the content of awareness campaigns would need to be expanded.

COMPETITION POLICY

The Approach Paper to the Eleventh Five Year Plan recognized the need for creating a competitive environment to stimulate private investment. It emphasized the need for increased reliance on competitive markets subject to appropriate, transparent and effective regulations. A major objective of the Eleventh Plan is to recommend policies that spur private sector investment while ensuring fair competition by guarding against restrictive business practices. A review of cross-country literature suggests that there is a positive association between GDP growth and competition. Empirical studies have suggested that compe-tition enhances productivity at industry level, generates more employment and lowers consumer prices.

A pro-competitive policy environment has been found to be positively associated with long-term growth. Competition-enhancing policies have pervasive and long-lasting effects on economic performance by affecting economic actors' incentive structure, by encouraging their innovative activities and by selecting more efficient ones from less efficient ones over time.

The positive effects of competition are well illustrated by the recent experiences in India in several sectors such as telecommunications, automobiles, newspapers and consumer electronics, where there has been a fall in real prices/tariffs and marked improvement in the quality of goods/services. This experience demonstrates the benefits of ensuring competition in other sectors of the economy. The reforms initiated since 1991 recognized the need for removing fetters on trade and industry with the view to unleash the competitive energies. The Industrial Policy Statement of 1991 emphasized the attainment of technological dynamism and international competitiveness. It noted that Indian industry could scarcely be competitive with the rest of the world if it had to operate within an over-regulated environment. To enhance competition in the domestic markets and to generate/promote a culture of competition in the country is part of this broader agenda on reforms.

The economic reforms undertaken by the government have been generally on a sector by sector basis and the progress across sectors has not been uniform. While some sectors have successfully imbibed a strong competition culture, relatively weak competitive pressure exists in a number of sectors, such as electricity, in India. There are several policies and laws that can have significant bearing on competition. These should be made competition-friendly as far as possible. To strengthen the forces of competition in the market, both competition law and competition policy are required. The two complement each other. The competition law prohibits and penalizes anti-competitive practices by enterprises functioning in the market; that is, it addresses market failures. Sector regulatory laws mimic competition in the areas of natural monopolies.

Other regulatory laws, such as those for intellectual property or anti-dumping or even capital markets, too have an important interface with competition. The aim of the competition policy is to create a framework of policies and regulations that will inform other policies to facilitate competitive outcomes in the market. Competition policy is a critical component of any overall economic policy framework. Competition policy is intended to promote efficiency and to maximize consumer/social welfare. It also promotes creation of a business environment, which improves static and dynamic efficiencies, leads to efficient resource allocation and consumer welfare, and in which abuse of market power is prevented/ curbed. It also pro-motes good governance by restricting rent seeking practices of economic actors.

During the Tenth Plan period, the Competition Act, 2002 was enacted. The Act established the CCI to eliminate practices having adverse effect on competition, promote and sustain competition in markets, protect the interest of consumers and ensure freedom of trade carried on by other participants, in markets in India. The Competition (Amend-ment) Act, 2007 passed by the Parliament in September 2007 has incorporated some changes in the Competition Act, 2002 including the establishment of a Competition Appellate Tribunal to hear appeals from the orders of the CCI. Until recently, as the substantive provisions were not notified, CCI was engaged, inter alia, in promotion of competition advocacy and creating awareness about competition issues. This activity will continue, even after the operation-alisation of the Competition Commission, which should happen soon.

During the mid-term appraisal of the Tenth Plan, it was recognized that there is an urgent need for articulating a National Competition Policy (NCP) in India, which should fully reflect the national resolve to accelerate economic growth, improve both the quality of life of the people of the country, national image and self-esteem. It further noted that NCP would bring about a competition culture amongst economic entities to maximize economic efficiency, protect consumer interests and improve international competitiveness. The Planning Commission, in the context of the formulation of the Eleventh Plan, constituted a Working Group on Competition Policy with wide representation of professionals from government and non-government organisations. As suggested by the Working Group, there is a need for the government to adopt a broad-based, overarching and comprehensive NCP to promote coherence in the reforms process, to establish uniform competition principles across different sectors and to harmonize all other policies keeping in view the competition dimensions.

The broad objectives of the NCP should be: (i) to preserve the competitive process and to encourage compe-tition in the domestic market so as to optimize efficiency, (ii) promote innovation and maximize consumer welfare,(iii) to promote, build and sustain strong competition culture within the country; (iv) to achieve harmonization in policies, laws and procedures regarding competition dimensions at all levels of governance, (v) to ensure competition in regulated sectors and to establish an institutional mechanism for synergized relationship between the Competition Commission and Sectoral Regulators, and (vi) to strive for a single national market.

The NCP should be based on the following principles:

- there should be effective control on anti-competitive conduct which undermines competition in markets in India;
- there should be competitive neutrality or a level playing field among all players, whether these be private enterprises, PSEs or government departments engaged in non-sovereign commercial activity;
- the procedures should be rule bound, transparent, fair and non-discriminatory;
- there should be institutional separation between policy making, operations and regulation;
- where a separate regulatory arrangement is set up, it should be consistent with the principles of competition;
- third party access to essential facilities on fair terms should be available;
- any deviation from the principles of competition should be only to meet desirable social, environmental, developmental or other national objectives which are clearly defined, transparent, non-discriminatory, rule based and having the least competition restricting effect. The above principles of competition should be applicable across all sectors of the economy and be incorporated in policies, which govern them.

Several existing policies, statutes and regulations of the Central Government restrict or undermine competition. A review of such policies, statutes and regulations from the competition perspective (this is referred to as 'regulatory impact assessment' in several countries) may be undertaken with a view to remove or minimize their competition restricting effects. Proposed policies, statutes, regulations that impact competition should also include a competition impact assessment through an internal mechanism which should form one of the inputs in any decision-making process in this regard. Regulatory impact analysis should be a pre- condition for introducing regulatory changes in any sector. Any disinvestment or privatization attempt should take into account the competition dimension. In a globalizing economy, incorporation of competition clauses in trade agreements will go a long way to check anti-competitive behaviour and potential anti-competitive cross-border transactions/mergers having an adverse effect in India.

The initiatives at the State Government level would require undertaking pro-competition reforms, keeping in mind the principles of NCP. There are many economic areas of State policies and regulations that impact or inhibit competition in the market. These restrictions also tend to fragment the national market and undermine the freedom of economic actors. The State Governments should be encouraged to undertake a review of existing policies, laws or regulations from the competition perspective and also undertake a competition impact assessment of proposed policy, law and regulations before these are finalized; while seeking expert assistance of CCI and other expert agencies. Similarly, the statutes, laws and procedures which govern the sub-State authorities need to be reviewed so as to align them with the principles of NCP.

All State Governments have, at the instance of CCI, established Nodal Points within their administrations to deal with the subject of competition; the State Governments are encouraged to give these Nodal Points an effective role in this regard. Given the wide canvas of NCP, a suggestion has been made by the Working Group on Competition Policy for setting up an institutional arrangement for monitoring the progress of the implementation of the policy. A small and compact Competition Policy Council of about 25 members could be set up which would be advisory, non- statutory and autonomous in its functioning and be headed by an eminent non-official person and comprising key officials from economic Ministries/ Departments, and non-officials from media, academia and civil society. The task of the Competition Policy Council would be to review the progress in the implementation of NCP such as reviews of policies, regulations and practices, and the competition impact assessment of new laws, regulations and policies.

An incentive scheme could be instituted by the government under which financial grants may be given to State Governments linked to the progress in aligning their policies and laws with the principles of NCP. The grants could be released based on the progress made by the various State Governments on the recommendations received from the Competition Policy Council. The interface between the Competition Commission vis-à-vis sectoral regulators is critical. The basic premise to be recognized is that sectoral regulators have domain expertise in their relevant sectors. The Competition Commission, established under the Competition Act, 2002 on the other hand, has been constituted with a broad mandate to deal with competition for which certain very specific parameters are laid down under the Act. A formal mechanism for coordination between the Competition Commission and the sectoral regulators is, therefore, of key importance. Coordination between sectoral regulators and Competition Commission should be made mandatory through suitable provisions in the Competition Act, 2002 and sectoral laws.

Regulation may be justified or warranted in sectors which have natural monopolies or network industries; more so where a universal service obligation exists. However, regulation may not be required where these features do not prevail. Such sectors should ideally be left to the forces of competition. Even in sectors where regulation is required, it should be competition based or competition driven. One of the objectives of the regulation should be to create a competitive market in so far as this is feasible. As competition in the regulated sectors expands, the regulation should ideally become lighter and ultimately economic regulation may not be necessary. Therefore, a sunset clause based on considered timelines appropriate to the regulated sector may be considered in all economic regulatory laws so as to leave the industry to market forces once effective competition is achieved. Any anticompetitive conduct can always be addressed by the Competition Act, 2002.

Successful implementation of competition policy and law largely depends upon its acceptance by the people. Competition advocacy buttressed by good enforcement plays a vital role in securing the willingness and acceptability of a competition policy and law. Competition advocacy can also be looked at as law enforcement without intervention. An important tool of advocacy is the ability of many competition authorities to give an opinion on proposed legislation and public policy on their own, so that the law makers and policy makers consider the competition dimension and give reasons for deviating from them for the benefit of the public. The assistance of CCI and other expert bodies could be utilized for conducting studies in this regard.

The concept and the role of competition are relatively new to the Indian business community. There is, therefore, a pressing need to increase the level of awareness about the benefits of competition and the contribution of the competition law in this respect among the public, more particularly among the business community. The Com-mission has been given, under the Act, the mandate to generate public awareness; its efforts in this area may be further strengthened. The Commission should formulate, publish and post in the public domain, guidelines covering various dimensions related to competition law for enhancing public awareness. Such guidelines will help enterprises by bringing greater clarity about the provisions of the competition law and the manner of its enforcement. The Commission should also engage in Compliance Education for business. There is strong commonality between competition policy and law on the one hand and consumer protection policy and law on the other. An effective competition policy lowers entry and exit barriers and makes the environment conducive to promoting entrepreneurship, which also provides space for the growth of small and medium enterprises and consequent employment expansion. Competition law concentrates in maintaining the process of competition between enterprises and tries to remedy behavioural or structural problems in order tore-establish effective competition in the market.

The consequence of this is higher economic efficiency, greater innovation and enhancement of consumer welfare. Thereby the consumer experiences wider choices and greater availability of goods at affordable prices. On the other hand, the consumer protection policy and law are primarily concerned with the nature of consumer tran-sactions, trying to improve market conditions for effective exercises of consumer choice. Thus, the two disciplines focus on different market failures and offer different remedies, but are both aimed at maintaining well functioning, competitive markets that promote consumer welfare. The two disciplines are mutually re-enforcing.

CONSUMER CITIZENSHIP

Recent decades have brought positive progress around the globe in many areas of life but dramatic social and economic disparities and far reaching environmental degradation have also occurred. These are in many cases the consequence of the impacts of governmental policies, commercial activities and individual lifestyle choices. In order to be better able to reflect upon the local, national, and global consequences of their choices, individuals need training in how to define issues; gather, handle and apply relevant information; consult; plan courses of action; make choices; analyse and assess their actions. This is particularly true in their roles as consumers.

Consumption is action taken in cultural contexts, strongly influenced by marketing, media and social expectations. Analyzing interaction with the market requires gaining insight into the person's or community's background, present relationships and their reactions to advertising and media. In Europe, as in many other parts of the world, communities are conglomerations of people from highly diverse backgrounds and cultures. Thus, the work carried out by the members of the Consumer Citizenship Network is concerned not only with general features of consumption and citizenship but also with the various perspectives on consumption and citizenship springing from the heterogeneous quality of European society due to immigration and mobility. Consumer citizenship is a universal responsibility as Europeans of all origins must deal with a complex market-dominated society.

Transdisciplinary Inquiry and Mobility

The Consumer Citizenship Network (CCN) was established in 2003 as an interdisciplinary network of educators, researchers and representatives of non-governmental organisations (as well as UNESCO, UNEP and Consumers International) who share a common concern about how the individual's role can contribute constructively to sustain-able development and mutual solidarity. Progress towards sustainable development and achievement of the Millennium Goals is slow for the European Community as well as the global community.

The European Parliament and the European Council have "the achievement of balanced and sustainable development and the recognition of the interrelationship and interdependency between economic, social and environmental aspects of growth" as one of their underlying objectives. The CCN participants represent 113 institutions from 37 countries and have worked to develop interdisciplinary approaches to sustainable development and sustainable, responsible consumption. CCN members represent disciplines from business and economics, social sciences, natural sciences, political science and the huma-nities. The network facilitates communication, dialogue and debate online and face to face. It promotes mobility by stimulating staff and student exchange between institutions in many of the countries within Europe.

Central Themes

Central themes which the CCN deals with can be summarized as follows:

- How can the individual deal with the ethical challenges of prosperity?
- How can the media and ICT be constructive tools for the consumer citizen?
- What are the individual's rights and responsibilities as regards food, transport, housing, energy use and personal finances?
- What contributions can the European consumer citizen make towards the eradication of poverty in the world?
- How can awareness and social involvement be stimulated in the individual?
- How can sustainable consumption be encouraged?

Theoretical Knowledge and Practical Experience

The Consumer Citizenship Network has tried to contribute to the process of preparing citizens for life in a complex, highly commercial, global society by increasing collaboration between research, higher education and civil society in order to better relate theoretical knowledge to practical everyday experience. Research, discourse and educational focus on sustainable development in general and sustainable consumption in particular involve examining, among other things, the interface between traditional habits and modern, commercially regulated lifestyles.

The CCN has held three international conferences and published books, proceedings and other material dealing with such topics as transparency, accountability, democratic participation, the family's role in modern society, cultural understanding of morals and values, freedom and responsibility, food and nutrition, consumer rights, welfare systems, business ethics, CSR, debt prevention, environmental assessment, ecological footprints, accessibility and inclusiveness. Copies/ printouts of articles about the research on these and other topics can be acquired both online and/or by contacting the Consumer Citizenship Network Core Unit.

The CCN network creates a bridge between universities/ colleges and the socio-economic organisations which are concerned with sustainable consumption and active citizenship. Thus CCN contributes to the reinforcement of links between teaching and civil society. Several of these civil society organisations concentrate on encouraging active citizenship in communities of immigrant groups. Others carry out in-service training for adults and youth from diverse backgrounds in which consumer citizenship is a central theme.

Social Responsibility on the Part of Business and Consumers

Although most religions, ethnic groups, commercial enterprises and governments have traditions concerning social responsibility, these vary extensively. Conflicts arising from differences in both definition and practice have fuelled antagonism in many parts of Europe in recent years. The Consumer Citizenship Network partners are concerned with the balance between material and non-material well-being and how one can translate ethical values into everyday practice through conscientious participation in the market.

The CCN has approached the task of stimulating the individual's awareness of the central role they play in forming society and assisting them in finding constructive ways of doing so by first acknowledging that *"a consumer citizen is an individual who makes choices based on ethical, social, economic and ecological considerations. The consumer citizen actively contributes to the maintenance of just and sustainable development by caring and acting responsibly on family, national and global levels.*

By focusing on social responsibility on the part of business and consumers, the CCN addresses the growing international concern for implementation of norms and behaviour which support sustainable development and global solidarity. In the international arena, the CCN contributes to the UN Decade for education for sustainable development as well as the International Standards Organisation's efforts to create guidance standards for social responsibility to be used by public and private organisations. On a regional level, the CCN concentrates on the development of consumer citizenship education.

Consumer Citizenship Education

Educators and researchers around the globe recognize the dilemmas of commercial persuasion, health and safety, ethical consumption, rights and responsibilities and sustainable development, but few systematic pedagogical approaches to these interrelated problems have been put into use. The CCN network participants have worked to develop consumer citizenship education as a relevant, interdisciplinary theme in universities and colleges. Consumer citizenship education deals with "empowering students to develop and evaluate alternative visions of a sustainable future" and motivating them to turn these visions into reality. The Consumer Citizenship Network has brought together expertise in the fields of citizenship, environmental and consumer education and provides channels for dialogue and cooperation in research and development work related to consumer citizenship education. The Network works to develop good practice for teaching and accessing consumer citizenship education.

Consumer Citizenship Education can be defined as:

- being based upon the concept of world citizenship which claims to provide a global ethic for sustainable development.
- addressing both the supply and demand sides of sustainable consumption in light of intra-generational equity.
- Analyzing the prerequisites for and the implications of sustainable consumption.
- Reflecting upon development in personal, local, national and international contexts.

- Tacilitating the locating and understanding of relevant scientific information.

In addition to the publication of The Consumer Citizenship Education Guidelines, the CCN has prepared and published numerous articles dealing with consumer citizenship education. These deals with aspects such as: identification of special needs, knowledge clusters, world citizenship, the internationalization of education, active learning, core life skills, experience-oriented education, problem-based learning, change management, cross cultural understanding, and moral education. A number of these articles take into consideration the perspectives arising from immigration and mobility within Europe. They analyze the changes in European society due to the effects of the single market, globalization and social mobility. Value-based social competences are steadily losing ground in Europe to instrumental competences whose goal is competitive advantage. The Consumer Citizenship Network has also recognized the need for curricula reform and integration of alternative teaching methods in order to further the development of competences which improve the individual's ability to function creatively and cooperatively in modern society.

Indigenous Knowledge and Social Innovation

An effect of immigration is that indigenous knowledge often moves to new localities or disappears completely. Modernization of communities is another cause of the disappearance of important, useful information and habits. The CCN project, Looking for likely alternatives (LOLA), launched in 2005, is a pedagogical tool for teachers and students which assists them in the process of identifying, evaluating and documenting cases of social innovation towards sustainable lifestyles. The LOLA pilot project aims to adapt to the needs of higher education the process of case collection initiated in the EMUDE European research project and contribute to the "catalogue of cases of sustainable daily life solutions" on the SEP web platform. This project not only brings forth new examples of sustainable lifestyles but also aids in reminding communities of the viable lifestyles which may exist but be in danger of disappearing.

The LOLA project allows teachers and their class to discover, approach and give visibility to sustainable lifestyles in their surroundings. It provides an opportunity to progress beyond the common pedagogical use of case studies and project work which tends to be limited to the imme-diate classroom context. The process brings the students into direct face-to-face contact with groups of people (the "creative communities") already implementing sustainable solutions in their daily life and thereby increases the learning potential of working with cases. It connects the work of teachers at several schools in a collective search for examples of universal value, thereby putting into action the goals of the UN Decade for Education for Sustainable Development. This consists in a process of integrating initiatives dealing with "learning to learn" and "learning for a sustainable future" with initiatives concerned with learning to be a critical, aware, consumer citizen.

The documentation and evaluation of this process is useful for other teacher trainers and schools – increasing their knowledge of what is actually happening in society in terms of initiatives for responsible lifestyles and sustainable development. The LOLA pilot project has been developing a "teacher training toolkit" and a "students' reporter book" to support the collection of cases of sustainable lifestyles by the students and the organizing of the activity by the teachers. These are now available in seven languages. A European catalogue of cases of sustainable lifestyles is progressively completed on the Sustainable Everyday Project web platform. Reports and mobile exhibitions are other available outputs.

Lifelong Learning

Issues affecting individuals in the modern consumer-oriented society change rapidly. Events occur such as pandemic diseases, food safety crises, climate changes etc, which challenge attitudes and habits of both new and established communities. Constant and close dialogue between researchers, teachers and civil society is necessary in order to provide individuals, from whatever cultural background they come, with updated, relevant information. The Consumer Citizenship Network has associated partners from Africa, India, Asia and the Americas. Their involvement provides opportunities for sharing expertise from Europe and gaining better insight into examples of solutions available elsewhere thereby helping consumers in Europe learn from the attitudes and behaviour of people in and from other parts of the globe.

ISSUES IN CONSUMER BEHAVIOUR

Generally, economic forums have tended to ignore the broader issues in consumer credit, preferring to focus on the valuation of more standard corporate financial claims. When the consumer is discussed, it is typically consumer consumption and savings decisions that are studied and analyzed. This neglect of consumer credit seems remarkable, given that debt owed by households represents over 25 percent of total credit market debt outstanding; that consumer credit, excluding mortgages, makes up over 10 percent of commercial bank credit; and that the outstanding volume of consumer credit, including mortgages, exceeds the volume of U.S. government debt. There is no single reason for the omission of consumer financial assets from the research agenda of the academic community, but I can offer a few rationalizations. The first is that macro-economists – even those who specialize in monetary theory – have had little interest in the detailed behaviour of asset choice at the consumer level. They prefer to concentrate on consumption theory and the associated empirical tests of these theories, rather than analyze the allocation of savings and wealth dynamics. Second, specialists in finance have tended to concentrate on firm-level behaviour because firms are viewed as more rational players than consumers and firms' behaviour is of more economic value.

Asset sizes are bigger; representative agents are more easily modeled; and market discipline seems to force the decision maker closer to the optimal economic choice. Only recently has this begun to change. With the emergence of the asset-based security markets, financial theorists and empiricists have begun to examine the behaviour of financial assets that have resulted from the aggregation of consumer debt. This is most obvious in the mortgage mar-ket, where the emergence of various types of securitized mortgage instruments fostered research on their valuation and time-series dynamics. This interest has recently been expanded into other types of asset-based securities, such as CARDs, CARs, and CLOs. In each case, to analyze the underlying asset, the researcher has to examine optimal decisions of a representative agent and the impact of aggregating individual claims on instrument behaviour. Another development that has helped spur interest in the microeconomics of consumer financial decisions is the intellectual shift that has taken place in macroeconomics toward a well-specified microeconomic foundation for macroeconomic theories.

It is now acknowledged that to under stand consumption and savings decisions on the macro level, we must model the behaviour of individual agents. And this interest in micro foundations has been accompanied by the development of new data sets, such as the Federal Reserve's triennial Survey of Consumer Finances, the Consumer Expenditure Survey, and the Panel Study of Income Dyna-mics, that present information at a disaggregated level to allow for testing of these micro theories. Yet, despite recent interest in consumer debt instruments, there is much work to be done. This conference is just the first of many efforts that we at the Federal Reserve Bank of Philadelphia plan to make to advance the consumer credit research agenda. We hope to shed light on the state of research and to spotlight areas of potential future contributions. In my comments I will try to put the current literature on consumer finance into context and explain why consumer credit should have a place in academic research between standard macro modeling and the valuation of standard financial assets. I will also try to set out a list of issues that must be studied to further our knowledge and understanding of one part of the financial landscape that continues to grow at double-digit rates.

CONSUMPTION THEORY

From the traditions of classical macro theory to the work of Keynes, standard macroeconomic models involved the representative economic agent who maximizes an expected utility function that summarizes well-behaved preferences, in a world with positive marginal productivity and a fixed discount rate. The agent's choice is constrained by a multiperiod budget or endowment sequence. Nearly all of us as graduate students could write down this problem's multiperiod first-order conditions and the appropriate transversality conditions associated with optimal behaviour. The representative agent maximizes expected utility by equating marginal utility across periods, subject only to a borrowing and lending condition that bounds the problem. Such models yield paths of consumption and savings over time that achieve maximum expected utility subject only to the aggregate interest rate, which itself can be solved for simultaneously in a general equilibrium setting. Once consumption behaviour had been characterized, economists turned to characterizing savings behaviour in a world where the agent's life span is uncertain. Here, the profession's attention centered on models that featured various types of risk aversion and their impact on both wealth accumulation and decumulation.

This work proved central to understanding the role of pensions on intertemporal consumption behaviour and remains an important part of our understanding of life-cycle savings behaviour. The credit market imperfections leading to liquidity constraints and the significance of the bequest motive in driving savings decisions have been studied. On the public policy stage the research offers important insights into the debate over both Social Security and the entire area of private pension programs. Others have also used it to relegated to micro finance theorists, who began where the monetary theorists left off. In these micro finance models the representative consumer maxi-mizes his expected utility, which is represented by a concave function of exogenously given wealth. The models are usually single period. Multiperiod considerations are some-times addressed with some intertemporal endogeneity, leading to some of the rich models of asset choice in a multi-period consumption framework.

Still, we are a long way from a sophisticated model of households' ultimately joint decisions about how much to save, how to divide savings among different types of assets, how much to borrow, and what types of debt to incur. The characteristics of the specific assets are typically not modeled beyond the first two moments of their underlying distributions. Uncertainty is characterized only in this most general way, usually by reference to normality and stationarity. Anything more specific understand the effects of the private sector's evolution to defined contribution plans and their associated actuarial risks to covered workers. Some have even discussed and modeled the role of inflation uncertainty in this multiperiod asset-choice problem. However, few researchers studying this problem attempted to explain the specific portfolio of risky assets that should be selected by economic agents over their life cycle or the appropriate vehicles to use to accumulate debt during periods of excess consumption.

These issues were is relegated to applied finance and its interest in state-dependent payoffs and their effect on valuation and time-series dynamics. In short, the detailed payoff patterns associated with the debt instruments issued by the agent were entirely too mundane for the theorists' consideration. So, a student of consumer credit and con-sumer choice was sent to the applied finance literature for the modeling and valuation of real consumer debt instru-ments. To some extent, the underdevelopment of this line of research probably reflects the relative simplicity of most U.S. households' portfolios before the 1990s. But an explo-sive period of financial innovation in the last two decades and the rapid growth in consumers' wealth in the 1990s has introduced many mor households to many more financial options. For example, today an increasing share of household wealth is held in financial assets, and a smaller share is invested in the household's primary residence.

More households participate in equity markets, with equity making up over half of households' financial holdings. These changes in the structure of household portfolios can be attributed to the stock market boom of the 1990s, the relatively slower growth in housing prices during the same period, a highly competitive mutual fund industry, and demographic factors. While the shift in household portfolios in the 1990s has been dramatic, what might be more surprising is that the shift hasn't been even larger. Households still seemingly prefer relatively simple and safe portfolios. Exactly why this is the case, however, is unclear, for as noted above little economic research has centered on consumer asset choice. Still less has investigated the characteristics unique to each financial product available to smooth consumption over a multiperiod uncertain horizon. To learn more about these issues the researcher is directed to the field of finance.

The Value of Consumer Financial Claims

Interestingly, applied finance is up to the task of modeling consumer assets. Its general theoretical construct of stochastic behaviour, using expected present value in a state-contingent framework, is well suited for the underlying uncertainty associated with consumer credit. With the rise of discrete-time models and binomial tree modeling techniques, the standard financial valuation techniques can be applied to consumer debt instruments characterized by time-specific default probabilities and multiperiod cash-flow uncertainty. But, as indicated earlier, consumer assets do tend to have small market values, and the field was traditionally viewed as extraordinarily "unsexy." As a result, the new techniques being applied to analyze corporate finance instruments have only rarely been applied to consumer debt, and there has been little interest expressed by the research community in understanding the nuances of the individual consumer markets.

As a result, the characteristics and time-series price

dynamics associated with different types of consumer debt instruments have never been seriously investigated. This void in the literature is important. Consumer debt of various types exceeds total U.S.

Treasury debt, and it is likely to be the only liquid market of the early 21st century. The economics and finance profession has been slow in concentrating on both the theoretical and empirical issues surrounding these instruments - with one exception, the mortgage market. Residential mortgages currently account for the majority of consumer debt, with an outstanding value of over $5 trillion, and represent the only area of consumer debt that has received significant attention.

Fostered by the development of various types of mortgage pass-through instruments, a large literature developed about their valuation. The aggregation of individual instruments added scale but also complexity. Prepayment risk, default modeling, and state-dependent cash flows led to the development of a rich literature. Interestingly this literature has not crossed over to other areas of consumer debt, even as the percentage of consumer debt represented by mortgage assets continues to decline. In fact, there is very little in the literature on various types of asset-backed securities, in spite of their growing importance, and we know little about the difference in yields across various types of asset-backed securities.

How can this seemingly important void in the literature be addressed? The research plan is fairly straightforward if one proceeds from first principles. The securitization vehicle can be understood as the aggregation of individual economic decisions made by a series of representative agents. Using consumption theory in a stochastic environment, one could model cash- flow dynamics, including default and prepayment variation. Present value valuation techniques could then be applied to the underlying aggregation, subject to the subtle but important covenant constraints that differentiate each instrument. Collateral, recourse, and seniority become key elements in the distinction between repayment timing and ultimate default probabilities associated with different consumer debt types. Issues of adverse selection, switching costs, borrower heterogeneity, and liquidity constraints also come into play, making the pricing of consumer debt instruments, such as credit cards, not a trivial exercise. However, with sufficient care, the techniques applied to mortgage debt, which were derived from multiperiod consumption behaviour, could be applied to CARs, CARDs, and CLOs. Price dynamics would follow directly.

Any such effort would immerse the research in the public policy debates that dictate terms and conditions. Just as "due on sale" clauses substantially altered mortgage dynamics in the 1970s, and regulations surrounding adjust-able rate mortgages altered the valuation of these instru-ments substantially, consumer protection policies have substantial implications for consumer credit instruments. For example, bankruptcy regulation alters repayment probability and valuation, as do access to collateral, privacy rules, and public disclosure regulation.

All of these policies alter credit risks and credit spreads. The public debate surrounding these consumer protection attributes would be enhanced by both the estimation and discussion of the implied costs of such regulations. The beneficial effect of the consumer rights acquired through such legislation must be weighed against the implied cost to the lender and the derived increase in credit spreads to the entire consumer class.

The Unfinished Agenda

There is much to be gained from the application of standard economics and finance to the valuation of consumer debt instruments. By modeling the uncertain cash flows and creditor rights associated with different debt instruments, we can obtain proper pricing and risk assessment. This will also facilitate arbitrage across markets and reaffirm the law of one price across various types of instruments subject to similar uncertainty. Such research will also illuminate the current policy debate regarding debtor versus creditor rights at the basis of various types of consumer right proposals. Valuation techniques can derive the costs of such legislation against which the benefits can be contrasted. This is a rich agenda that all of us share as researchers. And the Fed has a unique role to play, as both a center of financial knowledge and a supporter of various types of economic research.

The Fed has traditionally devoted significant resources to banking and financial market research, at a number of the Reserve Banks. We here in Philadelphia have a particular interest in this area. The Third District is the home of the credit card industry, with approximately 40 percent of all consumer credit cards emanating from the state of Dela-ware. To underscore our interest in this area and to address what we see as a mandate to understand this industry, we have established a Payment Cards Center within the Bank to investigate issues central to this part of the financial services sector. The value of various types of consumer debt instruments and their relative values under different the study of consumer transactions media finds a historical precedent in the traditional theory of money demand. The traditional theories of money demand – for example, the Baumol- Tobin inventory model – weren't specific about the medium used for transactions. And, as we know, financial innovations and deregulation effectively destroyed the empirical relationship between money and income.

We need to develop new theories if we hope to explain the economic rationale for and the impact of various transactions media,. like credit cards, debit cards, and smart cards, which are much more complicated than our traditional characterization of money. Debit cards and smart cards are relatively new developments, but there is much we still do not know about credit cards, which have been around public policies, including but not limited to bankruptcy rights, collateral access, and various types of consumer protection legislation, are clearly crucial issues, and they definitely belong on the Payment Cards Center's research agenda. Payments issues, as well, are on the Center's agenda. Clearly these too are central to understanding the payment cards industry and the evolving financial services sector. Just as one can tie the study of consumer debt instruments to a traditional literature, for years: why do so many consumers, even wealthy ones, borrow at the high rates on credit cards? Given the large number of credit card issuers, why are credit card rates so high and sticky? Why was there a large increase in delinquencies and bankruptcies when economic conditions were so favorable? A well-developed theoretical framework for solving these and related puzzles is a pressing task, which promises an interesting and rich research agenda.

THE CHANGING FACE OF THEAFFLUENT CONSUMER

While the travel preferences of the super rich and those who come from "old money" are well understood by the hospitality industry, the "emerging rich," younger affluent people, usually have a different mindset toward travel. This chapter explores their travel expectations and the approach that marketers should take to capture their business. Despite fluctuations in the economy, much of the world has spent the past few years in the midst of a luxury consumption boom. Luxury spending in the United States is growing more than four times as rapidly as spending overall, and there is an increasingly large appetite for luxury goods throughout Asia and Europe. In what Fortune magazine terms the "Goldilocks" economy, new wealth is being created at an unprecedented rate, and as a result, the face of the affluent consumer has changed. The challenge now posed to marketers of luxury goods and services is defining the demographics and psychographics of affluent consumers. Who are they? What are their buying habits?

And what is the most effective means to reach them? According to the book Luxury Fever, by Robert H. Frank, luxury travel (trips with perdiem spending of at least $350) grew by 130 percent between 1990 and 1995 and the occupancy rates for luxury hotels, which stood at 69 percent a decade ago, now stand at 76 percent. Luxury cars accounted for about

12 percent of all vehicles sold in the United States in 1996, up from 7 percent in 1986. Luxury "status symbols" are popping up everywhere across America from restaurant-style stoves in home kitchens to ultra premium wines, choice real estate, and even cosmetic surgery. But this growing taste for luxury is not indicative of purely American values. According to Frank, "Japan, with fewer than half as many people as the United States, consumes more than half the U.S. volume of luxury goods."

And while multi-millionaires are clearly prominent among the purchasers of these luxury products and services, recent large sales volumes imply the vast majority of buyers have less than six figure incomes. As puzzling as this may seem, it can be traced to human nature in that once basic needs for food and shelter are met, and as incomes continue to grow, it is instinctive for people to indulge their inner "desires" for the finer things in life.

The Affluent Consumer Grows Younger

Therefore, with the recent booming economy, one can no longer draw a picture of the typical affluent consumer as having "old family money." The face of the affluent consumer is changing across age, economic, and racial spectrums. Today, the affluent consumer can be anyone from an heir to a family fortune to an e-commerce millionaire who spends his days in Gap jeans and T-shirts. Moreover, when these individuals purchase a luxury good or service, they want more than just the product, they want "an experience." And in particular when it comes to travel, the affluent consumer wants to collect vivid and meaningful "experiences" to store as memories and exchange as "conversational currency." In a recent presentation at the annual convention of The Leading Hotels of the World, Ltd., Pamela Fiori, editor in chief, Town & Country Magazine, clearly defined who the luxury customer is, pointing out that she classifies four primary groups:

1. The Super-rich: those who live on an entirely different level, travel on private planes, collect works of the Old Masters; belong to royalty, etc;

2. The Bill Gates types/Industrialists/Rock Stars whose fortunes are less certain; money was earned fairly recently but in staggering amounts nonetheless, and there is nothing they cannot buy;
3. The Comfortably Rich, not royalty, but extremely well-off and well-traveled. They make their money the old-fashioned way, they earn it—but they want to reap the rewards. They are demanding and know the services they want and are extremely brand conscious; and
4. The Emerging Rich/Emerging Affluent who comprise the top-level of Generation X. According to Fiori, this is the most difficult group to define. They made their money fast. The way they live, everything is fast. They are venture capitalists and are diverse ethnically and racially.

Fiori believes there has never been a better time in history to market a luxury product. "As the majority of 'The Emerging Rich' did not grow up surrounded by the finer things, it is important for luxury travel marketers to enlighten them and expose them to the wonderful hotel experiences awaiting them, because once they experience the good life, they are not going to go backpacking again." Dr. Lalia Rach, dean, Preston R. Tisch Center for Hospitality, Tourism and Travel Administration, New York University, concurs. "Today change is the dominant feature of the affluent travel market. With the rise of the new economy, the Wall Street 'whiz kids' and the Internet revolutionaries have created a new generation of young entrepreneurs who have taken their ideas and skills and become millionaires seemingly overnight.

The most dramatic change in the affluent traveler's profile is the decrease in the average age and their different mindset toward travel." Dr. Rach continues to profile the new affluent traveler as follows:

"They are exceedingly absorbed by their work providing a true example of a 24 hours a day and 7 days a week lifestyle. They work exceedingly hard and expect their relaxation to be as challenging and demanding. When they do take time to relax and enjoy themselves, they want to do so in an atmosphere that reflects their earning status, provides a reward, and is fun and unusual. Exclusivity is but one aspect that interests them while on vacation. They are looking for products and services that allow them to define themselves and to celebrate their success, but in a manner that is not traditionally defined and in many cases is not understated. So whether the choice of a rental car, theatre tickets, or an afternoon activity, they want an unusual, out-of-the-ordinary experience. The affluent 20 something may wish to blend simplicity with extreme luxury such as a picnic with sandwiches, fruit, cheese, and a 100-year-old bottle of wine. Of course the picnic setting would be an ex-clusive island or the top of a mountain accessible only by helicopter. The scope of their interest is boundless, and they are looking for suggestions—but not what the traditional affluent traveler likes unless it is with a modern explosive twist."

Dr. Rach concludes by noting that "it is unusual to have a new niche develop within a narrowly defined market segment. The dichotomy of the new affluent traveler is captured in a single statement—the more they make, the more they expect from life, including their travel experience."

Selling the Dream

When it comes to luxury goods and services, you are selling the dream and therefore cannot always approach marketing to the affluent consumer with a basic scientific approach. Hérmes, perhaps the consummate luxury brand, is living proof of this belief. Addressing The Leading Hotels of the World Annual Convention, Christian Blanckaert, president, Hérmes-Sellier, spoke about "Marketing to the Luxury Customer." He believes that "Luxury is often associated with anything that gives attention, care, respect of the individual, and culture. The explanation of luxury itself is a paradox—it is a word of feeling, word of mouth, spirit, dreams, talent—and nothing to do with a marketing book. Today and tomorrow if we want to approach products and services in luxury, we should forget marketing and concentrate on dreams, magic, the irrational, rather than market research. If there is no concentration on magic and hopes, there will be no delivery of luxury." Blanckaert was also quick to point out that "Hérmes is not in the luxury business, Hérmes is in the dream business. Our object is to charm, to surprise, not to market."

With this in mind, how do luxury marketers identify and sell to the affluent consumer? At The Hotels of the World, for example, management has long believed that affluent consumers naturally gravitate toward luxury brand names that consistently deliver quality. Guests at a Leading Hotel undoubtedly drive luxury cars, purchase Louis Vuitton handbags and luggage, wear Christian Dior fra-grance, and consume any number of high-end products. Would it not be more prudent for the world's finest purveyors of luxury goods and services to come together and create a luxury brand network to jointly market to the affluent consumer? Seeing no such marketing initiative in place, the management of The Leading Hotels of the World, Ltd. developed the concept of the "Luxury Alliance" and partnered with Relais & Chateaux as the two founding members.

Launched in August 2000, the Luxury Alliance has already welcomed Crystal Cruises, eLuxury.com, and Vivre as partners. The objective of the Luxury Alliance is to conduct joint marketing programs to an exclusive group of high-end clientele who already consume member products or would have a strong predisposition to do so. The goal is to share customers, conduct cross-selling and promotional marketing efforts, and thereby create increased revenue opportunities for all Luxury Alliance partners. The Leading Hotels of the World, Ltd. also formed a joint venture partnership with consumer trend research expert Peter Yesawich, president & CEO of Yesawich, Pepperdine & Brown of Orlando to create Leading Marketing Services, a full-service marketing, advertising, and public relations firm.

The Leading Hotels of the World, Ltd. has a 73-year history of marketing to the affluent consumer, while YP&B is the recognized leader in full-service hospitality marketing communications as well as monitoring the trends and buying habits of consumers. As partners in this new joint venture, Leading Marketing Services is now in a unique leadership position to write the rules for affluent consumer marketing. YP&B, in fact, recently conducted a survey entitled "Portrait of Affluent Travelers" which debuted in conjunction with the launch of Leading Marketing Services.

The survey polled the opinions of a nationally representative sample of 500 U.S. adults who took at least one trip that required overnight accommodations in 1999, half of whom had annual household incomes between $150,000 and $199,999; the other half of whom enjoyed annual household incomes in excess of $200,000. One key finding of the survey is that fully eight out of every ten wealthy adults state that they always look for the best prices when making purchases. But don't expect them to be scouring the mall in search of the best bargains; they are far more likely to look online, and "prefer to buy brands with a reputation for quality."

Further research into the psychographics of the new affluent consumer creates a distinctive profile that is much different from the "typical" affluent consumer to whom many of us have marketed in years past. It would be wise to keep these facts in mind when you are planning your marketing efforts: the younger affluent consumer seeks life-enriching experiences; wants to be assured of style and quality; is stimulated by new and different situations; wants to be recognized as knowledgeable and worldly; is not afraid of the unfamiliar, offbeat, or exotic; has a global perspective; enjoys regionally authentic products; has a certain predisposition to nostalgic designs; does not purchase luxuries purely for materialistic reasons; has a social conscience and appreciates doing business with organisations that have a true social commitment; frequently socializes and therefore has a strong influence on the buying decisions of peers; considers spirituality and religion as an integral part of life; is quick to seek out information online; desires ways to simplify life; and is always pursuing more of life's most essential luxury—time.

When it comes to marketing travel to this new, younger affluent consumer, Rach notes "an active, coordinated marketing effort is necessary to inform and entice this segment. Advertising and communications should relate to their situation in life. An understated approach will most likely turn them off.

Marketing that is bold, aggressive, colorful, emphasizes relationships, fun, and imparted with some irony are concepts that attract this cohort. As well, the manner in which communications are distributed is important. Advertisements must be placed in publications that they read (business, specialized, and technology magazines), at events they attend (music concerts, sporting events), and on targeted Web sites (finance, trading, entertainment).

Affluent consumers—young and old—are purchasing in record numbers and they continue to seek information on the newest luxury goods and services available. Luxury marketers, however, need to recognize that a blanket marketing approach will no longer suffice. Much like the way the Internet has changed our marketing strategies, those targeting the "affluent consumer" must recognize that cookie-cutter campaigns will no longer work and a more targeted approach speaking to the various audiences within this niche must be applied if marketing efforts are to be effective.

6

Consumption
Expanding the Discourse on Social Change

Perhaps the most disturbing trend in our public debates over issues like economic globalization and development, democracy and human rights, is the very framing of the issues themselves. Four hundred years into the scientific, rational experiment, this method of discourse has effectively come to dominate how we envision and address the way we live in our world. Though such 'social engineering' has its material merits, it lacks a complete view, such as one that takes into account the very basis of material development, which is human happiness. Religious and spiritual viewpoints of personal and social transformation are important resources in expanding the arena of discussion on social issues. To assert the importance of a religious perspective is not to argue for committing to Buddhism or some other traditional faith.

The point is simply that we cannot escape religious questions insofar as we cannot escape the deepest questions about the meaning of our lives and where we derive that. Rather than dismiss religion as a narcotic for the politically-unaware, we should not overlook the potentials for self-transformation that reside in its traditional teachings and institutions. A truly human, loving politics has in itself an important spiritual aspect, one that can be immensely empowering if not subsumed and lost under concerns of power, means, and ends. Religion and politics are not anta-gonistic but rather are complementary, overlapping and inter-penetrating. Religious engagement, therefore, remains an enormously powerful social force that should not be surrendered to fundamentalists.

This highlights the importance of self-transformation (including techniques to assist that) as much as group or structural transformation. To pursue the latter without the former is to risk re-enacting the social tragedies of the last two centuries, in which revolutions merely replaced one gang of thugs with another. From an 'engaged Buddhist' perspective, it is critical to look beyond mechanistic approaches to the larger question of the role of consumption in the way we construct the meaning of our lives. Today we cannot talk about consumption without discussing consumerism, that way of living which locates the meaning of one's life in acquisition and consumption. The problem is not simply that our present economic system exploits people in underdeveloped countries and destroys their traditional economies.

From a Buddhist perspective, globalization is far more insidious than that. In that sense, the problem of most underdeveloped societies today is not so different from the problem of the 'developed' world: an impoverished world view which privileges consumption over other values and meaning-systems. We may be skeptical about religion, and there is good reason to be suspicious of most religious institutions but we also need to realize that consumerism functions as a religion for a rapidly increasing number of people worldwide.

THE DISTORTIONS OF CONSUMERISM

Buddhism is unique among the major religions in the way it focuses on demystifying the construction of the ego, or 'self'. This anatta (not-self) teaching has been problematic to western sensibilities, and it has often come off as a nihilism. Yet conceptualizing anatta as a method of understanding rather than as a static state of existence reveals a way of slipping between the polarities of egomania and nihilism to experiencing life free of narrow, self-interested perspectives. Seeing how this sense of self is constructed is the first step in an unfettering process. Buddhism takes the western psychological sense of repression (like fear of death) one step further. Fear of death is fear of what will happen in the future; but fear of not-self – that my sense-of-self is not real – is fear of what 'I' am (or am not) right now.

Perhaps all of us have some sense of this problem, but our feeling of being 'unreal' is repressed. In other words, our sense of self, because it is a fragile construct, is inherently insecure and uncomfortable.

The result is that we become obsessed with constructing our own identity – that is with making ourselves real in one or another symbolic fashion. In other words, my fear of death recurs as a preoccupation with symbolic immortality, with making my mark on history so that I will not be forgotten. The relevance of this for consumerism becomes obvious. In the past self-identity was usually a matter of one's religion, community race, class, occupation, etc. All of these markers have been intimately tied to place and often formed an important form of personal and social grounding.

Yet as they have also involved intolerance of other religions, communities, races, etc., we can be pleased that such forms of self-identity seem to be declining, mostly in the more developed parts of the world. This does not mean, however, that what is replacing them is satisfactory. Today, increasingly we are conditioned to construct our self-identity through consumption. From a Buddhist perspective, our lives are now constantly saturated with a religious message that promises a different kind of salvation – that is, a different way to become truly happy. The primary agent of its proselytizing is, of course, advertising which now envelops us so completely that we tend not to be aware of its effects. The basic problem, however, is that consumerism doesn't work and can't work, in the deepest and most important sense, as a way to give our lives satisfactory meaning. Essential to any solution, therefore, is the process of becoming more aware of how the false promise of consumerism distorts our own lives and the lives of those around us.

Buddhism sees desire or 'greed' as a fundamental motivating factor in our consumer societies. Through the ever-increasing domination of 'market' values like competition and hyper-individualism, the principal way of relating to the world comes through the acquisition and conquering of things and people. With the market perpetually designing new 'needs' for the individual, the terms 'need' and 'want' have become virtually synonymous. Poverty has taken on a purely quantifiable meaning of material underdevelopment. Those in poverty suffer from under consumption of the essentials of a developed lifestyle, i.e. cars, TVs, expensive university education, etc. We have become blind to what our real needs are. So we see teenagers in the United States living on food stamps acquiring $150 Nike basketball shoes, or squatter families living in corrugated steel shacks in Jakarta owning televisions and motorbikes.

Buddhist psychology sees that greed naturally leads to 'dispersion' and 'delusion'. With the loss of a discriminating mind which distinguishes between need and desire, the door is open to the ocean of delight and numbness in consumer goods and experiences. The media, principally TV, is the foremost component of this dispersion and delusion. It not only offers myriad worlds of entertainment without depth or meaning, but it is fuelled by advertising dollars that spread the ethic of greed incessantly through commercials. The consumption of experience in the booming leisure industries another major area of delusion and dispersion. From mega-media to tourism to sports, leisure activities have become a major component of most national economies. The foreign exchange made by governments on tourism and the building of entertainment empires like Time-Warner and Disney make the business of dispersion and delusion key components to solidifying ever more centralized power structures.

The consequences of this dispersion and delusion are thus twofold. First, it leaves us distracted and disconnected from our surroundings. With so many games to watch, so much shopping to do, so many trips to take, we have less and less time to check in on our families, our relationships, our neighbours and, most importantly, ourselves. From turning on the TV first thing in the morning to spacing out to the car stereo or walkman on the way to work to collapsing in front of the TV at night, the time to constructively ponder and plan a more meaningful life is washed away. Then, with the ever increasing speed of technology, the disconnections deepen into the next level in the Buddhist causal chain, despair and disempowerment. There remains little hope for changing our lives when the 'democratic' politics of 'developed' countries involve image adjustment rather than policy adjustment, and from Bangkok to New York people fear for their livelihoods as corporations shed employees in the race for a competitive edge. The political effect of this consumer world dominated by market and state leads ever more deeply into the dispersion and numbness of consumer experience.

Transforming from the Personal

Buddhism has a number of integrated practice systems for the 'structural adjustment' of the spirit. Perhaps the most straightforward yet profound encapsulations are the three interconnected practices known as sila-samadhi-panna (proper conduct-mindfulness-wisdom). First, in the face of unlimited greed and the loss of qualitative distinctions between needs and desire, sila offers a starting point in a system of discipline and ethics. This is a quite detailed system in Buddhism, yet one powerful aspect for our present consumer societies is the idea of 'renunciation'. Renunciation is an experience rich in diversity from culture to culture. Its essence is letting go of certain pleasures for the chance to experience a higher meaning or to perform a higher task. A travelling musician renounces a settled home in search of the muse. A student limits his/her 'partying' to graduate on time. The expressions are endless and beyond the stern admonishments of the starving recluse in the woods.

The purpose of Buddhist practice is not extremism but instead a middle way of moderation. By adopting basic practices of renunciation, we begin to reassert the value of simplicity into our societies. When those in 'poverty' are no longer seen as half-human under consumers who paternalistically must be brought into the fold of consumer values, they may discover an identity of self-worth and self-empowerment to form true priorities in their quest towards material and spiritual stability. The rich are transformed as well. Traditional Buddhist society evaluated a person of wealth not by how much they had accumulated personally but by how many soup kitchens or shelters they had established. With renunciation as an active social value, it becomes clearer to the rich what they actually need for a comfortable life. The rest is excess to be shared with others, especially those of lesser means among one's associations and community.

In the space and simplicity created from a life with a certain level of renunciation, the second component of Buddhist practice enters, namely, samadhi, a key aspect of which is mindfulness. With the Walkman and TV cleared away or used only at certain times, the reality of our place comes streaming in. We begin to notice how other family members spend their time. Intricacies in a loved one's state of being become apparent. Neighbours become like colleagues or extended family rather than faces next-door. Most centrally, our body, mind, emotions and our interactions with the world become more conscious. Connections between physical well-being and emotional and mental well-being arise. In short, connections in a disconnected world begin to be restored. In the most basic method of Buddhist meditation, mindfulness with breathing (anapanasati), long, slow breathing yields greater mind-fulness, awareness and well-being. As a very basic awareness technique, we can experience that the action films, multimedia entertainment, caffeine and nicotine, sports excitement, and shopping mall dazzlement of our consumer culture all make our breathing shorter and quicker and in turn make our thoughts faster, less connected, less aware.

With the building of some restraint (renunciation) and some mindfulness, the third component of the practice develops, panna or wisdom. Renunciation opens our life up to deeper experiences in the present. Mindfulness enables us to penetrate them ever more deeply. When this occurs, we begin to see the delusion of events surrounding us. We begin to see the bite of our greed and dispersion which had seemed so pleasurable before. We begin to see the non-lasting nature and instability of these pleasures and the frustrations they concoct as they fade and as we squirm and writhe to re-light them. Wisdom, however, does not end just here. Buddhism may seem like some value free system for gaining mental power.

The system is indeed a very powerful tool for becoming aware of values and attachments and cutting them. However, a Buddhism which uses sila and mindfulness to train corporate workers to accomplish their tasks more ruthlessly does not lead to true wisdom. Wisdom may enable us to see the causes and conditions of events in our environment, yet it also includes the critical use of this wisdom for the benefit of others. Wisdom in the service of greed or power is not true wisdom. True wisdom harnesses the operative imperative of the human being, to spend a life in supporting others as a vehicle free of defilement. Being free of attachments allows us to help ourselves as we help others.

Moving from the Individual to the Community

A truly beneficial global society can only arise where community, bio-region, land mass, continent and world are united in a cooperative social project. In Thailand, the dislocations of rural communities by economic globalization are myriad. The people have lost their traditional mode of livelihood, farming, through the development of corporate agriculture and the exposure of their food staples to the pressures of international markets and the distortions of government policy. Further the invasion of consumer products like electronic appliances and soft drinks have broken down traditional systems of cultural sharing and health while further enticing villagers to abandon their farms for the bright lights and wage labour of Bangkok. Traditionally, Buddhist monks have been leaders of the community while their temples have acted as community centres. In the past twenty years, a charismatic group of 'development' monks have begun to apply the Buddhist system of practice as outlined above to the social level. Working with groups of dedicated lay followers, they have sought to regain a modicum of community autonomy by using the power of consumption.

Based at the village temple, the establishment of buffalo banks and rice banks has enabled villagers to disengage from purchasing unnecessary mechanized farming equipment and chemical fertilizers from national and international corporations as well as seed rice at inflated prices from their own government (sila). The financing systems for acquiring these goods made necessary by outside economic manipulations of the local economy had further indebted the farmers, forcing them into deeper poverty and eventually off their land. Such temples have integrated these community initiatives with personal development of the community (samadhi). By establishing meditation classes, gambling and the consumption of expensive (and economically debilitating) national and Foreign liquors have been reduced.

By adapting traditional social events at the temple, such as robe offering ceremonies for the monks, monks and lay leaders use these occasions to raise the awareness of villagers. They also use them to raise funds for community development projects. Such initiatives like cooperative stores divert money back into the community in a twofold form of right consumption. They promote the diversion of excess money into community projects as opposed to competitive, private consumption, and also develop and maintain locally run businesses which can be accountable to the community (panna). Finally, the expansion of such a vision beyond village empowerment can be seen in the co-ordination of the 'development' monks into an emerging national network called Para Sekhiyadhamma. The network at present co-ordinates and shares material and spiritual resources, mostly on local and regional levels, while national co-ordination beyond yearly meetings is just developing. Concerning consumption specifically, the network has campaigned throughout the country on the destructive use of Styrofoam.

Moving Beyond Skepticism

The results of such 'Buddhist' initiatives towards community regeneration and social transformation still present a number of questions. The above examples from Thailand largely constitute rural responses from relatively lesser economized societies. Further, such attempts and others like the well known Sarvodaya initiative in Sri Lanka have not been immune from the powerful forces of market dissolution and advertising. Two important questions, therefore, remain. How effective can religious, and specifically Buddhist, responses be in fully economized societies? And what is the actual place of this kind of engaged Buddhism in the larger world of institutionalized Buddhism?

In more economized Buddhist societies, the prospects of such Buddhist engagement seem more doubtful. In Japan, although a number of consumer movements exist, they are rarely related to or informed by Buddhist teachers or communities. In general, Japanese Buddhism is more of a supporter of modern consumption patterns with expensive and elaborate funerals (Japan's third largest industry) and temple tourism. Indeed, throughout the Buddhist world, both east and west, mainstream Buddhism is usually a supporter of the present drive for material wealth and spiritual sanctification through conspicuous consumption. From massive donations to temples and monks for religious blessing in Southeast Asia, to 'meditative consumerism' in expensive retreats and ritualistic paraphernalia in the West, to the rise of new schools which teach that material gain is a sign of spiritual blessing (Sokka Gakkai from Japan internationally, Fu Kwan Shan in Taiwan, and Dhammakaya in Thailand), Buddhism as a practice for personal and social transformation of our present economic and social injustices seems highly specious.

Yet Buddhism is not alone in this situation. The co-opting of every aspect of our humanity and spirituality by this consumer 'religion of the market' raises questions about how much any method of social transformation can resist market and consumer forces. This highlights the importance of religion and spirituality generally, because religions offer visions of life that can serve as meaningful alternatives to the religion of consumerism. One of the strengths of the engaged Buddhist approach is its basically non-sectarian character. Engaged Buddhism has formed within itself a nurturing ground for people of other faiths as well as people lacking any faith to discover a systematic method of personal and social transformation.

Engaged Buddhism has been able to link with and to be enriched by similar movements in other religions and other secular forms of human interaction. In conclusion, consumption and consumerism is a vital issue whose implications are as much religious as economic and political. Buddhism as a spiritual resource has much to offer this issue. When we move from engineering towards transforming, we see that consumption cannot be treated as an isolated variable. Once we begin to examine engaged Buddhism and other spiritual approaches we begin to see how transforming consumption patterns is part of a much more complete and fundamental transformation of our human psyche and society.

FINANCIAL SECTOR IN INDIA

While the trigger for the global developments in the financial markets during the recent past was the rising default rates on sub-prime mortgages in the US, the source of the problem was perhaps not the macro-global imbalances but significant mispricing of risks in the financial system. Easy monetary policy in major financial centres, globalisation of liquidity flows, wide-spread use of highly complex structured debt instruments and the inadequacy of banking supervision in coping with financial innovations, contributed to the severity of the crisis. The persistent under pricing of risks was suspected by several central banks for quite some time, but it was felt by many that these risks were widely dispersed through financial innovation and that they would not pose any serious problems to the banking system. When the sub-prime crisis did occur, however, it triggered a wide contagion affecting many of the large global financial institutions. Banks, in particular, appear to have ceased to trust each other's creditworthiness leading to difficulties in the money markets in the US, Europe and the UK resulting in drying up of liquidity, since each financial institution attempted to shore up its own liquidity to meet its obligations.

The problems of maturity mismatch in the conduits or structured investment vehicles (SIVs) created by the banks for purposes of securitisation manifested themselves in sudden spurt in demand for liquidity from banks to meet their liquidity support obligations to the SIVs or to fund the assets of the SIVs that were taken on to their balance sheets. It is now realised that the relevant banks have leveraged excessively and had not fully recognised the risks or had seriously under priced them, thus warranting large capital infusion. Uncertainty about the possible losses yet to be disclosed by several of them has not yet ceased. These developments have brought forward several new realities that pose severe challenges to macro-economic management, in particular to monetary and regulatory policies globally.

First, concerns relating to the US slowdown and its intensity have mounted in view of the potential spill over on to the global economy. Second, threats to the global economy are emanating from advanced economies in sharp contrast to earlier crises which stemmed from the emerging world. Third, there are indications that protectionist tendencies have increased around the world in anticipation of the growing possibilities of slower growth in advanced economies. Fourth, linkages between financial sector developments and the real sector have become more worrisome than before, with apprehensions that financial turmoil may spill over to the real sector with adverse implications for employment and growth. With tightening in lending standards, deterioration in asset quality and deceleration in consumer loan demand, there are indi-cations that events in the financial markets are beginning to have a persisting impact on the real economy as well. Fifth, higher and more volatile prices of food, energy and other commodities have compounded the problem, causing a significant upside bias to inflation and inflation expectations across the world, complicating the conduct of monetary policy at a time of severe financial stress.

Further, while rising energy prices may be an exogenous shock for several countries, for the global economy as a whole it is endogenous. Sixth, terms-of-trade losses due to soaring commodity prices not only reduce the capacity of a re-balancing of the world economy but also impact several countries in different ways but essentially in an adverse fashion. In fact, it is possible that new global economic imbalances are emerging on account of large movements in commodity prices, especially oil. Seventh, Emerging Market Economies (EMEs) are exhibiting resilience until now in the face of the global financial turmoil reflecting relatively stronger macro-economic framework and sustain-able macroeconomic balances. However, until how long and to what extent it will persist is uncertain. On the other hand, inflationary pressures appear to be common to mature economies and EMEs but the latter are under greater stress.

The central banks in major countries have had to take recourse, in appropriate mix, to three instruments to avoid serious spill-over of these issues in money or credit markets into the wider economy:

i. Adjustment of interest rates for borrowing and lending;
ii. Money market operations designed to inject special liquidity in order to avoid a break-down in payment systems among banks; and
iii. To put in mechanisms for financial transactions among the largest of the financial intermediaries which auto-matically impact the second and third rung inter-mediaries.

Central banks in major industrialised economies, by and large, responded with injection of liquidity for a longer period than is usually done; they also resorted to dilution in the quality of collateral required for liquidity support. Most of these operations have not been conducted at the penal rates expected in such situations. This is an unprecedented package which, some observers believe, is indicative of the seriousness of the underlying problems. In addition, there were some specific-institution oriented operations, namely, in the United States, Germany and the United Kingdom. While there have been inflationary pressures in most economies, the USA has been faced with a threat of serious slowdown in growth warranting a series of cuts in policy rates in recent months.

In recent weeks, concerns over inflationary pressures globally have taken the centre-stage even while there are no indications as to whether threats to financial stability have been fully resolved and whether persistent threats of recession in USA have abated. Consequently, the policy dilemmas have become more acute at the current juncture.

The most urgent and short-term priority for central bankers at the current juncture seems to be to calm the nerves about inflation or to anchor inflation expectations, with an implicit recognition that a somewhat elevated headline inflation in the short-term may be difficult to avoid. Further, high inflation rates when accompanied by higher variability of inflation, raises greater uncertainties.

These acute policy dilemmas at the current juncture between growth and inflation have to be faced in the background of financial turbulence which is yet to calm down. There are also calls for fundamental re-think on macro-economic, monetary and financial sector policies to meet the new challenges and realities, which perhaps represent a structural shift in the international financial architecture demanding potentially enhanced degree of coordination among monetary authorities and regulators.

A review of the policies relating to financial regulation, in a way, needs to address both the acute policy dilemmas in the short run and a fundamental re-think on broader frameworks of financial and economic policies over the medium-term.

Market Failures

What are some of the identifiable sources of market failures that led to the current financial turbulence? First, the prolonged benign macroeconomic conditions gave rise to complacency among many market participants and led to an erosion of sound practices, resulting in adoption of poor credit risk appraisal standards. Second, some of the standard risk management tools and models used by market participants were not equipped to estimate the potential impact of adverse events for structured credit products and high uncertainty around model estimates that largely missed the underlying combination of risks. Further, these risk models, generally tended to induce the market participants to adopt a unidirectional approach. Third, many investors, including institutional ones, with the capacity to undertake their own credit analysis, did not undertake sufficient in-house examination of the risks in the assets underlying structured investments. Fourth, the role of credit rating agencies (CRAs) in the recent market developments has attracted attention.

Fifth, the distortions in incentive structures can be seen from various perspectives namely incentives for originators, arrangers, distributors and managers in the originate- to-distribute model; the compensation schemes in financial institutions not distinguishing between realised and unrealised profits; encouraging financial structures tailored to obtaining high ratings etc. Sixth, weaknesses in public disclosures by financial institutions on the type and magnitude of risks associated with their on- and off-balance sheet exposures are noticeable. Seventh, large commercial banks and investment banks have assumed increasingly similar risk profiles, use similar models to assess and are subject to the same risk-management challenges under the given circumstances. Eighth, there is a new dimension to bank liquidity, with the shifting emphasis to a market based wholesale or purchased liabilities. This makes banks increa-singly dependent on the market for raising liquidity, while markets may have a tendency to shy away from providing liquidity when they are most needed.

Regulatory Shortcomings

While the foregoing brings out the failures of the markets and of the market participants, some of the regulatory shortcomings identified are as follows. First, the regulators recognised some of the underlying vulnerabilities in the financial sector but failed to take effective action, partly because they may have overestimated the strength and resilience of the financial system or they assumed that the risks were well distributed among entities outside the banking system. Many analysts and policymakers had raised concerns about excessive risk taking, loose underwriting standards, and asset overvaluations, all of which have in the absence of timely effective actions laid the seeds for crises. Second, the limitations in regulatory arrangements, including the capital adequacy framework, contributed to the growth of unregulated exposures, excessive risk-taking and weak liquidity risk management. Third, weaknesses in the application of accounting stan-dards and the shortcomings associated with the valuation and financial reporting of structured products played a significant role in the current turbulence through pro-cyclical valuations and lack of full disclosure of banks' true risk profile through the cycle. Fourth, the crisis revealed the need to adapt some of the tools and practices of central banks to manage system liquidity in the light of banks' cross-border operations.

The recent experiences have highlighted the differences in emergency liquidity frameworks of central banks, on aspects such as range of collateral, range of eligible counterparties; and the differences in central bank practices. Fifth, supervisors did not adequately address deterioration in risk management standards in the regulated entities, which did not fully reckon the risks associated with new financial instruments, and there were shortcomings in consolidated supervision. Sixth, deficiencies in crisis management and bank resolution frameworks, including deposit insurance, have been observed, especially where central banks do not have a central supervisory role. Seventh, the complex interrelationship between regulation, the inappropriate accounting practices, and regulators' excessive dependence on external ratings may have exacerbated the market turbulence.

Menu of Solutions

The above underlying factors clearly demonstrate a need to enhance the resilience of the global system and consider some of the prescriptions that have been proffered for the consideration of the policy makers. The recent developments in the global financial markets have been closely followed by many. These include market participants, central bankers, supervisors, multilateral institutions, political leaders, analysts, academicians, and also the layman. With so much attention being focused on the ongoing turbulence, by so many stakeholders, we have a wide menu of solutions and prescriptions. I will quickly run-through some of these. First, risk management frameworks including the governance arrangements in banks and financial institutions need to be reviewed by the managements in the light of the recent experiences. Second, supervisors need to play a more active role in scrutinizing the risk management practices, including stress testing and governance arrangements, off balance sheet entities and structured products. At the same time, it is crucial to recognize that risk management cannot be achieved solely by regulation. Consolidated supervision and prudential reporting should be applied to off balance sheet entities associated with financial institutions and to loans sold with implicit or explicit recourse.

There is a need to review the prudential norms linked to external ratings assigned by the CRAs. Third, supervisors should encourage institutions to develop more robust models which use more prudent and reliable assumptions and stress testing methodologies; and monitor more closely the internal processes, and controls for managing risk. Fourth, there is a need to rationalise the regulatory and supervisory prescriptions with a view to reducing the scope for arbitraging. This also calls for closer coordination of the relevant supervisors/ supervisory arms. Fifth, it is necessary to correct the imbalances in the incentive mechanisms at various levels. Sixth, greater transparency is not only necessary to make the markets more efficient and to optimise the allocation of capital, but it is also considered to be the best insurance policy against irrational herd behaviour and unjustified contagion in times of stress.

Seventh, there is a need to collectively review and resolve the element of pro-cyclicality in prudential regulations, accounting rules, and the attitude of the authorities that tend to apply these. Eighth, it is necessary for the CRAs to improve their governance and rating methodologies. Ninth, arguably it is useful to re-visit the relevant accounting standards and explore the scope for applying fair value accounting through the cycle so as to mitigate pro-cyclicality. Tenth, supervisors should have clear authority to intervene at the first sign of weakness, preferably much before the institution's net worth turns negative. Finally, deposit insurance systems should aim to limit the likelihood of retail depositor runs in troubled banks through adequate coverage, and have the capacity to pay depositors quickly.

INDIAN EXPERIENCE

Ensuring Financial Stability

In contrast to the above global scenario, India has by-and-large been spared of global financial contagion due to the sub-prime turmoil for a variety of reasons. The credit derivatives market is in an embryonic stage; the originate-to-distribute model in India is not comparable to the ones prevailing in advanced markets; there are restrictions on investments by resident in such products issued abroad; and regulatory guidelines on securitisation do not permit immediate profit recognition. Financial stability in India has been achieved through perseverance of prudential policies which prevent institutions from excessive risk taking, and financial markets from becoming extremely volatile and turbulent.

As a result, while there are orderly conditions in financial markets, the financial institutions, especially banks, reflect strength and resilience. While supervision is exercised by a quasi-independent Board carved out of the RBI Board, the interface between regulation and supervision is close in respect of banks and financial institutions, and on market regulation, a close coordination with other regulators exists. Let me recount this experience which, in some ways, reflects a policy that aimed to assure financial stability while maintaining growth momentum at reasonable levels and giving a high priority to price stability.

Investment Portfolio

In the year 2000 the Reserve Bank of India (RBI) conducted a stress test of the banks' investment portfolio in an increasing interest rate scenario, when the general trend then was decreasing interest rates. At that time, banks in India were maintaining a surrogate capital charge for market risk, which was at a variance from the Basel norms. On the basis of the findings, in order to equip the banking system to be better positioned to meet the adverse impact of interest rate risk, banks were advised in January 2002 to build up an Investment Fluctuation Reserve (IFR) within a period of five years. The prudential target for the IFR was 5 per cent of their investments in 'Held for Trading' (HFT) and 'Available for Sale' (AFS) categories. Banks were encouraged to build up a higher percentage of IFR up to 10 per cent of their AFS and HFT investments. This counter-cyclical prudential requirement enabled banks to absorb some of the adverse impact when interest rates began moving in the opposite direction in late 2004. Banks have been maintaining capital charge for market risk as envisaged under the Basel norms since end-March 2006.

The regulatory guidelines in India require banks to classify their investments in three categories, similar to the international standards. The investments included in the Held to Maturity (HTM) category was capped at 25 per cent of the total investments and banks are allowed to carry the investments in the HTM category at cost, subject amortisation of premium, if any. With the change in the direction of the movement of interest rates in 2004, the cap on the HTM category was reviewed in the light of the statutory prescriptions (referred to as statutory liquidity ratio (SLR) in India) requiring banks to mandatorily invest up to 25 per cent of their Demand and Time Liabilities (DTL) in eligible government securities.

In view of the statutory pre-emption and the long duration of the government securities, banks were permitted to exceed the limit of 25 per cent of total investments under Held to Maturity (HTM) category provided the excess comprised only of the SLR securities, and the total SLR securities held in the HTM category was not more than 25 per cent of their DTL. Such shifting was allowed at acquisition cost or book value or market value on the date of transfer, whichever is the least, and the depreciation, if any, on such transfer was required to be fully provided for. The above transition is consistent with international standards that do not place any cap on HTM category, and was considered advisable taking into account the statutory nature of the SLR while ensuring prudence and transparency in valuation on transfer to HTM category. While the earlier prescription for this category was relatively more conservative, the changes in September 2004 recog-nised the dynamic interface with the interest rate cycles and were counter-cyclical.

Capital Adequacy - Risk Weights

In view of the increase in growth of advances to the real estate sector, banks were advised to put in place a proper risk management system to contain the risks involved. Banks were also advised to put in place a system for ensuring proper checking and documentation of related papers before sanctioning / disbursing of such loans. In June 2005, the RBI advised banks to have a board mandated policy in respect of their real estate exposure covering exposure limits, collaterals to be considered, margins to be kept, sanctioning authority/ level and sector to be financed. In view of the rapid increase in loans to the real estate sector raising concerns about asset quality and the potential systemic risks posed by such exposure, the risk weight on banks' exposure to commercial real estate was increased from 100 per cent to 125 per cent in July 2005 and further to 150 per cent in April 2006.

The risk weights on housing loans extended by banks to individuals against mortgage of housing properties and investments in mortgage backed securities (MBS) of housing finance companies (HFCs), recognised and supervised by National Housing Bank (NHB) were increased from 50 per cent to 75 per cent in December 2004. However, on a review, banks were advised to reduce the risk weight in respect of exposures arising out of housing loans up to Rs.30 lakh (USD 75,000 approx) to individuals against the mortgage of residential housing properties from 75 per cent to 50 per cent, in view of the lower perception of risks in these exposures. In the light of the strong growth of consumer credit and the volatility in the capital markets, it was felt that the quality of lending could suffer during the phase of rapid expansion. Hence, as a counter cyclical measure, we increased the risk weight for consumer credit and capital market exposures from 100 per cent to 125 per cent.

Provisions against Standard Assets

The prudential norms relating to income recognition, asset classification and provisioning, introduced during 1992-93 are being continuously monitored and refined to bring them on par with international best practices. In keeping with this, several measures were initiated in 2005-06. The provisions for standard assets were revised progressively in November 2005, May 2006 and January 2007, in stages in view of the continued high credit growth in the real estate sector, personal loans, credit card receivables, and loans and advances qualifying as capital market exposure and a higher default rate with regard to personal loans and credit card receivables, which emerged as a matter of concern.

The standard assets in the following categories of loans and advances attract a two per cent provisioning requirement (i) personal loans (including credit card receivables); (ii) loans and advances qualifying as capital market exposure; (iii) real estate loans (excluding residential housing loans); and (iv) loans and advances to systemically important non- deposit accepting non-banking finance companies (NBFC-ND-SI). In order to ensure continued and adequate availability of credit to the highly productive sectors of the economy, the provisioning requirement for all other loans and advances, classified as standard assets was kept unchanged, viz., (i) direct advances to the agricultural and SME sectors at 0.25 per cent; and (ii) all other loans and advances at 0.4 per cent.

Exposure to Inter-bank Liability

In order to reduce the extent of concentration of bank's liabilities the RBI had issued guidelines to banks in March 2007 placing prudential limits on the extent of their Inter-Bank Liability (IBL) as a proportion of their net worth (200%). Those banks which had a higher capital adequacy ratio of 125% of the regulatory minimum were allowed a higher limit of 300% of net worth. In addition, prudential limits have also been placed on the extent to which banks may access the inter-bank call money market both as a lender and as a borrower. The RBI has been strengthening the regulatory and supervisory framework for non-banking finance companies (NBFCs) since 1997 with the objective of making the NBFC sector vibrant and healthy. The focus was initially on deposit-taking NBFCs. These efforts were pursued further during 2006-07, when a major thrust was on strengthening the regulatory framework with regard to systemically important non-banking financial companies so as to reduce the regulatory gaps. At that time, the regulatory focus was also widened to include systemically important non-deposit taking NBFCs and prudential norms were specified for these entities. The application of different levels of regulations to the activities of banks and NBFCs, and even among different categories of NBFCs, had given rise to some issues relating to uneven coverage of regulations. Based on the recommendations of an Internal Group and taking into consideration the feed-back received thereon, a revised framework to address the issues pertaining to the overall regulation of systemically important NBFCs and the relationship between banks and NBFCs was put in place in December 2006.

Securitisation Guidelines

The RBI has issued guidelines on securitisation of standard assets in February 2006. The guidelines are applicable to banks and financial institutions, including non- banking financial companies (NBFCs). These guidelines provide for a conservative treatment of securitisation exposures for capital adequacy purposes, especially in regard to the credit enhancement and liquidity facilities.

The regulatory framework encourages greater participation by third parties with a view to ensure better governance in the structuring of special purpose vehicles (SPVs), the products, and the provision of support facilities. A unique feature of these guidelines, which may be at a variance with the accounting standards, is that any profits on sale of assets to the SPV are not allowed to be recognised immediately on sale but over the life of the pass through certificates issued by the SPV. We believe that these guidelines, as a package, have ensured an appropriate incentive mechanism for securitisation transactions.

Banks' Investment in Non-SLR Securities RBI had emphasised that banks should observe prudence in order to contain the risk arising out of their non-SLR (i.e., non government) investment portfolio, in particular through the private placement route. Detailed prudential guidelines on the subject were issued in June 2001, which were reviewed and revised in November 2003. These guidelines, inter alia, address aspects of coverage, regulatory requirements, listing and rating requirements, fixing of prudential limits, internal assessments, role of Boards, disclosures, and trading and settlement in debt securities. Banks were specifically advised that they should not be solely guided by the ratings assigned to these securities by the external rating agencies but that they should do a detailed appraisal as in the case of direct lending.

Marking-to-market

The Indian accounting standards are generally aligned to the International Financial Reporting Standards, though there are some differences. In India, we are yet to fully adopt the marking to-market requirements as available in the international standards. The Indian standards are relatively conservative and do not permit recognition of unrealised gains in the profit and loss account or equity, though unrealised losses are required to be accounted. Banks are required to mark-to-market the investments in the Held for Trading (HFT) and Available for Sale (AFS) categories at periodical intervals, on a portfolio basis, and provide for the net losses and ignore the net gains. This has proved to be a stabilising factor, in as much as it has not induced an imbalance in the incentive structures and has also proved to be less pro-cyclical. Moral Suasion and Supervisory Review Moral suasion and public articulation of concerns has helped in achieving a desired re-balancing of suspected excesses in risk-taking among banks. Some of the areas where moral suasion has been used are the need for banks to monitor unhedged foreign currency exposures of their corporate clients, adoption of appropriate incentive mechanisms by banks for encouraging disclosures of derivative exposures by their corporate clients, banks' reliance on non-deposit resources to finance assets, their excessive reliance on wholesale deposits and uncomfortable loan-to-value (LTV) ratios in respect of housing loans etc.

A supervisory review process (SRP) was initiated with select banks having significant exposure to sensitive sectors, including reliance on call money market, in order to ensure that effective risk mitigants and sound internal control systems are in place. In the first round, a framework was developed for monitoring the systemically important individual banks. The second round of SRP was directed to analyse banks' exposure to sensitive sectors and identify outliers. Based on the analyses of these outlier banks, guidelines were issued to all banks indicating the need for better risk management systems in banks at operating levels. In brief, in India the focus is on regulatory comfort, going beyond regulatory compliance. In a choice between emphasis of regulations on saving capital and protecting depositors' interests or reinforcing financial system stability, the latter have always prevailed.

Indian Experience of Financial Sector Liberalisation and Development

It is necessary to clarify that while the measures mentioned above are aimed at fostering financial stability, in order to enhance efficiency several other initiatives have been taken to liberalise the macro-policy environment in which banks operate through a re-orientation of regulatory prescriptions by replacing micro regulations with macro- prudential regulations, providing an enabling environment for universal banking, improved corporate governance in private sector banks, and enabling consolidation of banks in the private sector.

Some other important measures that promoted a vibrant and robust operating environment and framework for the banking system that promoted growth and business opportunities include a reduction in pre-emption through reserve requirements; shift to market determined pricing for government securities; disbanding of some of the administered interest rates; auction-based repos-reverse repos for short-term liquidity management; facilitation of improved payments and settlement mechanism; setting up of the Clearing Corporation of India Limited (CCIL) to act as central counter party for facilitating payments and settlement system relating to fixed income securities, money market instruments and foreign exchange transactions; setting up of INFINET as the communi-cation backbone for the financial sector; introduction of Negotiated Dealing System (NDS) for screen-based trading in government securities; introduction of Real Time Gross Settlement (RTGS) System; debt recovery tribunals, asset reconstruction companies, settlement advisory committees, corporate debt restructuring mechanism, etc. for quicker recovery/ restructuring of stressed assets; promulgation of Securitisation and Reconstruction of Financial Assets and Enforcement of Securities Interest (SARFAESI) Act, 2002 and its subsequent amendment to ensure creditor rights; setting up of Credit Information Bureau of India Limited (CIBIL) for information sharing on defaulters as also other borrowers. These growth oriented initiatives have appropriately complemented the stability oriented initiatives.

Development Orientation

In the context of the rapidly evolving financial landscape, the RBI has also been suitably reorienting its regulatory and supervisory framework to meet the needs of the common man. It has also been the endeavour of the RBI to improve credit delivery and customer service by banks. The RBI has simultaneously focussed on financial inclusion and extension of banking services to the unbanked areas of the economy. The guidelines on lending to the priority sector included improvement of credit delivery to those sectors of the economy that impact large segment of the population, the weaker section and to the sectors which are employment-intensive such as agriculture and tiny and small enterprises.

In order to improve credit delivery to micro and small and medium enterprises (MSMEs), the RBI has urged banks to review their institutional arrangements for delivering credit to the SME sector, especially in identified clusters in various parts of the country, and to take measures to strengthen the expertise in and systems at branches located in or near such identified clusters with a view to providing adequate and timely credit. The RBI has taken several measures in recent years aimed at providing customer service at reasonable cost. These measures include enhancing customer protection and disclosures, code of ethics and grievance redressal, among others. The RBI's broad approach to financial inclusion aims at 'connecting people' with the banking system and not just credit dispensation; giving people access to the payments system; and portraying financial inclusion as a viable business model and opportunity. The RBI has been initiating measures to improve the outreach of banks and their services, and promote financial inclusion in less developed states and union territories.

Monetary Policy

As a part of the conduct of monetary policy, the RBI monitors, inter alia, monetary and credit aggregates. It uses both liquidity and interest rate instruments to achieve the monitory policy objectives. Pre-emptive actions have been taken since 2004 to withdraw monetary accommodation which was reinforced with measures aimed at moderating early signs of over-heating. Further, appreciation of the possible permanent and temporary components with regard to oil prices has been articulated in the policies. While undertaking a nuanced approach to managing aggregate demand recognising the elements of shock and consequent impact on inflation expectations, the underlying demand conditions warranted several interest rate and liquidity measures in recent weeks.

While monetary policy influences aggregates, reality is often dis-aggregated. Hence, the RBI uses prudential regulatory policies to complement the monetary policy measures and objectives. It is pertinent that the lender of last resort function is not separate either from monetary and liquidity management or from financial regulation. Thus both monetary policy and prudential regulations are used as complementary tools to achieve the central bank objectives and they both support and reinforce each other.

Concluding Remarks on Broader Issues

The detailed account given above of the developments in the global and the Indian financial sector would be incomplete without devoting some attention to the broader issues. These issues need to be reckoned and debated widely lest the response to recent developments be construed as internal to the financial sector, warranting only such sector-specific solutions. First, whether the benefits of financial liberalisation and financial globalisation need to be reevaluated? It is possible to argue that liberalisation of trade in goods has contributed more to growth and price stability than financial sector initiatives. In particular, it may be argued that the incentive frameworks for financial intermediaries appear to be disproportionate to their conceivable contribution to the economy. The arguments in favour of persevering with financial innovation and urging regulators to continue to give priority to facilitate innovations should be viewed in this context.

Second, whether the regulators have placed greater emphasis on savings of capital in banks rather than on the interests of the depositors and on systemic stability? The recent compulsions for shoring up of capital by some of the global financial institutions in advanced economies seem to suggest this. What induced the regulators to permit such excesses in leverage and savings of capital? Does this also involve issues pertaining to governance and accountability of regulators? Third, whether there is a beginning of fiscalisation of the financial sector in view of the intensification of the links between the two? For example, the recent episodes of participation of the sovereign wealth funds in the re-capitalisation of banks tantamount to fiscal support. Further, large doses of liquidity support to financial markets by regulators against collateral may also involve quasi-fiscal costs, under some circumstances.

Fourth, whether there is, what may be called, financialisation of the political economy? The attractiveness of finan-cial intermediaries in terms of high profitability, significant growth - especially cross-border, massive spread of investors, and the inadequate scope for application of principles of rules of origin in the financial sector could have resulted in enhanced clout for these intermediaries in the political economy. Incidentally, Professor Jagdish Bhagwati's reference to Wall Street - Washington links is relevant in this context. Fifth, whether there has been excessive financialisation of corporates, in the sense that large corporates take significant positions in the financial markets through their treasury operations? Increasingly, many of the positions of the corporates in the financial markets may not be related to their underlying business. Do we have an issue when such activities of corporates in the financial markets, unrelated to their underlying business, are not regulated the way similar activities of financial market intermediaries are regulated? To conclude, on the way forward, to exit the current financial turbulence and fortify against future similar episodes, we may need to look beyond reforms within the financial sector and address broader related issues that impinge on the balance between the sovereign, the regulators, the financial institutions and the markets.

INDIAN RETAIL INDUSTRY

Retailing is still in its infancy in India. In the name of retailing, the unorganised retailing has dominated the Indian landscape so far. According to an estimate the unorganized retail sector has 97% presence whereas the organized accounts for merely 3%. Industry has already predicted a trillion dollar market in retail sector in India by 2010. However, the retail industry in India is undergoing a major shake-up as the country is witnessing a retail revolution. The old traditional formats are slowly changing into more complex and bigger formats. Malls and mega malls are coming up in almost all the places be it - metros or the smaller cities, across the length and breadth of the country. A comparative change can be seen with the help of graphical study given below. A McKinsey report on India (2004) says organized retailing would increase the efficiency and productivity of entire gamut of economic activities, and would help in achieving higher GDP growth.

At 6%, the share of employment of retail in India is low, even when compared to Brazil (14%), and Poland (12%). Government of India's plan of changing the FDI guidelines in this sector speaks of the importance attached to retailing. Recently moves by big corporate houses like Reliance Industries has further fuelled the major investments in retail sector. A strategic alliance, land acquisitions in prime areas give the essence of the mood in this sector. Both MNCs and Indian firms want to get their share of this burgeoning pie. Notable in Indian firms are Pantaloons Retail & Big Bazaar, Trent's Westside, Shopper's stop, Reliance and Subhiskha, Wills Lifestyle stores, Café Coffee Day, which are present in India in different retail formats. Wal-Mart stores have just started operations in India. Some leading retail coffee chains of the world like Starbucks, Barnies are planning to expand in a major way in India.

The Indian Retail Sector

India is the country having the most unorganized retail market. Traditionally it was a family's livelihood, with their shop in the front and house at the back, while they run the retail business. More than 99% retailer's function in less than 500 square feet of shopping space. Global retail consultants KSA Technopak have estimated that organized retailing in India is expected to touch Rs. 35,000 crore in the year 2005-06. The Indian retail sector is estimated at around Rs. 900,000 crore, of which the organized sector accounts for a mere 2 per cent indicating a huge potential market opportunity that is lying in the waiting for the consumer-savvy organized retailer. Purchasing power of Indian urban consumer is growing and branded merchandise in categories like Apparels, Cosmetics, Shoes, Watches, Beverages, Food and even Jewellery, are slowly becoming lifestyle products that are widely accepted by the urban Indian consumer. Indian retailers need to advantage of this growth and aiming to grow, diversify and introduce new formats have to pay more attention to the brand building process. The emphasis here is on retail as a brand rather than retailers selling brands.

The focus should be on branding the retail business itself. There is no doubt that the Indian retail scene is booming. A number of large corporate houses —Tata's, Raheja's, Piramals's, Goenka's — have already made their foray into this arena, with beauty and health stores, supermarkets, self-service music stores, new age book stores, every-day-low-price stores, computers and peripherals stores, office equipment stores and home/building construction stores. Today the organized players have attacked every retail category. The Indian retail scene has witnessed too many players in too short a time, crowding several categories without looking at their core competencies or having a well thought out branding strategy.

The growth rate of super market sales has been significant in recent years because greater numbers of higher income

Indians prefer to shop at super markets due to higher standards of hygiene and attractive ambience. With growth in income levels, Indians have started spending more on health and beauty products. Here also small, single-outlet retailers dominate the market. In recent years, a few retail chains specialised products have come into the market. Although these retail chains account for only a small share of the total market, their business is expected to grow significantly in the future due to the growing quality consciousness of buyers for these products.

Numerous clothing and footwear shops in shopping centres and markets operate all over India. Traditional outlets stock a limited range of cheap and popular items; in contrast, modern clothing and footwear stores have modern products and attractive displays to lure customers. With rapid urbanization, and changing patterns of consumer tastes and preferences, it is unlikely that the traditional outlets will survive the test of time. Despite the large size of this market, very few large and modern retailers have established specialized stores for products.

There seems to be a considerable potential for the entry or expansion of specialized retail chains in the country. The Indian durable goods sector has seen the entry of a large number of foreign companies during the post liberalization period. A greater variety of consumer electronic items and household appliances became available to the Indian customer. Intense competition among companies to sell their brands provided a strong impetus to the growth for retailers doing business in this sector. Increasing household incomes due to better economic opportunities have encouraged consumer expenditure on leisure and personal goods in the country. There are specialized retailers for each category of products (books, music products, etc.) in this sector. Another prominent feature of this sector is popularity of franchising agreements between established manufacturers and retailers. A strong impetus to the growth of retail industry is witnessed by economic boom and driver of key trends in urban as well as rural India.

Opportunities In Various Segments

These are different segments concerned with food, beverage, grocery, fashion & life style etc. It can be discussed separately.

Food Retailing Segment

The Food World (FW) supermarket chain has been one of the pioneers in organized food retailing in India. Before FW entered the food retailing market, it carried out an extensive survey in consumer attitude towards retailing. An important finding of the survey was that in terms of overall satisfaction, traditional Indian grocery stores scored 5 - 6 on a 10-point scale. FW believed that this was largely due to the absence of organized retailing and low brand proliferation. The company thus decided to offer people a pleasant shopping experience and work towards making grocery shopping less cumbersome. The main challenge for FW was to alter the existing mindset of Indians with respect to price and value and add excitement to grocery shopping.

On the basis of the above information, FW defined its objective as: "To offer the Indian housewife the freedom to choose from a wide range of products at a convenient location in a clean, bright, and functional ambience without a price penalty."

Initially, the target markets were identified as neighbourhoods that had at least 4,000 households with an average monthly income of more than Rs. 4,000. For this kind of customer base, FW needed to start operations in a metropolitan city. Considering the fact that the cost of real estate was low in Southern India, FW chose Chennai, Hyderabad and Bangalore as initial locations for setting up FW stores. FW adopted a self - service format for its stores, which typically had around 4500 sq ft of selling space. The designing of the stores was given special attention and a uniform look was adopted for all the stores. The colors red and yellow were used liberally while designing the stores. To give the outlets an up market look, the interiors were kept completely visible to the public by using huge glass panes for the frontage. The interiors were kept brightly lit and emphasis was given to creating a clean, pleasant ambience. All the outlets were air - conditioned and played po-pular music continuously. All this was done with the objective of providing an enjoyable and refreshing shopping experience to customers. The merchandise primarily comprised groceries, personal care products, kitchenware and tableware. Over the years, this list was expanded to include music, magazines and a few other product categories to cater to a wider customer base. Every item in the store was marked individually with both price and bar codes. Separate payment counters were set up for people planning to pay through credit/debit cards and for people buying only 3 - 5 items. FW also entered into alliances with the fast food major, Pizzas Corner and the satellite radio broadcasting company, World Space. While Pizza Corner sold pizzas from FW outlets. World space displayed and sold its services and products at the stores. Such tie - ups and promotional exercise have become a routine feature for FW.

Retailing of Lifestyle Products Segment

Shopper's Stop Limited (SSL) is the pioneer in India's organized retail revolution. SSL redefined the concept of 'shopping' by making efforts to provide the Indian consumers with an international shopping experience. In 1991, SSL set up its first outlet in Mumbai, Maharashtra, with a floor space of around 4,000 sq ft. Since then, SSL has established its stores in all major cities in India with store space ranging from 18,000 sq ft to 60,000 sq ft. SSL stores provide a complete and in - depth range of fashion and lifestyle products and accessories to meet the lifestyle pattern of every shopper. Around 85% of SSL's merchandise is branded and it stocks more than 150 national and international brands. Within a short period, SSL emerged as the largest single retailer for Levis, Pepe, Lee, Arrow, Zodiac, Reebok, Nike, Parker, Ray Ban, Swatch, Chambor, Revlon, Lego, Mattel and many other leading brands. The company closely monitored the movement of all brands, and if any brand failed to meet customer expectations, it was phased out. SSL also launched a range of private labels like Life, Kashish and Karrot in the premium classic, value classic and value fashion segments.

A team of designers were recruited from India's premier fashion design institutes to develop private labels. Earlier, Indian customers were used to shopping for their apparel and accessories at various shops (as no shops offered all the products at one place), which paid little or no attention to the ambience or the comfort of their customers. SSL, apart from offering a complete range of garments and accessories, included central air - conditioning, impeccably maintained trial rooms, beautiful rest rooms, play area for children, large car parking, in - store café, and other services such as alterations, goods exchanged without any questions and gift wrapping. As a part of differentiating its product offerings from that of other major lifestyle stores such as Life Style and Globus, SSL also began conducting many events and promotion campaigns to combine entertainment with shopping. These included the 101 - day Seven Wonders of the World Festival, Surprise Sale, Salon Streets, and Men in Vogue, Great Store Robbery, Campus Stoppers and Valentine Promotion. One of the major events offered by SSL, which attracts hoards of customers, is *Parikrama* a crafts fare aimed at showcasing the diverse ethnic arts and traditions in India.

Barista and Café Coffee Day

Being a traditional tea consuming country, the average coffee consumption in India was quite low at 10 cups per person annually. However, in the late 1990s, a silent coffee revolution was sweeping urban India. Coffee drinking was increasingly becoming a statement of the young and upwardly mobile Indians. Coffee bars, an unheard concept till the mid 1990s had become big business. There was a transition from the conventional and outdated coffee house to more sophisticated and trendy coffee bar chains like Barista, Café Coffee Day, Qwiky's and Café Nescafe. By the turn of 20th century, nontraditional coffee retailing outlets like coffee bar chains, coffee vending machines and specialty coffee powder shops succeeded in making coffee one of the most desirable beverages in urban India. The coffee parlors were an instant hit across all major metros and cities in India, as they offered an entirely new experience to customers. Barista entered the Indian coffee retailing market in 2000 and decided to position itself as a lifestyle brand. The company targeted the premium segment youth, as it realized that it wasn't only coffee that its target segment was looking form, but also for a place to hang around comfortably, where they could be themselves and do whatever they wanted, such as reading a book, writing a letter, or simply chilling out. Hence, it recreated the ambience and experience of the typical Italian neighborhood espresso bars in India, with bright, trendy and comfortable interiors. It promoted a social and interactive environment, where one can play games like chess and scrabble, read books, listen to music, enjoy arts, surf the Net and sip an Espresso Italiano, or Iced Café Mocha. Fun posters, message boards and TV screens with music videos, all set the right mood. An open kitchen behind the bar enables one to watch the coffee actually being made.

To ensure superior quality of its product offerings, Barista used only top grade Arabica beans to make coffee and also invited brew masters from Italy to create new blends. The employee orientation program at Barista specially focused on enabling the team to understand and avoid the attitudes and behaviours in traditional restaurants that restrain customer from being himself/herself. Since 2002, as a part of differentiating its services, Barista began offering Italian food at its outlets and also entered into tie - ups with Planet M, Crossword and Ebony to set up Espresso Corners at these places. During this period, to expand the reach of its services, the company also opened outlets in banks (ABN - Amro), movie theaters (PVR in Delhi), offices (HSBC and GE), airports and in hotels.

Nescafe, Cadbury E-Cuba and Tata Tea

Nestle popularized the coffee kiosk concept in India, where

it offered coffee through its vending machines. Nestle installed hundreds of Nescafe kiosks at places such as shopping malls, cinema halls, food centers and office buildings. Its vending machines came in different sizes and styles to match the needs of consumers at different locations. For instance Nestlé's high capacity multitask vending machines provided snacks, drinks and confectionery items. The kiosk model enabled consumers to have hot coffee instantly, whether they were shopping or at office, just by the click of buttons. Most offices buy the Nescafe vending machines to provide their employees with free coffee.

Cadbury India, with the help of telecommunications companies – BPL Mobile and E-Cuba India, launched chocolate vending machine operated by mobile handsets in select corporate and congregation points in Mumbai. Since 2002 the concept of vending machines to retail has picked up momentum in India. The Tata were the first in India to establish vending machines for tea, followed by HLL 'Taj Mahal' and Lipton vending machines and coca-cola international tea brand 'Georgia' vending machines. These vending machines were placed at many strategic places such as airports, railways stations, shopping malls and complexes, restaurants and food outlets.

Beauty and Healthcare Retailing Segment

The Shahnaz Hussian group founded and led by Shahnaz Hussian has been one of the pioneers of organized beauty care retailing in India. The group offers exclusive salon treatment geared to individual needs as well as a number of commercial formulations for the treatment of specific problems like acne, pimples, pigmentation, dehydration, alopecia, etc. It employs about 4200 people in 650 salons spread across 104 countries with a strong pre-sence in Asia, US and the Middle east. The group formulates and markets over 400 products for all age groups and for a variety of beauty and health problems or needs. The group sophisticated R&D units develop the products and put them through stringent quality control tests. These products are environment friendly and no testing is done on animals. All the products offered by the group are entirely natural and carry the guarantee of purity and safety.

Key Trends in Urban India:

- Retailing in India is witnessing a huge revamping exercise.
- Estimated to be US$ 200 billion, of which organized retailing (i.e. modern trade) makes up 3 percent or US$ 6.4 billion.
- Ranked second in a Global Retail Development Index of 30 developing countries drawn up by AT Kearney.
- India is rated the fifth most attractive emerging retail market: a potential goldmine.
- Food and apparel retailing key drivers of growth.
- Organized retailing in India has been largely an urban phenomenon with affluent classes and growing number of double-income households.

Key Trends in Rural India:

- Rural markets emerging as a huge opportunity for retailers reflected in the share of the rural market across most categories of consumption
- ITC is experimenting with retailing through its e-Choupal and Choupal Sagar - rural hypermarkets.

The Hidden Challenges

Modern retailing is all about directly having "first hand experience" with customers, giving them such a satiable experience that they would like to enjoy again and again. Providing great experience to customers can easily be said than done. Thus challenges like retail differentiation, merchandising mix, supply chain management and competition from supplier's brands are the talk of the day. In India, as we are moving to the next phase of retail development, each endeavor to offer experiential shopping. One of the key observations by customers is that it is very difficult to find the uniqueness of retail stores. The problem: retail differentiation.

The next problem in setting up organized retail operations is that of supply chain logistics. India lacks a strong supply chain when compared to Europe or the USA. The existing supply chain has too many intermediaries: Typical supply chain looks like:- Manufacturer - National distributor - Regional distributor - Local wholesaler - Retailer - Consumer. This implies that global retail chains will have to build a supply chain network from scratch. This might run foul with the existing supply chain operators. In addition to fragmented supply chain, the trucking and transportation system is antiquated. The concept of container trucks, automated warehousing is yet to take root in India. The result: significant losses/damages during shipping.

Merchandising planning is one of the biggest challenges that any multi store retailer faces. Getting the right mix of product, which is store specific across organisation, is a combination of customer insight, allocation and assortment techniques. The private label will continue to compete with brand leaders. So supplier's brand will take their own way because they have a established brand image from last decades and the reasons can be attributed to better customer experience, value vs. price, aspiration, innovation, accessibility of supplier's brand.

Employment Opportunities

Urban Employment: Employment opportunities for youth, According to PricewaterhouseCoopers (PwC) it is said that retailing will create additional eight million jobs though retailing In India and will benefit population by employing local (Urban) youth and others directly or indirectly. But it is feared that our friendly neighbourhood kirana shops where, one can make purchases in small quantities and return the goods if not found good and many more friendly services, will be on the verge of disappearance there by creating a vacuum which cannot be filled by the big organized one.

Rural Employment: Contract Farming is the new mantra of organized retailing in India. There is no doubt that the farmers are in some way benefited by contract faming where in, the latest technology and equipment and scientific farming is done by farmers with the help of retailers there by increasing the productivity in agriculture, and uniform payment for their produce through out the crop irrespective of fluctuations in market price. But one should also focus on the freedom of farmers to sell their produce at will. It is evident in India that rich farmers who possess vast lands are the beneficiary but farmers who have little land and dependent on other trades are marginally benefited by this kind of business. Similarly, Selva Kumar, who runs a kirana 100 meters from a Reliance outlet in Chennai, says, "We have lost 40 percent of our business, and that's the future. We're not closing, but there'll be no growth." "It's good value here, better than other supermarkets, but there are difficulties with the quality, especially apples and papayas," says Rama Tibrewal, a middle-aged Reliance shopper in Hyderabad.

Competition

The organized retailers are financially sound in investing in Big Business promotion, aesthetic looks, technology and Supply chain management etc. Its business principle "The bigger the better". The Bigger retailers the better it can counter competition from small retailers and sustain business. But the unorganized retailer cannot compete and are trying fight hard against organized retailers however they cannot afford to invest heavy on technology and other inputs. Due to tough competition, Customer have lot many opportunities and choices to go for, unless local retailers offer them best prices they won't be interested to come back, unorganized retailers stores are finally waking up to become competitive and try to attract more consumers.

Competitive Trend

"Small pharmacy stores have teamed up to implement steps to fight back the competition from large chains. The All-India Chemist and Druggist Association (AIODC) are conducting talks with several companies such as Dr. Lal Path Labs, Dr Reddy's Labs and Thyrocare Pathology to offer diagnostic facilities". "Metro Cash & Carry will be starting a training school for kirana stores, in an effort to strengthen them and their business practices to take on the competition from organized retailers". Geraro Monzillo, the deputy managing director.

Government's Contribution

Government of India permitted up to 51% foreign direct investment in single-brand retailing in the country. This rule, to some extent saved the existence of unorganized retailers but in the long run there is a possibility that Indian Government may allow 100% FDI there by permitting to setup multinational retail operators which may wipe out the existence of unorganized sector. Government's ignorance towards the needs of the unrecognized retailers and in one way discouraging them by not giving enough support in the form of financial, infrastructural, distribution, storage, transport, trade centers and other facilities makes it an awful situations for unorganized retailers and this may lead to catastrophe.

Growing Economic Disparity

In India more than 60% population is engaged in farming, which is major chunk of income generated and it is the equivalent to half of other sectors but disparities in income levels in India specifically rural India remain as wide as ever. Nevertheless employment will grow in all sectors and which will be of labor incentive. However, Work force of women in agricultural and services sector will enhance pressure on rural jobs in near future. "Much of India is still mired in poverty, but just over a decade after the Indian economy began shaking off its statistic shackles and opening to the outside world, it is booming.... The growth of the past decade has put more money in the pockets of an expanding middle class, 250 million to 300 million strong, and more choices in front of them".

Strategies

Right Positioning

The effectiveness of the mall developer's communication of the offering to the target customers determines how well the mall gets positioned in their minds. At this stage, the communication has to be more of relative nature. This implies that the message conveyed to the target customers must be effective enough in differentiating the mall's offering from that of its competitors without even naming them. The message should also clearly convey to the target audience that the mall offers them exactly what they call the complete shopping-cum-entertainment point that meets all their expectations.

The core purpose is to inform the target customers about the offering of the mall, persuade them to visit the mall and remind them about the mall. The mall developer can create awareness about the offering among the target customers in a number of ways. Various communication tools available to the mall developer for this purpose may include advertising, buzz marketing (WoM), celebrity endorsement, use of print media, press releases and viral marketing .Once the message is being conveyed through these channels, the mall developer must add a personal touch to his message by carrying out a door-to-door campaign in order to reinforce the message.

Effective Visual Communication

Retailer has to give more emphasis on display visual merchandising, lighting, signage's and specialized props. The visual communication strategy might be planned and also be brand positioned. Theme or lifestyle displays using stylized mannequins and props, which are based on a season or an event, are used to promote collections and have to change to keep touch with the trend. The merchandise presentation ought to be very creative and displays are often on non-standard fixtures and forms to generate interest and add on attitude to the merchandise.

Strong Supply Chain

Critical components of supply chain planning applications can help manufacturers meet retailers' service levels and maintain profit margins. Retailer has to develop innovative solution for managing the supply chain problems. Innovative solutions like performance management, frequent sales operation management, demand planning, inventory planning, production planning, lean systems and staff should help retailers to get advantage over competitors.

One of the most important challenge in organized retail in India is faced by poor supply chain and logistics management. The importance can be understood by the fact that the logistics management cost component in India is as high as 7% -10% against the global average of 4% - 5% of the total retail price. Therefore, the margins in the retail sector can be improved by 3% - 5% by just improving the supply chain and logistics management.

In India, with demand for end-to-end logistics solutions far outstripping supply, the logistics market for organised retail is pegged at $50 million and is growing at 16%. It is expected to reach $120-$130 million by 2010. Organised retail on the other hand is growing at 400% and is expected to reach around $30 billion by 2010. Even supply chain and logistics firms like Hong Kong based Heng Tai Consumables and ABS Procurement Co and ACM China (the greenhouse specialist) is also eying the opportunity for managing the supplies.

The supply chain management is logistics aspect of a value delivery chain. It comprises all of the parties that participate in the retail logistics process: Manufacturers, Wholesalers, Third Party Specialists like Shippers, Order Fulfillment House etc. and the Retailer.

Here, logistics is the total process of planning, implementing and coordi-nating the physical movement of merchandise from manufacturer to retailer to customer in the most timely, effective and cost efficient manner possible. Logistics regards order processing and fulfillment, transportation, warehousing, customer service and inventory management as interdependent functions in the value delivery chain. It oversees inventory management decisions as items travel through a retail supply chain. If a logistics system works well, the retail firm reduces stock outs, hold down inventories and improve customer service - all at the same time.

Logistics and Supply Chain enables an organized retailer to move or store products more effectively. Efficient logistics management not only prevents needless movement of goods, vehicles transferring products back and forth; but also frees up storage space for more productive use. Retail analysts say on-time order replenishments will become even more critical once the Wal-Mart/ Bharti combine begins operations - the American retailer works almost entirely on cross-docking and is likely to demand higher service levels, including potential levies for delays in shipment.

The efficiency and effectiveness of supply chain and logistics management can also be understood by the fact that m odern retail stores maintain lower inventories than traditional retail. In India, generally in the traditional kirana stores, three weeks inventories are kept; while in a modern retail store like Hypercity, it's nine days and it's under two weeks for Food Bazaar. Now, it is beneficial for both the manufacturer as well as the retailer. If we go through the following food supply chain in India, we find that a lot can be improved by maintaining the supply chain and logistics.

Changing the Perception

Retailers benefit only if consumers perceive their store brands to have consistent and comparable quality and availability in relation to branded products. Retailer has to provide more assortments for private level brands to compete with supplier's brand.

New product development, aggressive retail mix as well as everyday low pricing strategy can be the strategy to get edge over supplier's brand. In their preparation to face fierce competitive pressure, Indian retailers must come to recognize the value of building their own stores as brands to reinforce their marketing Positioning, to communicate quality as well as value for money. Sustainable competitive advantage will be dependent on translating core values combining products, image and reputation into a coherent retail brand strategy.

With the generous use of Global and Local Experiences, Indian retailers are going to improve their bottom lines with efficient management of Supply Chain and Logistics. At the same time, Indian Retailers like Future Group with retail stores like Big Bazaar, Pantaloons and Reliance Retail are also going to show the world as to how it can be managed in a more innovative and efficient manner. The retail sector in India is witnessing a huge revamping exercise as traditional markets make a way for new formats such as departmental stores, hypermarkets, supermarkets and specialty stores.

Western style malls have begun appearing in metros and second-rung cities which introduced the Indian consumer to a shopping experience like never before. Rated the fifth most attractive emerging retail market, India is being seen as a potential goldmine. It has been ranked 2nd in Global Retail Development Index of 30 developing countries drawn up by A.T. Kearney. Government of India has also opened the door for the retailing giants to enter into the markets. Many foreign investors are also showing keen interest to enter into the Indian market. With the flow of FDI, retail sector will have to see a many changes in the coming years.

Bibliography

Bragg, R. J. (1991). *Trade Descriptions: A Study of the Trade Descriptions Act, 1968, and Part III Consumer Protection Act, 1987.* Oxford: Clarendon Press.

Fairest, P. (1988). *Guide to the Consumer Protection Act, 1987.* London: Croner CCH.

George, Linda K. (1992)."Economic Status and Well-Being: A Review of the Literature and an Agenda for Future Research," in Aging, Money, and Life Satisfaction, Springer.

Giliker, P. and Beckwith, S. (2004). *Tort* (2nd ed. ed.). London: Sweet and Maxwell.

Guttentag, Jack. (1975). "Creating New Financial Instruments for the Aged," New York University, Graduate School of Business Administration, Center for the Study of Financial Institutions.

Hodges, C. (1998). "Development risks: Unanswered questions". *Modern Law Review* 61: 560.

Jacobs, Bruce, and William Weissert. (1987). "Using Home Equity to Finance Long-Term Care," Journal of Health Politics, Policy and Law, Spring.

Kutty, Nandinee. (1995). "The Scope for Poverty Alleviation among Elderly Homeowners in the United States through Reverse Mortgages," Cornell University.

Mayer, Christopher, and Katerina Simons. (1994)."Reverse Mortgages and the Liquidity of Housing Wealth," Journal of the American Real Estate and Urban Economics Association, Summer.

Merrill, Sally, Meryl Finkel, and Nandinee Kutty. (1995). "Potential Beneficiaries from Reverse Mortgage Products for the Elderly," AREUEA Journal, 22(2):257-99.

Mildred, M. and Howells, G. (1998). "Comments on 'Development risks: Unanswered questions'". *Modern Law Review* 61: 570.

Nelson-Jones, R. and Stewart, P. (1987). *Product Liability: New Law Under the Consumer Protection Act, 1987*. London: Fourmat Publishing.

Owles, D. (1988). *The Unsafe Product: Manager's Guide to the Consumer Protection Act, 1987*. London: Kogan Page.

Phillips, William and Stephen Gwin. (1993). "Reverse Mortgages," Transactions (Vol. XLIV), Society of Actuaries, Schaumburg, IL.

Rasmussen, David, Isaac Megbolugbe, and Barbara Morgan. (1995) "Reverse Mortgages: Private Incentives, Market Constraints, and Public Policy," Fannie Mae.

Rasmussen, David, Isaac Megbolugbe, and Barbara Morgan. (1995). "Using the 1990 Public Use Microdata Sample to Estimate Potential Demand for Reverse Mortgage Products," Journal of Housing Research, Vol. 6, Issue 1.

Rasmussen, David. (1995). "The Demand for Reverse Mortgages: A Survey of Elderly Homeowners," Florida State University.

Redfoot, Donald L. (1993)."Long-Term Care Reform and the Role of Housing Finance," Housing Policy Debate, Vol. 4.

Redfoot, Donald L. (1996)."The Role of Housing Finance in Long Term Care Reform," Lusk Review.

Scholen, Ken and Yung-Ping Chen (1981) (eds.).Unlocking Home Equity for the Elderly, Ballinger Publishing, Cambridge, MA.

Scholen, Ken, Maurice Weinrobe, Bruce Jacobs, Jay Greenberg, and William Weissert. (1986)."The Role of Home Equity in Financing Long Term Care," Minnesota State Housing Finance Agency.

Scholen, Ken. (1982). "Final Report of the Home Equity Conversion Project," State of Wisconsin, Bureau on Aging.

Scholen, Ken. (1986)."An Analysis of the HUD Report on Reverse Mortgage Insurance," AARP Federal Affairs.

Scholen, Ken. (1987).""Using Home Equity To Pay For Long Term Care," State of Connecticut Governor's Commission on Long Term Care Financing.

Scholen, Ken. (1993)."Consumer Response to Reverse Mortgage: A Blueprint for Product Development," National Center for Home Equity Conversion.

Scholen, Ken. (1996). Marketing Reverse Mortgages: Keys to Market Growth, NCHEC.

Scholen, Ken. (1997) (ed.). Model State Law on Reverse Mortgages, AARP Foundation.

Shears, P. *et al.* (2001). "Food for thought - What mad cows have wrought with respect to food safety regulation in the EU and UK". *British Food Journal* 103(1): 63–87.

Szymanoski, Jr., Edward J. (1994)."Risk and and the Home Equity Conversion Mortgage," AREUEA Journal, 1994, 22(2):347-99.

Theresa R. Venti, and Ming H. Chow. (2000). "Understanding Reverse Mortgage Cash Flows: A Hazard Model of HECM Loan Terminations," Paper presented at AEA/ASSA Conference. Boston, MA, January 7-9.

U. S. Department of Housing and Urban Development. (1985)."Home Equity Conversion Mechanisms," December, Washington, DC.

U. S. Department of Housing and Urban Development. (1995). No Place Like Home: A Report to Congress on FHA's Home Equity Conversion Mortgage Program, Washington, DC, 2000.

U. S. Department of Housing and Urban Development. (1995).Evaluation of the Home Equity Conversion Mortgage Insurance Demonstration, Washington, DC.

U. S. Department of Housing and Urban Development. (1995).Evaluation of the Home Equity Conversion Mortgage Insurance Demonstration, Washington, DC.

Van Gerven, W. *et al.* (2000).*Cases, Materials and Texts on National, Supranational and International Tort Law*. Oxford: Hart Publishing.

Index

A

Affluent consumer, 214, 215, 217, 218, 219, 220.

Assertiveness, 51

Attitudes toward marketing, 57, 58, 59, 60, 61, 62, 64, 65, 66, 67, 68, 73, 75, 77

B

Barista and café coffee day, 253

Beauty and healthcare, 255

Birth of copra, 11

Broom stick, 16

Business ethics, 81, 99, 104.

C

Capital adequacy, 239,

Competition policy, 183, 192, 193, 194, 198, 199.

Competitive trend, 258.

Comprehend consumers, 34.

Consequentialist Approach, 101.

Conserve clients, 23, 24, 32, 41, 43.

Consumer alienation, 52.

Consumer behaviour, 23, 25, 26, 36, 45, 49, 142, 206.

Consumer bonding, 153.

Consumer citizenship, 199, 200, 201, 202, 203, 204, 206.

Consumer education, 2, 9, 10, 11, 21, 149, 150, 157, 161, 170, 184, 185, 188, 203.

Consumer financial claims, 210.

Consumer needs, 3, 4, 136, 150.

Consumer protection, 10, 11, 13, 14, 21, 148, 149, 157, 159, 163, 168, 170, 183, 184, 185, 186, 187, 188, 191, 192, 199, 212, 214.

Consumer protection act, 11, 21, 148, 149, 157, 163, 170, 184, 185, 186, 187, 188.

Consumer protection laws, 164, 168, 169, 170, 173

Consumer responses, 50, 52, 53, 54, 68, 77

Consumer responsibility, 1, 60, 151, 152, 153, 155, 172

Consumer rights and responsibility, 139.

Consumerism, 23, 25, 26, 27, 57, 58, 59, 60, 61, 62, 64, 65, 73, 74, 77, 79, 162, 164, 166, 175, 176, 177, 178, 180, 222, 223, 224, 229, 230
Consumers day, 184
Consumption theory, 206, 208, 211
Content degradation, 7
Cross-cultural comparison, 26, 48, 58, 60
Cultural dimension, 22, 23, 27

D

Deontological approach, 101
Development orientation, 245
Discourse on social, 221
Distortions of consumerism, 222

E

Economic disparity, 259
Effects of content degradation, 6
Employment opportunities, 257
Enhancing consumer awareness, 192
Ethnicity, 25
Ethno consumerism, 23, 25, 26, 27
Ethno marketing, 22, 23, 24, 25, 31, 33, 34, 36, 37, 38, 40, 41, 43, 44, 45, 46, 47
Ethno marketing trategic matrix, 23, 33
Ethno marketing strengths, 47
Ethnography, 23, 32, 45, 46
Extortion, 109, 110, 116, 117
Extortion as justification, 109

F

Financial sector, 230, 231, 233, 235, 244, 246, 247
Financial sector liberalisation, 244
Financial stability, 233, 237, 238, 244
Food retailing segment, 251
Food security, 140, 141

G

Global reputation, 13, 14
Globalization, 60, 164, 166, 167, 173, 178, 204, 221, 222, 227
Globalization, liberalization and Consumerisation, 166
GM food 144, 145, 146
Growing economic disparity, 259

H

Hidden challenges, 256

I

"Ideal" consumer behaviours, 22
Indian retail industry, 248

Indian retail sector, 248, 249
Indigenous knowledge, 204
Individualism/collectivism, 51
Inter-bank liability, 241
Investment portfolio, 238, 242

J

Junk food, 147, 153, 154
Justification for bribery, 116

L

Law and globalize world, 167
Legislative jurisdiction, 169, 170
Liberalisation, 148, 166, 244, 246
Lifelong learning, 205
Lifestyle products, 252

M

Market failures, 164, 193, 199, 234
Market oriented, 25, 29, 30, 32
Marketing ethics, 77, 81, 82, 85, 88, 89, 90, 97, 101, 117, 118, 119, 120, 121, 122, 123, 125
Marking-to-market, 242, 243
Mature consumer society, 80
Menu of solutions, 236
Mobility, 28, 184, 200, 201, 204
Monetary policy, 230, 232, 245, 246
Moral free space, 92, 94, 96, 107, 119, 120
Moving beyond skepticism, 229

N

National consumer, 173, 191, 192
Normative frameworks, 118
Normative moral foundation, 81

O

Organisational cultures, 25, 29

P

Paradox of profitable piracy, 5
Policy on conformity, 191
Protected informed consent, 92

R

Recalling unsafe goods, 17
Regulatory shortcomings, 235
Reliability, 65
Retailing segment, 251, 255
Right to basic needs, 140
Right to boycott, 12
Right to choice, 147
Right to redress, 149
Right to safe environment, 142
Right to safety, 2, 9, 21, 143, 144, 165, 184
Risk weights, 239, 240

S

Safer products, 152
Securitisation guidelines, 242
Selling the dream, 217
Social change, 221
Social contract theory, 81, 82, 85, 86, 87, 88, 89, 105, 120, 121, 125
Social innovation, 204
Some ethno marketing, 47
Standards for safeguarding, 143
Strong supply chain, 256, 260

T

Theoretical knowledge, 201
Transitional economies, 58, 59, 62, 64, 65, 67, 74, 75, 76, 77, 78, 79, 80
Transitional economy, 57, 58, 59, 65, 74, 76, 79

V

Validity issues, 65
Visual communication, 260

W

Women consumers, 156

Y

Young consumers, 1, 153, 154, 155